WINGS OF WAR

EX LIBRIS

WINGS OF WAR

The ninth ranking United States ace in all wars, Walker M. "Bud" Mahurin is the only man to score victories against the Germans and the Japanese during World War II and against the communist air forces during the Korean War—and to be shot down by all three adversaries. Having savored both the exaltation of victory and the despair of long, brutal imprisonment, Mahurin is uniquely qualified to write not only about the tactics and strategy of aerial warfare, but also about the strength and unbelievable tenacity of the human spirit. This book's title, *Honest John*, derives from his radio call sign in Korea, where he commanded the famous 4th Fighter Interceptor Group; it also perfectly describes his narrative style, which is frank, soul-searching, and fundamentally true.

Mahurin embarked upon his unparalleled career in typical fashion, melding a youth's love affair with flying and the opportunity suddenly offered by the U.S. Army Air Forces' aviation cadet program, which he entered in September 1941. Assigned to fly the Republic P-47 in the European theater in 1943, he became a scourge to the Luftwaffe, scoring twenty-one victories with an aggressive style. "I closed astern (the Me 110) and let loose. As soon as the shots began to pepper him he rolled over on his back," he writes of one encounter. "I could observe many hits all over his machine, which by this time began to disintegrate."

In the process of scoring the last of his kills in Europe, Mahurin was shot down by the enemy bomber's tail gunner. Bailing out of his stricken P-47, he landed in Occupied France and was sheltered by the Underground until he could make his way back to England.

Mahurin was then sent to the Pacific theater, flying North American P-51s on long-distance raids against the Japanese, during which he scored one victory. On a later mission, when his Mustang took hits from ground fire, he had to bail out into the ocean, fifty miles from the nearest land. To add insult to his precarious predicament, a fish bit his hand before he was rescued by an air-sea rescue boat.

TIME
LIFE
BOOKS

TIME-LIFE BOOKS INC., ALEXANDRIA, VIRGINIA 22314

In Korea, Colonel Mahurin first flew a North American F-86 in the 51st Fighter Interceptor Wing, commanded by the famous Colonel Francis "Gabby" Gabreski. Mahurin adapted quickly under Gabreski's tutelage, and soon began downing MiGs with the same technique that had worked against Messerschmitts—by firing only at point-blank range. "His beautiful MiG was a shambles," he writes, describing one engagement. "As I looked into the cockpit I could see the pilot slumped over against the instrument panel."

After scoring three aerial victories on his own, he shared in a fourth, and probably destroyed a fifth enemy plane. Then, during a daring strafing mission, Mahurin's F-86 was forced down by ground fire. This time there was no escape. He would endure more than a year of barbarous imprisonment, during which he was starved, beaten, and maltreated by his Korean and Chinese captors. The story of his incarceration is that of a man's triumph over evil, of the spirit's triumph over adversity; no matter how badly he was treated, Mahurin resisted with fortitude. When, worn down by months of starvation, isolation, and beatings, he was presented with a choice of life or death, he managed to outwit his Chinese adversaries by concocting a patently absurd story about germ warfare, one that managed to fool the enemy but was obviously a stratagem to Western observers.

After his return from his third military campaign, Mahurin left the service to begin a highly successful career in the aviation industry. He continues to both fly and write, and currently is at work on a new memoir.

Walter J. Boyne

This volume, like every book in Wings of War, has been reproduced photographically from an original edition. It thus preserves the authenticity of the original, including typographical errors and printing irregularities.

HONEST JOHN

HONEST JOHN

The Autobiography of

WALKER M. MAHURIN

G. P. Putnam's Sons   New York

MANUFACTURED IN THE UNITED STATES OF AMERICA

VAN REES PRESS • NEW YORK

Contents

Foreword

I THOUGHT long and hard before deciding to put this story into book form. I am not literary nor am I an author, two facts that will be evident to any reader. For sixteen years I was a devoted career military officer. Six years ago I became an executive for a major aircraft corporation, then a salesman for an electronics corporation, and recently a development planner for still another corporation. I find that I am happy in civilian life for the first time since leaving the service in 1956. This book could possibly result in the destruction of that happiness.

This story has been difficult for me to tell. It does not reflect to my credit and could revive strong sentiments that I have long sought to suppress. Then, too, while writing I had to relive many tense and painful moments. Those who read this book will either agree with what I have said and done or violently disagree. I don't expect in-between feelings. I decided to tell the story as plainly, simply and truthfully as I could remember it, then stand back and let the reader judge my actions. The title *Honest John* has a double meaning.

The actual mechanics of the book began in March of 1956, when the officers of the 27th Air Division at Norton Air Force

Base prevailed on me to tell them the story of my capture and imprisonment in North Korea during the Korean War. I talked to them for four and a half hours and my conversation was recorded. Later my words were transcribed into some eighty typewritten pages. Often after I left the Air Force I ran into people who questioned my decision to give up service life, apparently thinking that I had either been forced out or had elected to leave because of prison-camp experiences. This story will explain my reasons.

In retrospect I think that I would behave the same if faced with the same set of circumstances—with one exception. Should events unfold so that I face capture by the same enemy, I will never let myself be captured alive. At the time I felt I did the only thing I could do, and the outcome was as it should have been.

In this book I have made what I consider to be rather startling revelations. Because I work in a defense industry I had to be sure that what I was saying would not be objectionable to my service friends scattered throughout the Department of Defense. My book has been read by both Major Gene Gurney and Major James Sunderman of the Office of the Secretary of the Air Force Information Services. Fortunately, they did not disapprove. I also felt obligated to show many portions of the book to General Frank Everest, recently retired Commander of Tactical Air Command and a personal friend. He, too, expressed no objection. Since time has been limited, I have made no effort to show pertinent parts of the book to all who have been mentioned. I sincerely hope that none is offended.

When the reader has reached the last page he will have been exposed to words that I wanted to say in the way I wanted to say them. I hope that I will have made a point or two, because that is why I wrote the book. Another author, a man I have not yet had the pleasure of meeting, has written a great book about his experiences during World War II. He concluded with the statement, "Show me a hero, and I'll show you a bum." He may be right, but I must leave it to the reader to decide which fits me.

Part I: The Little War

1.

WHEN the Korean War broke out I was assigned to Headquarters United States Air Force in the Pentagon. My job, as assistant executive to the Secretary of the Air Force, consisted largely of answering correspondence addressed to the Secretary by people seeking favors—pretty slow duty for a guy who had spent the major portion of his life in the cockpit of an airplane. But once in awhile we got a letter that would brighten up the day.

Once a man wrote to tell of his invention: an engine that would enable an airplane to fly nonstop several times around the world without refueling. His letter appeared to be plausible— he claimed to have the engine in his garage, in working order— and we directed him to the proper developmental agencies in the Pentagon. After their evaluation he was informed that his invention was a little ahead of its time, whereupon the man wrote to me in rather abusive terms, threatening to turn his engine over to either the Russians or to *Life* Magazine if we didn't snap it up immediately. This sounded odd, and I decided to have a real investigation run on him. He turned out to be a retired railroad engineer who spent his time rocking back and forth in a rocking chair, working up supercharged dreams and putting them down on paper.

Another inventor in the general crackpot group was a man who claimed to have developed an all-plastic guided missile. On the heels of his correspondence he invaded the Pentagon and my office with a ten-foot guided missile. It had a wing span which could hardly be maneuvered through the doorway. He claimed to have invented a new and superior type of plastic for aircraft construction, and he wanted the Air Force to give him $50,000,-000 to set up factories and a business for him. We had other fish to fry.

More monotonous than screwball inquiries were those from harassed Congressmen on the Hill. Usually these revealed the legislators to be the rope in a tug of war between organized pressure groups and the voters back home. I became a real poison-pen pal with one Congressman who bedeviled us more than the rest. One day he wrote to the Secretary of the Air Force, asking, "Please give me the official Air Force position on cotton linters." The letter came to me for action. It took me a week to find out what cotton linters were, let alone find out what one did with them. The answer from the Department of Commerce, which had also been asked: "They are used to stuff pillows."

There were many other queries. "Why had the Air Force opened SNARF Air Force Base?" "Why had the Air Force closed BARF Air Force Base?" We tried to answer them all as politely as possible.

It wasn't easy to get away from paper pushing; higher brass usually outranked me for available aircraft. Quite a few of my World War II cronies, however, were still in active tactical outfits, and once in awhile I could con someone into letting me try the new jets, just to keep my hand in. After all, the Air Force had invested many thousands of dollars in me as a flyer, and I wanted the investment to draw interest.

Colonel Gordon Austin, head of the Fighter Policy and

Tactical Employment Branch of Headquarters USAF, and Colonel Randy Holzapple watched my activities with jaundiced eyes. I am sure they felt that this junior officer was getting a little out of hand, sneaking in all that jet flying time. One day when I walked past their office with a hand full of correspondence they jumped out from behind the door with a large canvas mailbag, tackled me, and shoved me feet first into the bag, tying the open end around my neck. Then they threw me out into the corridor. It took me over an hour to escape from the thing. Whenever people passed—and there were generally officers among them—they would merely snicker and proceed merrily down the hall. By the time I got loose I never knew I had so many friends who were enemies in that damned building.

There were other diversions too. A friend of mine, Colonel Joe Bryan, who worked for the Central Intelligence Agency, called one day to invite me to go for a ride on an aircraft carrier. It seemed there was to be a symposium of Naval Reserve Intelligence officers at Norfolk, Virginia, and the climax of the trip was to be a three-day junket on the aircraft carrier *Franklin D. Roosevelt*. I was invited to go along with another good friend, Colonel Corey Ford, now a successful author. Just about this time someone had inadvertently driven the mighty battleship *Missouri* into the mud off Fort Mason in the harbor at Norfolk, and much to the consternation of the Navy it had been dubbed Fort Truman by members of the Air Force. The *Missouri* is a tremendous vessel and unfortunately could be seen all over the harbor area. Armed with this knowledge, Corey and I hunted Washington for a suitable present to give the commander of the carrier when we went on board. We had been taking plenty of ribbing from the Navy officers en route to the carrier, and we pressed on to the captain's cabin as soon as we arrived. When Captain Swede Ekstrom greeted us at the door we handed him a depthometer—a small reel with seventy-five feet of string and a lead weight attached. We told him that it might be useful to him when we steamed out of the harbor past the *Missouri*. He could measure the depth of the water on the way. Swede accepted our present without a trace of a smile, saying, "And I have a present for you too." With that he handed us each a box of Mother Sill's Seasick Pills!

When the Korean War broke out, this sort of horseplay stopped in a hurry. And with headquarters on a wartime footing, I itched more than ever to fly. We began to hold situation briefings every morning for the benefit of the general officer staff in the Pentagon. Mike Moore and I usually attended, to make progress charts for Air Force Secretary Thomas K. Finletter. We also took phone calls from Congress and answered questions about the war. Every time Colonel Mike Michealus gave his briefings I felt a yen to be sprung from the Pentagon and join a tactical flying outfit. Here was a shooting war and I wasn't even near it. Still, initially, there wasn't too much to the air war in Korea: lots of dive-bombing ground-support action, but very few enemy aircraft. That is, until the day when the Migs entered the picture.

From time to time in our command briefings we had heard of the possibility that the Russian-built Mig-15 fighter might come into action, but none had ever been seen. Suddenly one day a group of Republic F-84 fighter bombers, performing a ground support mission, were attacked by many swept-wing enemy aircraft, and immediately the whole complexion of the air war changed. All United Nations-operated aircraft in Korea were either straight wing jets, or propeller jobs with limited performance. Usually a straight wing jet is limited to about 600 miles per hour, and a piston-engined aircraft to even lower speeds. Because of it's swept wings, our most conservative intelligence estimates predicted that the Mig-15 would be capable of at least 660 miles per hour, an appreciable advantage. Immediate action was required. Obviously the answer was the North American Aviation Sabre, the F-86.

I had two friends stationed at Langley Air Force Base, Virginia; Brigadier General George Smith, Commander of the 4th Fighter Interceptor Wing, and Colonel J. C. Meyer, Commander of the 4th Fighter Group. J. C. was one of the nation's leading fighter pilots during World War II and a great guy. Just after the Migs were sighted the Air staff in the Pentagon decided to move the entire 4th Wing to Korea with their F-86s, and within the shortest period of time J. C. led his men and aircraft to the West Coast, put them aboard an aircraft carrier, and shoved off for Japan. A short time later he was ensconced at an air base called Kimpo by the Koreans and K-14 by the Allies, located just outside of Seoul, the capital of South Korea.

Being a professional soldier and having tasted some degree of success as a fighter pilot during World War II, I took all of this activity pretty hard. And it began to be real binding when reports of aerial combat between the Migs and the F-86s started coming back, especially when J. C.'s pilots began to shoot down a few of the enemy. I almost had a heart attack when J. C. got two Migs himself. Major Jimmy Jabara scored one victory after the other, finally becoming the world's first jet ace. Colonel Glen Eggleston, Colonel Bruce Hinton, Colonel Dick Creighten, Major George Davis and a host of others, were out there really shooting them up. Although I was happy for them, especially because I knew them all personally, I could see them passing me by, qualifying as jet combat leaders, and gaining fine reputations while I sat at home, shoving papers back and forth between Capitol Hill and the Pentagon. It just wasn't right.

I began to lay my groundwork. The normal tour in the big building is four years; I had been there only one. First I wrote a note to a friend, Brigadier General Hugh A. Parker, then deputy commander of Western Air Defense Force at Hamilton Air Force Base, asking him if he had any positions open for unit commanders. I wrote another letter to Major General Frederic H. Smith, Vice Commander of Air Defense Command at Colorado Springs, to see if he had any ideas. I finally went down to the officers personnel section in headquarters to talk to Colonel Herbert Grills, Chief of the Full Colonels' Assignment Division, to see how he would feel about allowing me to leave the Pentagon before my tour was up. Herb dealt only with full colonels, and he couldn't help me unless there were some changes—changes that didn't seem to be in the wind. No encouragement there. A reply from Lefty Parker said that he could use a full colonel as a group commander, but didn't have a slot for a lieutenant colonel. No encouragement there either. But just then I got about the biggest break of the century.

The Air Force decided to have a promotion cycle to promote lieutenant colonels to full colonels, since, with Reserve and Air National Guard units being called to active duty, there was need for a much larger officer corps. Rumor had it that there were to be 750 promotions to full colonel out of a total of 3,000 lieutenant colonels considered eligible, selections to be made on the basis of "exceptionally well qualified," rather than on the old standard of seniority. I was eligible, but just barely, so I set to work seeking advance information for many of my better-qualified friends. Being in the office of the Secretary, I was in a good position to put my hands on the promotion lists, and when word got out that Mahurin was more or less informed, telephone calls began to come in from all over the country. Guys I hadn't seen or heard from for years wanted to know where they stood. We all had to wait over the Christmas holidays, knowing we were being considered, and it wasn't until about the 12th of January that a friend, Major Jack Bernstein, who worked in the Secretary's mailroom, caught a glimpse of the list as it passed from the Air staff to the Secretary for signature. Jack gave me a few of the names, and I spent the whole day passing the word along. I finally made out a list of my own for Jack to check on, and, prior to the 19th of January, spent almost my whole month's salary on long-distance calls to spread the good word. Jack told me early in the game that my name was on the list, but I didn't believe him. In the first place, I was sixth from the bottom in seniority, and in the second place I was twelfth from the bottom in age. I had just turned thirty-two. Nor could I honestly say that I had been the best officer in the office of the Secretary, let alone on the Pentagon staff.

One of the names on the list was Lieutenant Colonel Francis S. Gabreski. At the time Gabby was commanding the 56th

Fighter Interceptor Group at Selfridge Air Force Base. I had visited him several times during the past year, mostly for flying time in his Lockheed F-80 jets, and I had also been his host when he led his entire fighter group in an aerial parade during the funeral of General Hap Arnold. I knew both he and his wife Kay would be thrilled to find that he had been one of those blessed—that he was now a "full bull"—and when I called him long distance he was so pleased he forgot to thank me for telling him the good news. Lieutenant Colonel Charles Terhune was elated too. Chas and I had worked together in Japan at the end of the war, and I had turned the 3rd Air Commando Group over to him when I left Japan for home. Both he and his wife Bea had been sweating out this big promotion for years. There were many others.

The promotion list came out officially on January 19. To our amazement and disbelief, Mike Moore and I had made it. Later that day, walking down the halls of the Pentagon, I met Harold Stuart, who at that time was Assistant Secretary of the Air Force, for Reserve and National Guard Affairs. Hal wanted to know where my eagles were. I told him that I still didn't believe the list, and besides I was too damn cheap to buy new brass. Half an hour later Hal's secretary came into my office and presented me with two shiny new insignias and a note from Harold saying: "Now, damn you, will you believe it?"

That same day I got a call from Gabby at Selfridge, giving me hell for not telling him that I was on the list too. We had a celebration party that night at my home in Falls Church, and right in the middle of it the door opened and Selman and Mary Ledbetter, old friends of ours since our first days in the Pentagon, came in with two live chickens which they immediately put on my shoulders. As a city boy, I can now speak with authority when I say that it is tough as hell to get rid of two live chickens.

The promotion made me double my efforts to get out of the Pentagon. I called Lefty Parker, who came through with a teletype stating he had a vacancy in the 1st Fighter Interceptor Group at George Air Force Base in Victorville, California. Herb

Grills produced a memo stating that he would release me for the new job. I went in to see the big boss, Thomas K. Finletter himself, and since he barely knew who I was and couldn't care less, he approved readily. Following this I took all my documents to my immediate boss, Colonel H. C. "Sam" Donnelly.

I really pulled out all the stops with Sam: how unsuited I was for the papermill (I am sure he agreed); how I wanted to be in a fighting unit; how I had spent so many, many years in the big building; how my children were in ill health and needed desert air; and finally how I now outranked the man who was my boss. I showed him the note from Lefty, the note from Herb, and finally the approval from the Secretary. I've never seen a man so mad. It wasn't that Sam hated to see me go, nor was it that I had been doing a superb job. It was just, as he put it: "God damn you, Mahurin, you've finally maneuvered me into a position . . . get the hell out of here." I was on my way.

I arrived at George Air Force Base with my wife Pat and the two kids in the middle of February, 1951, to report to Colonel Dolf Mulheisen, Commander of the 1st Fighter Interceptor Wing. Delightedly I found myself in command of one of the most famous fighter groups in the history of the Air Force. Further, three of the most famous fighter squadrons were in the group. The 94th Squadron was Captain Eddie Rickenbacker's old unit, and Captain Eddie had always been a hero to me, even as a kid. Long before I joined the Air Force I had read the pages of *Ace of Aces*, the story of Rick's life, and now here I was in command of his old outfit. Not only was I a step farther on the road to Korea, but I was also working in the best job in the Air Force: group commander. I was pretty proud of my new outfit. Many of the pilots were seasoned in fighter aircraft, they had plenty of experience and plenty of get up and go, and best of all they were eager to get into action if the need arose. I had been advised that my 188th Squadron, an air National Guard unit from Albuquerque, would be re-equipped with F-86s as soon as possible, so prior to the time we moved to the Long Beach Municipal Airport in California, I began to

18

check out our pilots in the T-33 Jet Trainer, anticipating the conversion to F-86s. This, however, was not to be. Whenever we would get a few of our lads jet qualified a commitment would come down from higher headquarters to send piston-engined pilots to Korea. Since the 188th was about the only pistoned-engined squadron in the Air Force, we finally ended up with only six qualified pilots.

Although I thought very highly of the 188th, they put me through agony one day. Lieutenant Colonel Tom Queen was in command of the squadron, and in accordance with existing alert regulations, many of his ships were spotted on the line in front of Squadron Operations, so that pilots on Air Defense Readiness could get into the air as quickly as possible. We had to have four aircraft, completely armed and manned with stand-by crews, stationed on the ramp at all times.

Customarily each morning, the aircraft engines are revved on the ramp to make sure they are functioning properly. Further, all systems are checked to assure each pilot that he will have 100-percent operation when he gets his machine into the air. I had tested our readiness several times, and in fact had made a few speeches to the community about how glad we were to be in Long Beach and how that fair city was now safe from enemy attack. All of a sudden we pulled the biggest goof of the century.

One Sunday morning about seven o'clock the mechanics were performing system checks when one of them accidentally touched the machine-gun firing switch on one of the Mustangs. Six 50-caliber machine guns let go with a roar, the combined fire directed toward the most exclusive residential section of Long Beach. The mechanic was so flustered by the noise that he completely forgot how to turn off the guns, and finally ended up by shooting 1,500 rounds of explosive ammunition all over town. I was at George Air Force Base at the time, and immediately received a call from Tom Queen, describing the episode—information which I passed on to my deputy wing commander, Colonel Robert F. Worley. Bob figured he had better wait until all the information was in before he passed the word to Major General Herb Thatcher, who at that time commanded Western Air Defense Force. The next morning, when Herb casually began to read his morning newspaper at Hamilton Air Force Base just outside San Francisco, he was confronted with big, black headlines describing the incident. He almost had a stroke on the spot, but before he could get his hands on a telephone to give us hell he, himself, received a call from General Hoyt Vandenburg, Chief of the Air Force, who wanted to know exactly what in God's name was going on out there on the Coast. All in all, Herb wasn't too happy, especially when he read a statement attributed to me which said that any time the 188th Squadron didn't have things to do on Saturday night they'd go in and shoot up the town. Fortunately no one was injured, and, as is the custom, we painted a grand piano, two Cadillacs, a bicycle and ten houses on the side of the aircraft.

Sending men to Korea was not just a one-way street. We began to receive pilots who had finished operations in Korea. Under the popular rotational policy of 5th Air Force in Korea, a pilot who had flown one hundred combat hours was eligible for rotation to the United States. Most of the pilots returning had jet combat experience, although it consisted largely of dive bombing and strafing on ground-support missions. Many of them had seen the Mig-15, although few had actually shot at the swept-wing aircraft. Most of them came back with hair-raising stories of the war: stories of downed airmen killed in their parachutes by the Communists as soon as they hit the ground; of prisoners who had been trussed up and killed on the way to prison camp; of other atrocities which I am sure did not lack in vivid imagination. Often accounts of primitive living conditions—as the front lines moved back and forth—were woven into the stories, and equally as often returning pilots reported intense and accurate groundfire around all important targets.

One of my returning pilots, Captain Lester Arrasmith, turned out to be a sort of a poor man's George Gobel. Les is one of the funniest men in the Air Force and he had a million stories to tell about the war. He claimed he always flew his combat missions with bombs and rockets hanging under one wing and his big Air Force-issue clothing bag under the other. He said that when the order came to evacuate Korea he didn't want to get caught in Japan without a proper change of clothes. I've heard from other pilots who were stationed at Air Base K-2, Taegu, at the same time as Les, that it was the damndest sight in all Korea to see his Mustang taking off to do battle with the mighty enemy with a suitcase under one wing and a 1,000-pound bomb under the other.

Even though the flyers who came back to the 1st Fighter Group were experienced headliners like Major Frederick Blesse, Captain Ralph Parr and Captain Joe McConnell, I still had to give them briefings and direct missions while lacking their Korean background. About all I had experienced combatwise in the last five years had been the Battle of Long Beach. One way I could attempt to impress them, though, was through flying ability, and I tried to get in at least one flight per day in the F-86. Each time I went up I would hang over the air base until someone else took off. Then I would attack him from above, and we would tear all over the sky in an effort to get on each other's tails. It was fun and also damn good training. I could hold my own pretty well with the younger pilots, but Boots Blesse, who eventually became one of our nation's leading jet aces, was really hard to whip. And the only way I could beat Ralph Parr, also a leading jet ace, was to use a better aircraft than the one he was flying.*

We were all learning and enjoying ourselves while doing so, but it still didn't seem to be quite enough. There was only one way to do what I thought really necessary, and that was to get actual experience. However, the demand for full colonels was low in Korea, and furthermore, all such assignments had to come from the Pentagon. Obviously the colonel's assignment

---

* Ralph ultimately shot down the last aircraft destroyed during the Korean War. It was a C-47 type loaded with Russian military and civilian dignitaries. Although the Russians complained bitterly in the UN that the action had taken place in Manchuria, Ralph's gun-camera film proved conclusively that the Russians were over North Korea at the time.

branch wouldn't stand for another change in assignment so soon. I knew, too, that I'd have quite a battle with Pat if I worked out anything that obvious.

In the meantime the complexion of the war was changing. Intelligence information indicated that the Communists were bringing many more Mig-15s into Manchuria, and large air battles involving many hundreds of enemy aircraft were taking place; it also appeared that the skill of their pilots was improving. Comparisons between the F-86 and the Mig-15 indicated that the Mig had a better rate of climb and a better combat ceiling, while the two aircraft were at a standoff in all other aspects. North American Aviation had developed a new version of the F-86 called the F-86E. This machine had what the aviation world called a Slab Tail which gave it a decided increase in performance and maneuverability at higher speeds when compared to the older A model being used in Korea.

Because of developments in the skies over North Korea, the Pentagon had decided to re-equip the 4th Fighter Wing with the F-86E. Most of the original commanders had returned to the United States, and now the wing was being directed by Colonel Ben Preston. My friend Gabreski, who by that time had been assigned to Korea with the 4th Wing, received orders to transfer to the 51st Wing at K-13, Suwon, about thirty miles south of Seoul. The 51st had been doing ground-support work with two squadrons of Lockheed F-8os. It had been decided to re-equip this unit with F-86Es, and Gab was needed to make the conversion and put the wing in shape. I received orders to transfer all of my new aircraft to the Alameda Naval Air Station at Oakland, California, so that they could be placed aboard an aircraft carrier bound for Japan. We had to nominate qualified pilots to go along with the aircraft. Bob Worley, Dolf Mulheisen and I put our names on the list, but higher headquarters bounced the paperwork back to us almost before the ink was dry. They simply didn't want high-ranking men.

On the 19th of November I took all of my aircraft to Oakland and was at shipside when the carrier, with 75 pilots and 100 aircraft, departed for the Far East under the command of

Colonel Levi Chase, who had flown with the Eagle Squadron in the Royal Air Force during the Battle of Britain. It was a tough blow to see them go. The worst was knowing that Gabby, already the nation's leading living ace, was going into action with the best aircraft, undoubtedly to build his score even higher. When I said good-bye to the gang I told them that I would see them soon. I had finally figured out a way.

As soon as I returned to the base I wrote a long letter to Lefty Parker. In essence I said that it was most difficult for a commander to exert influence on men who had vastly more experience. There was a big air war going on, and the only way to learn about it was to participate. I knew that Lefty didn't want me to leave his command, but I asked him to consider my going to Korea, possibly for 30 days on temporary duty. I would return to my own command as soon as the 30 days were over. In this way I could fly a few missions, find out what was going on, and be a better leader as a result. When I ended the letter I made sure that Lefty would send his answer to my office rather than to my home, because it would be certain death if Pat got wind of what I was doing.

While I was waiting for a reply, the international situation began to change. The United Nations and the North Koreans agreed to negotiate for peace, and it seemed that the war might shortly be over. I was as anxious as anyone that the conflict be brought to a close as quickly as possible, but I still hoped to get to Korea in time to fly a couple of combat missions, or at least be there for the windup of hostilities. If I could get into a fight with the Migs just once, I would be a better commander in the future should war break out elsewhere in the world.

About a week later the reply came. Lefty thought I had a good idea, and he had talked to Air Defense Command about it. They, too, thought the idea had merit. Would I please re-write the letter, requesting 90-days duty instead of 30? I'd heard the old military axiom about not volunteering for anything, and I should have been able to see what was coming. But I didn't. I'm probably the only guy in history who went out of

23

the house for a loaf of bread and came home 22 months later. Yet at the time I was only too happy to write the letter, and off it went to Western Air Defense Force.

2.

ON December 2, 1951, orders arrived from the Air Defense Command assigning me to the Far Eastern Air Force in Tokyo for a period of 90 days. Going along with me would be several other officers: Colonel Jack Hayes, Commander of the 78th Fighter Group at Hamilton Air Force Base; Colonel Bill Schaeffer, a squadron commander from Selfridge Air Force Base; and Major Van Chandler, from Otis Air Force Base. Our instructions were all the same: depart the United States on December 14, travel by military air, and arrive at the earliest possible date.

Only one more problem remained—but it was the worst of all. How was I to break the news to my wife? I kept quiet about the orders until my birthday on December 5. Pat had invited friends over to celebrate, and I figured this would be the time to break the news. She couldn't give me too much hell in front of all those guests. I was pretty proud of her—all she said was, "Damn you, I'll bet you rigged this one."

What she hated most was my being away over the Christmas holidays, but my obvious answer was that I had nothing to do with the situation. These were orders which must be obeyed; we had to follow orders, regardless of the time of year. One thing which kept her from actually exploding was that the war would probably be over in the shortest possible time—perhaps before I could get to Korea. Or so it appeared.

Finally, after a tearful departure at Fairfield-Suizan Air Force

Base, I boarded a military air transport flight bound for Japan. We arrived at Haneda, outside of Yokohama, on December 16, and four of us took a cab to the Imperial Hotel to be near Far Eastern Air Force Headquarters in the morning. As we checked in I ran into two old friends who were on permanent duty in Japan and living at the Imperial. Colonel O. B. Johnson and Colonel Bob Friedman had served with me in the Pentagon and they felt free to get on an insulting basis with us right off the bat. When we told them what we were doing in Japan they burst into ribald laughter. These two guys, as well as all the rest of the officers of Far Eastern Air Force, felt that peace would come at any moment. Obie Johnson was convinced I shouldn't even get on an airplane for Korea, because I'd only get there in time to turn around and come back. I listened to them with mixed emotions. I had come a long way for a fight. Although we all wanted the war to end, still I wished it would go on just long enough for me to get in one or two missions. When Obie made his comments all I could think of was that he was looking for a replacement for his current job so that he could return to the States. I am sure he had me in mind.

After one day in Japan, making the necessary arrangements, we left for Korea. Our destination was K-16, the Seoul City Airport, but when we arrived over the base the weather was terrible and we were forced to proceed to our alternate, K-13, Suwon. It had been raining for some time, but our pilot made a good approach and landing and we were finally on Korean soil. Although I had visited that faraway country in 1945 after World War II, I had forgotten just how desolate a place it was. Our aircraft was parked away out in the boondocks, with no way to disembark but to slide down the side on a rope hanging from the afterdoor. We all went about halfway down the rope and then fell off—bags, coats, clothes and all—into the worst mud pile I have ever seen. After sloughing to base operations through miles of mud, we were informed that there were no quarters available and that we would have to take a jeep into Seoul to find a place to stay. I suddenly happened to notice a sign in front of base operations, giving names of prominent people assigned to K-13. Colonel Francis S. Gabreski topped the list. He and his 51st Wing were co-owners of the base, along with the 8th Fighter Wing, commanded by Colonel Jim Tipton, another renowned fighter pilot from World War II days in England. I immediately put in a call to Gab, who showed up in a few minutes with the damndest rig I had ever seen. He arrived in a jeep that was completely enclosed in aluminum—top, doors, sides and all. On the left front fender he had mounted a gigantic chromium siren, and on the right front fender was a huge, red spotlight. Everything that wasn't chromium was painted a fire-engine red, and the whole was topped off with a big white sign just under the windshield which read: THE CHIEF.

Gab seemed genuinely glad to see me. He was curious about why I was in Korea and anxious to know to what unit I would be assigned. He said he wanted to give me a little of the history of the 51st Wing, and if I wanted to be assigned with him he'd call Brigadier General Jim Ferguson, the vice commander of 5th Air Force, to see if I couldn't be made special assistant to the wing commander.

By this time, Gabby had been in Korea for about six months, most of the time with the 4th Fighter Wing. He had recently been assigned as wing commander of the 51st, and he now had two squadrons which had just been equipped with the F-86Es I had sent him from the United States, along with a third squadron flying the Lockheed F-80 out of Okinawa. Most of his pilots had been flying the older F-80s and thus had had little experience against Russian Mig-15s.

In contrast, the 4th Wing had been the only Sabrejet outfit in Korea for almost a year. On the 20th of May, 1951, Major James Jabara had destroyed his fifth and sixth Migs to become the world's first jet ace. In the following months five other pilots had also achieved this distinction. Just before I arrived in Korea on December 13, the pilots of the 4th Wing had destroyed 12 Migs, probably destroyed another, and damaged three. Altogether the 4th's record was an enviable one.

Although Gab had prevailed on Colonel Harry Thyng at the 4th Wing to allow a few experienced pilots to transfer with him to the 51st, he was nevertheless having trouble shaping his unit into an effective combat team. He thought I could help them along, and asked if I would stay to work with him. Hell yes, I would. It looked like a great opportunity for a green hand to join a green team. All of us could grow up together. As soon as I had expressed my opinion Gab called Jim Ferguson, and within a very few minutes I was in business.

Altogether there were a total of 125 F-86s in Korea: 50 in the 51st Wing and 75 in the 4th. Both wings had converted from some other type of aircraft, and conversions of this kind always cause supply problems. In this case the situation was even worse than normal because Korea was at the end of the line. About the best any squadron could do for a given mission was to put 12 out of a total of 25 aircraft into the air. Something had to be done.

When a part is needed the normal procedure is to requisition it through supply channels, then wait for it to arrive. This took time. We decided we could wait no longer because, although the wing had submitted requisition after requisition, the parts just weren't coming through. On my way to Korea I had visited North American Aviation to talk to George Welch and Bill Wahl, both of whom had informed me that they intended to make a trip to the combat zone as soon as possible. George was chief test pilot for the company and had done most of the initial flying on the F-86. Bill, on the other hand, was one of the leading aeronautical engineers in the country, a man who had been giving technical briefings to members of the air staff in the Pentagon for many years. Both of these men had briefed me on North American Aviation's products in the Pentagon from time to time, and I liked them very much. They were coming out to the war area to try to learn what they could to improve the combat equipment being produced by North American.

When we found out the date they intended to visit us in Korea we had the wing maintenance officer list all of the parts we needed to put all of our aircraft in commission. We also had him list what he would need to keep them that way. We then placed a collect call to the United States to talk to Ray Rice, who was then the chief engineer at North American. We read the list of parts to Ray—some 250 items—and asked him to send all of them along with Welch and Wahl. Poor Ray. I am sure he was completely baffled. When he started to consider the cost of the phone call, plus the cost of the parts, plus the cost of air freight to Korea, the total came to an astronomical sum—much more than the company would even dare to foot. About all he could do was to call the Air Materiel Command in Dayton, Ohio, to suggest they pick up the tab for what we had requested. This was an unprecedented situation which the Indian level in the command found impossible to handle, and our request went right to the top. Within a week we were deluged by a staff of general officers straight from Dayton, men who had been ordered to Korea just after Ray had hung up the phone. They didn't have any parts, but they did have a nose for trouble. They figured we must be hiding equipment all around our air base, because their records showed there should have been plenty of parts on hand. They snooped all over, looking for stuff we didn't have. (Actually we did have a few bootleg parts, but Major Bill Lacey, the engineering officer of the 25th Squadron, had them so well hidden they were never found.) Then the generals, having decided they had given us a thorough going over, started back up the supply chain, taking bits and pieces out of every officer they could find who looked as if he wasn't doing his job. They finally ended up back at the factory where we had started. With this kind of attention the situation began to improve rapidly, and Gab and I gained our objectives. We had both found it convenient to be in Tokyo when the inspection team arrived, and we later heard that they didn't have too high a regard for those two smart-aleck colonels from the 51st Wing.

Now we had little reason for not shooting down enemy aircraft, but still our record did not improve. Something else must be wrong, and I tried to analyze my own feelings, now that I was exposed to combat again after a layoff of over six years. Perhaps our other pilots would feel the same. Maybe we were all too apprehensive; maybe we were pushing too hard. We had to find out.

First, Korea was scarcely a paradise. Almost every town had been leveled by ground combat, and the standard of living was extremely low, most of the peasants living in mud huts with thatched roofs. We were there in the wintertime, and winter weather in Korea is about as foul as can be imagined. Our air base was new and thus totally lacking in modern facilities. Everywhere one looked there was mud, just mud. Our living quarters were adequate but Spartan, and about the only place the officers and men could have some semblance of social life was at the officers' or enlisted men's clubs. All in all it was pretty grim.

Morale was obviously a most important factor, and morale can be improved with little things. We decided to paint the wings of each of our aircraft with a large yellow stripe bordered in black, in order to set our wings apart from those of the 4th. Next we sent to Japan for neck scarfs for the pilots. These were jazzy red affairs with the insignia of each squadron brocaded in the middle and the name of each pilot placed conspicuously on the bottom. We issued instructions that the installation officer should make available to each unit the necessary materials and equipment to build adequate pilots' lounges with adequate briefing rooms; to provide places where the crews could loaf in comfort instead of spending all off-duty hours in the sack, for lack of other facilities. Lastly, we managed to send an occasional aircraft to Okinawa to bring back supplies of fresh vegetables and fish, so that our men could have a few meals per week above the standard being served in most of the mess halls in Korea.

All of this helped, but the biggest problem we faced involved the emotional aspects of combat flying. What we were looking for was that little touch of bravery above the normal call. A military pilot is taking a risk every time he flies his high-performance machine and an additional risk when he goes into combat. It could be argued that he is handsomely compensated for this risk, but financial compensation is not enough. He is also rewarded by having a high sense of duty, a high sense of comradery, and a high sense of competitive spirit. If he lacked these forms of inspiration, he would soon recognize the dangers of his trade and say to himself, Why not play it safe and stay away from this flying game? Why take the risk?

A jet-fighter pilot is responsible to himself alone. He is alone in his cockpit. He has but one engine to depend on, and should it stop running he will be in trouble. At the speeds he travels he is going to be in trouble fast if anything happens. He must develop a super alertness, must be prepared for any emergency. Suppose his engine stops just as his aircraft reaches a height of fifty feet. He has but one alternative, he must put his ship back onto the ground at about 150 miles an hour directly into whatever lies in front of him. His worries are manifold. Will the ship break up or blow up? When he hits will his ejection seat malfunction and shoot him through the canopy, or will his back be broken on impact with the ground? Suppose his engine quits just as he is turning on the final approach for landing. He will be too low to bail out. Can he crash land? What if he tries to stretch his glide and stalls out short of the runway? Will the aircraft start to burn? What if he is trapped in the cockpit and the fire trucks can't reach him in time? Suppose he's flying at high speed in formation with his fellow pilots and one of them runs into him. Will his machine tumble around the sky so much that he will lose control of his senses? What if he tries to eject, and a part of the aircraft strikes him? Maybe the parachute won't open. Suppose he goes into a high-speed dive and a part of the aircraft breaks off. Can he pull out? Will the whole machine break up into little pieces? If anything happens he is going to come down and hit the ground at tremendous speed. And whatever happens will happen fast.

The fighter pilot in combat is out for the really big game. He is never sure how good the enemy aircraft is, but each fighter pilot is confident he possesses such superior pilot ability that he can lick anything in the sky. All fighter pilots are egomaniacs. None of them feels he can display fear in front of his fellow men. Still, each time he goes into combat the pilot is scared to death.

Outwardly the fighter pilots at the 51st Wing were reacting with the bravado of ancient swashbucklers, and they wanted everyone to know it. Most of them told long stories about combat experiences, and none of them let the truth discolor the stories. They drank hard and played hard, and usually the bar at the officers' club rang at night with songs about fighter pilots and their deeds. Most of them had developed a veneer to cover up the fact that they were well aware of the dangers of combat flying, and, like everybody else, were more than just a little insecure.

Gabby and I had seen two wars and were familiar with the problem of combat fatigue. Thank God the doctors were also aware of the limits of human endurance and gave us a ration of combat whisky to be used at the completion of every mission. Had it not been for the whisky ration and rest leaves in Japan, we would have had frequent mental crack-ups. The strongest men usually saved up the whisky ration to use in Tokyo on leave. The weakest could be found opening up the bar at the officers' club at the end of the working day and closing it at the last possible minute. These were the men we watched, maintaining that no one could do an adequate job of combat flying when floating on Cloud Nine or suffering from a hangover.

Gabby and I usually kept pretty close tabs on the men during our pre-mission briefings. We tried to make each briefing different from its predecessor by bringing up any new point of tactics which might enable us to shoot down some Migs. As a result the meetings were usually well attended, and I could generally count on an audience of 100 men every time I briefed. Out of that number I could pick, say, 18 who could actually be depended upon to mix it up with the enemy and perhaps do some shooting. Another 70 would fly into the combat zone, but for some strange reason would never see the enemy or fire a gun. The rest would inevitably develop some sort of mechanical, mental or physical difficulty sufficient to cause them to turn back home.

Gabby and I were not head-shrinkers; we couldn't do much about the mental problems of fighter combat. We tried to treat each man as an individual; we needed them all and thought they needed us. We held out for the possibility that once we began to shoot down enemy aircraft the morale of our pilots couldn't help but improve. A little of the mystery of the enemy would be destroyed if we could get at them and get at them good.

As far as I was concerned personally the worst thing about going into action for the first time was my uncertainty about the enemy. I had worried like the very devil the first time I flew in England during World War II, because I'd had no idea what the German pilots would do, how good their aircraft were, or what that aircraft looked like. All were unknown quantities. I didn't know whether my plane was as good, and I especially didn't know whether I could fly as well. I knew for sure that our tactics couldn't compare, simply because we didn't have any. I was thoroughly frightened. And the first time I saw a German fighter airplane in the air over Europe I really got clobbered. Afterward many of my fears disappeared. At least I knew the general form of aerial warfare. I had actually seen German aircraft, with their frightening swastika markings. I knew they could shoot and shoot well, because they had hit me. Later when I got into a fight with several of the enemy, managing to shoot down a couple of them, my mental attitude changed completely. They were not invincible, they were not supermen, and besides I had a pretty good aircraft under me, after all. On that occasion I had seen German fighters, flying through our large formation of B-17 bombers, shooting furiously as they passed. As I watched, all I could think was that those bastards were hurting Americans. It made me mad, and in my anger I forgot to be afraid. Even after I had shot two of them down and possibly destroyed another while running out of ammunition, I was still mad. After that episode I was in business every time I went up.

I went through the same mental anguish over a year later when I went to the South Pacific to fight against the Japanese. Again, I didn't know anything about Japanese pilots. I knew a little about their aircraft but not enough to make me feel at ease. My fear persisted until I fought a few battles with them

32

and got over the fright of seeing those big, red meat-ball insignias on the sides of the fuselages.

Now that I was in combat again, here were all the familiar unknowns, only this time I was older, and somehow they bothered me even more than they had in the past. Instead of seeking the exuberant shoot-em-up spirit of youth, I now merely wanted to be skillful. I had a family to think of. I did have a bit more background than I'd had in World War II: I'd become an aeronautical engineer. This time I knew that aircraft are designed by specific formulas. Nothing is left to chance, even though speeds, altitudes and designs had changed dramatically over the years. The basic formulas would always apply. There is a formula for minimum turning radius, a formula for best rate of climb, a formula for stalling speed, and so on. As a result I attributed very little to the comments of hot young fighter pilots who insisted that the Mig was superior in every way. We knew the following information: the F-86 would approach a maximum speed of .92 Mach number, or about 720 miles per hour, while the Mig-15 would do slightly less—.915 Mach. The Mig-15 could reach a much higher altitude than the F-86, and attain that altitude more rapidly. It had a better acceleration. But we could outturn the Mig at high speeds because of the slab tail on the F-86E. We could roll over faster because we had hydraulic flight controls, and, because we were heavier, we could dive down and zoom up faster than the Russian-built machine.

There were reasons for the differences in performance. The Mig-15 had more power in relation to weight because the Russians had skimped on many things we considered mandatory. Heavy armor plate, bulletproof glass, adequate cockpit pressurization and temperature controls, radar-ranging gun sights, hydraulic controls, and long-range fuel tanks, were all items that North American Aviation had considered to be more important than lighter weight when the F-86 had been designed. Since the Migs lacked these important features, they were bound to be lighter. We were driving Cadillacs while they had Fords. There were many times when we felt that we would rather be driving

Fords, but every time one of our pilots brought a shot-up F-86 home for a safe landing we were damn glad we had the Cadillacs.*

3.

GABBY assigned me to fly with the 25th Fighter Squadron, commanded by Major William Whisner. Bill was a capable and versatile officer who had destroyed sixteen German aircraft during World War II. As expected, like every other new pilot, I had to go through escape-and-survival indoctrination training, as well as fly familiarization missions. Until these training phases were completed, no new pilot was allowed to fly above the front lines.

This was the time to become familiar with the items included in the escape-and-survival gear each pilot carried with him on combat missions. We were all issued a standard kit, and each pilot added or subtracted what he wanted. For my part I added two pair of heavy white sox, a change of underwear, a .22 caliber Savage folding rifle, and, for some reason now obscure, a roll of toilet paper. The Intelligence officers had no specific instructions for us if we were downed behind enemy lines, because little was known of the enemy reaction to fallen airmen. There were no known friendly civilians above the bomb line, and none of our pilots had returned to friendly territory after

* After the war in Korea was over, a North Korean pilot named No-Kum-Sok escaped from the Communists in a Mig-15 and landed on K-14 intact. Air Force test pilots had a chance to evaluate his plane against the F-86. Lt. Col. Charles Yeager, famous as the man who first flew at supersonic speeds, flew the Mig-15, as did Col. Pete Everest, the first man to fly twice the speed of sound. All of our estimates of performance were confirmed. From an over-all standpoint, we had a much better piece of equipment than the enemy.

being shot down. We were advised to hide out until there were no human beings in the vicinity, then strike out for water in the hope of launching a one-man life raft. Once in the water the airman could paddle away from land and hope to be sighted from the air by Air-Sea Rescue Service planes or helicopters.

Fifth Air Force had selected prominent land features in North Korea as geographical checkpoints. Each checkpoint was given a code name so that if, during a big aerial battle, our pilots became separated from their flights, they could head for a certain location, openly broadcast the code name, and wait to rejoin formation until others flew to that location. For example, the Sui-Ho reservoir on the Yalu River, separating North Korea from Manchuria, was called the Mizu, the Japanese word for water. There was an area over the Yellow Sea, just off the mouth of the Chong-Chong River in the middle of North Korea, called Hey Rube. This spot was a great rallying place. Many times did I find myself alone in a fight, fly directly to Hey Rube and wait until someone else came along to join me. We called an area just south of the large Manchurian city of Antung Hot Spot, because several airfields, loaded with enemy aircraft, surrounded the city. The center of North Korea was called Race Track because the enemy formations always seemed to circle around and around in this area. We kept in radio contact with the ground through two reporting points. The Air Force had a large radar site just above K-14, and its controllers used the call sign Dentist. During the drive north early in the war the United Nations forces had captured a small island in the Yellow Sea called Cho-Do, and the Communists had never been able to take it back. We had a small radar site and an air-sea rescue operation on this island, which used the call sign Dentist Charlie.

The air war in Korea had taken on an unusual form because the enemy was able to keep all of his aircraft in a sanctuary north of the Yalu River. Our State Department treated Communist China as a noncombatant, and any flight into Manchuria by United Nations aircraft constituted a border violation of a neutral nation. We seemed to ignore the fact that the enemy flew from this neutral nation to kill our men. Fifth Air Force

35

was specifically prohibited from violating the border, and thus the Communists could operate in the air with impunity as long as they didn't cross the Yalu into North Korea. Also, they could maintain all their aircraft in the open without fear of strafing by United Nations aircraft; they could conduct all the training and ferrying flights they wished; and they could take off and land at any time, knowing they were safe from interference. To allow a foe the luxury of preparing for the conduct of war knowing that he is impervious to attack until he penetrates enemy territory is ridiculous to the extreme, in a strictly military sense. The basic ground rules in Korea were established by State Departments instead of qualified military leaders. The United Nations forces lost thousands of men because of the political, as opposed to the military, solution to the problems of the Korean War.

The Manchurian sanctuary was not only advantageous to the Communists in their air, but also on the ground. They could amass huge stockpiles of rolling equipment, supplies and men in Manchuria, then when night fell and it became difficult for our air force to attack ground targets, start moving down into North Korea. Hiding by day and moving by night, the supplies and men eventually arrived at the front lines, to be used against our soldiers. Had we been allowed to strike above the Yalu River at Manchuria this would never have happened.

There were many essential targets on both sides of the Yalu worthy of attack by heavy aerial bombardment. Those on the north side of the river were untouchable, those on the south side extremely difficult to approach. When 5th Air Force attempted to destroy targets on the south side it was necessary to fly parallel to the river, just on the North Korean side, in the bombing attempts. All the protecting escort fighters were required to take positions on the bomber formations either to the front, to the rear, or to the south side, to avoid straying into Manchuria. Thus the north side of our bomber formations would be wide open and vulnerable to enemy attack. The enemy, leisurely massing his fighters in his sanctuary well in sight of our own fighters, could make a quick attack on the unprotected flank of the bomber formations, shoot at several bombers, and dart back into the sanctuary unharmed. When 5th Air Force tried to bomb in daylight, the loss rate on the large bombers mounted so high that daylight attacks had to be abandoned.

The fighter pilot found the situation even worse—it was exactly as though one professional boxer were asked to fight another with one hand behind his back. The Communists would send many flights of aircraft up from different airfields in Manchuria whenever our friendly fighters penetrated North Korea. The enemy would climb in larger and larger circles while more units joined formation. As soon as the whole mass of aircraft had reached a desired altitude, usually higher than that of the United Nations fighters, they would drop external fuel tanks, dive down to pick up speed, and turn south into North Korea. Thus the Communists gained three advantages: superior speed, superior altitude and advantageous position. Until the enemy actually penetrated North Korea, the United Nations forces were unable to do anything but fly along at cruising speed and watch the Communists work their way into a superior tactical advantage.

Unfortunately the sanctuary worked to still another advantage for the enemy. Since the pilots of the Mig-15s were always able to gain superior altitude and speed before crossing the border, and since the friendly fighter pilots had to use low-power settings to stay in the air long enough for the enemy to come south to fight, the enemy always appeared to be faster and to have better climbing ability. There was no question that the Mig could reach a higher altitude than the F-86, but our pilots came home time and again with complaints about the performance of the Sabre. Sometimes the complaints were valid, but most of the time they were based on emotion and not on scientific fact. Our press got wind of our pilots' opinions, and the story was played up in American newspapers just when we most needed a boost in national morale.

There were two very large airfields in Manchuria from which the majority of Mig-15s operated: Antung, just across the Yalu

River from the North Korean city of Sinuiju, and Ta-Tung-Kao, about 15 miles west of Antung on the mouth of the Yalu. There was a third base, about 30 miles north of the Sui-Ho reservoir, called Fen-Chen, and several large bases near Vladivostok in Russia in a complex called An-Shan. There were many more bases near the large Manchurian manufacturing city of Mukden, about 200 miles north of the Korean border, and several more on the Shantung Peninsula. It was estimated that the enemy had well over 1,500 Mig-15s at his disposal at any given moment, while we had a total of 125 F-86s.

It was common knowledge that all of North Korea and most of Manchuria was covered by enemy radar stations. The Russians had captured some excellent equipment from the Germans during World War II, reproduced it and equipped all of their air defense units with improved versions. Our photographic reconnaissance aircraft had taken pictures of all of North Korea, enabling the intelligence people to come up with rather accurate descriptions of these installations. When United Nations aircraft ventured north of the battle lines we were sure they were picked up immediately by radar and plotted forward to a control center at Antung in Manchuria. It was almost impossible to achieve the element of surprise.

Most of our F-86 flights followed the same pattern. All aircraft on a combat mission would taxi out to the runway in pairs to line up two by two on the take-off end. The formation leader would give the engine run-up signal, and all pilots would advance the throttles to 100-percent power for an emergency fuel check, thus consuming a lot of fuel even before take-off. The formation leader would then signal his wing man, and the two would start off down the runway. Thirty seconds later the Three and Four men would start, followed in thirty seconds by Five and Six and so on. As soon as the entire formation was airborne the leader would throttle back to allow all others to join up with him. Then he would set course for the Yalu at a power setting substantially below that required for best fuel consumption. It is characteristic of jet aircraft that they climb

38

best, use less fuel in reaching altitude, and reach cruising altitude more rapidly at full power. The 51st Wing seemed to be using fuel needlessly, and thus our planes were unable to stay in the combat zone for sufficiently long periods of time.

While I was going through my indoctrination period I heard many other things I felt were wrong too. All formations flew to the combat zone in what was called Show Formation. Individual aircraft flew within 3 or 4 feet of each other, while flights of 4 aircraft each flew within 50 or 75 feet of each other under the theory that flying close formation required less fuel consumption because less trottle movement was required. Upon arrival in the combat zone the leader would signal to spread out into tactical formation, and all units would open up until there were several hundred feet between each aircraft. In my view, if the Communists actually had the radar equipment we gave them credit for having, a large gaggle of fighter aircraft would be the easiest thing in the world to spot and track. Since large formations were completely unmaneuverable, it would be easy to assemble an attacking force on the sanctuary side of the Yalu, then at the proper moment send the formation leader on a heading which would take him directly into the force of F-86s. To further complicate matters, our formation leaders were climbing their aircraft so slowly that all the F-86s arrived at combat altitude at an indicated air speed just above stalling. When all aircraft leveled off at cruising altitude they would pick up speed, but never enough to attain the high performance of which the F-86 was capable. Naturally, when the really large formations of Mig-15s, which had assembled and climbed to a superior altitude in the sanctuary, crossed over the Yalu to intercept the F-86s, they looked fast because our boys were on the verge of falling out of the sky.

At this time the 51st Wing was flying two combat missions daily, usually one in the morning and one in the afternoon. The light-bomber and fighter-bomber units flew at the same time, attacking various targets above the front lines. It was normal procedure for the F-86s of the 4th and 51st Wings to fly directly to the Manchurian border to set up a patrol pattern up and down the Yalu.

When I completed training my name finally appeared on the schedule to fly combat as wing man for Gabby. This was a challenge in a couple of ways: Gab liked to have the best young pilots flying his wing, and it meant we would really be forced to perform to show the young pilots that these two old duffer full colonels could fly with the best of them.

On my first mission the group took off as usual to fly north to the Yalu. We had been briefed to maintain radio silence, so that we might possibly take the enemy by surprise. However, we had been climbing for only about ten minutes when we heard a broadcast from Dentist which said: "Bandit flight Number One now in the Antung area." (Since the early days of World War II enemy aircraft have always been referred to as Bandits.) This broadcast from our radar site obviously meant that the enemy had taken off in Manchuria and was climbing to altitude, gaining speed to do battle with us. I once heard it said that every man has his clutching point, and hearing a call like this on the radio hardly helped to put mine further away. As we flew farther and farther into North Korea we heard repeated calls from Dentist until we knew that at least 8 bandit flights were airborne. Since we knew from experience that the Communists usually flew in flights of about 16 aircraft each, we were reasonably certain of encountering at least 128 Mig-15s with our little formation of 24 F-86s. Soon we were too far to the north to hear the communications from Dentist, and now Dentist Charlie, on Cho-Do Island, began feeding information. "Bandit Flight Number One now on a heading to Race Track," "Bandit Flight Number Two at Angels thirty-five over Antung." (Angels was the code name for altitude in thousands of feet.) "Bandit Flight Number Three over the Mizu." Information on the enemy came pouring in to us in our cockpits as we approached the combat zone. Then Dentist Charlie called that a flight of bandits was on a heading which would take them directly into our flight path as we approached the Yalu. Sure enough, we met them head-on just a few minutes later.

At long last I had my chance to come to grips with the Communists in this brand-new jet-propelled war. Although my fears had been increasing every moment on the way north, especially in view of the increasing number of enemy aircraft rising to meet us, now was the time to calm down and get into action.

I was able to get a good, solid look at the Migs as they whistled through our formation. The big red stars on their sides loomed larger than minor suns. Once past us we could see them turning around to gain position, and I suddenly realized that this was it all over again—combat in its purest form.

Gabby and I found ourselves in a big fight immediately. We began to turn and twist to avoid some of the enemy and to gain an advantageous position. Both of us were shot at from behind, but fortunately the Mig pilots appeared to have more *esprit de corps* than ability, and each time we were able to avoid being hit. There was plenty of chatter on the radio from others who were fighting: "Watch it, Blue Leader, you've got one on your tail," or "Nice shooting, Red Three, you nicked him." Each time that it seemed we were clear of the enemy, more dropped down from above. After more than thirty such fruitless minutes we at last reached so low a fuel state that we had to head for home. As we turned south I noticed a Mig several thousand feet below us and to my right, and I asked Gabby for permission to attack. He agreed, saying he would cover me, and I promptly dove down behind the Mig, opening fire from long range with my six machine guns. I could see no apparent results. With full throttle I closed in, still firing while reducing range. All of a sudden the light in my gun sight went out and I found myself without an aiming device. In desperation I kept blazing away, blindly hoping that one stray bullet might hit the Mig. Then Gabby came on the radio to warn me that other enemy aircraft were closing in and that I had better break off and head out of the combat zone. I still didn't see any damage to the Mig. Just then I heard someone on the radio say: "Look at 'em go!" I turned back to look toward the airfield at Antung just in time

41

to see three long trails of black smoke falling through the sky. All three of the Migs hit the ground and exploded within a radius of five miles from the enemy-held airfield. At least some of the guys had scored, even if I had missed mine. Gabby and I finally cleared the combat area and made an uneventful trip home.

As usual, practically the whole base was lined up on the side of the runway, waiting for us to land. Some of the guys had heard us jabbering in the air after the fight, and the first few aircraft had landed with black smoke from the guns all over their noses. Smoke from heavy 50-caliber ammunition will always blow back over the fuselage and wings and leave a distinguishing black mark that can be seen from quite a distance. Each time a ship returns to the flight line with this black marking the mechanics swarm to the spot. It is a rewarding experience for these men if their efforts culminate in some form of success, especially rewarding if the aircraft they have been servicing is known to be a hitter. The crew chief takes special pride if his baby brings home the bacon. By the same token, crew chiefs seem to revere the pilots who are flying their aircraft and baby them every chance they get, carrying their parachutes, strapping them into the cockpits, helping them climb out of the cockpits at the end of every mission, and in general treating them like local heroes on the college football team. When the crew chief climbs up the side of the aircraft to ask "Did you get one?" it is especially nice to be able to say Yes. When you do you can always bet that while you are celebrating the victory in the officers' club that night someone will be celebrating the same victory in the enlisted men's club.

This time when Gabby and I landed, my crew chief, who had noticed the black gun smoke all over the side of my ship, crawled up to ask me how many I had shot down. I hated like the devil to say that I had only fired but missed, and especially hated the look of disappointment on his face. But when I finally reached the personal equipment shack, to put my flying gear away, many of the other pilots who had returned before I did came up to pound me on the back in congratulation. I couldn't tell what for until Captain Jim Utterback, the operations officer of the 25th Squadron, came up to relate what he had seen. When I had called to Gabby about going after the Mig, Jim had been in a position to watch me go down to the attack and open fire. He had seen me break off combat and head south, and in fact he had figured he could get in a shot at the Mig himself. Just as he had worked his way into position the Mig had burst into flame and dived into the ground just south of the Antung airstrip. I was completely flabbergasted. To this day I think that Mig developed engine trouble and fell apart on its own, yet when the official orders arrived, recognizing the destruction of an enemy aircraft, I have to admit I didn't send them back.

After my first few missions Gabby and I set up a sort of *modus operandi* in an effort to solve our combat problems and increase our effectiveness. Each night we would review the combat events for the day with our key people, and then get down to the serious business of working out new tactics and techniques. Colonel George Jones, the group commander, had experienced a little combat during the days of World War II, but not really enough to satisfy him. Now he was so eager to get his hands on the enemy that he could hardly stand to rest between missions, and he was a nightly visitor. Wing Commander Robert Baldwin of the Royal Air Force, an extremely successful fighter pilot in England during the Battle of Britain, had been sent to Korea to gain combat experience, and became a permanent member of our discussion group because of his notoriety as a tactician. Lieutenant Colonel Ben Long, who had been my classmate in flying school, was usually on hand along with Bill Whisner, Van Chandler, Bill Schaeffer and a host of others. Any pilot who had destroyed an enemy aircraft during the day would be invited so that we could pool his knowledge with ours.

Looking back on those days I now realize that we had an entirely different attitude about this war than about World War II. As a country in 1941, we had been able to develop a real sense of hatred for the enemy. The much-publicized atrocities served to fan the flame of hatred, a hatred already intense because most of us felt that the Germans and Japanese had started it. I know I felt World War II personally, considered both the Germans and the Japanese mortal enemies who needed to be taught a lesson. When I fought against them on a combat mission my heart was really in it and I couldn't do enough damage to them. In 1943 I meant business.

Somehow Korea was different. It wasn't a question of knowing or not knowing what we were fighting for—all of our pilots had a pretty good idea. It was rather that, in view of the many restrictions placed on our combat activities, we felt that our nation wasn't really serious about winning. I couldn't get too steamed up over risking my life to contain Communism; Communism ought to be defeated instead of just contained. Nor do I think any of us knew enough about the North Koreans or the Chinese Communists to develop a killer instinct toward them. Thus many of us old-timers on the group and wing level and higher were apt to be somewhat cynical about the Korean War.

Two factors motivated us to succeed: *esprit de corps* and personal challenge. Most of us looked at the war as professional soldiers. We had been given a job to do and it was up to us to do the best we could with the tools at hand. Any results achieved by the United Nations forces from now until the end of the war could never be classed a victory because, under the ground rules which had been established, victory was impossible. We, as officers and pilots, could only benefit by doing a thorough professional job in order to be recognized in later years when it came time for promotion cycles again. This mean that there would be competition and plenty of it, but not competition between the enemy and the friendly forces. The commander whose unit flew more missions, dropped more bombs, destroyed more enemy aircraft, and had fewer losses, would be the man who gained the most from the war.

We approached our discussions and critiques like an All-American football team about to play the Rose Bowl. We wanted to find out all we could about the enemy team, what his best plays were, what his coach thought, and who were his best

44

players. We wanted to devise plays of our own to keep him on the defensive and off balance. We began to plan end runs around mountains in North Korea, hoping the enemy radar might have trouble picking us up. We ran missions far out into the Yellow Sea, making feints in all directions before our penetration runs into the combat zone. We sent some flights high and others low. And eventually we began to see signs of success.

Usually we took our fight to the enemy about 200 miles away from our bases. Thus we were always short of fuel, and we devised a method of knowing the fuel state of each pilot in the formation. The code word Bingo was used to signify that a pilot had reached a fuel level of 1,800 pounds, or just enough fuel to return safely to home base. After we had used this signal many times the enemy caught on and would wait until our first man called "Bingo" to send his fighters up, hoping to catch us when we were so low on fuel that we couldn't fight. Of course we slipped a few over on him by having some of our men call "Bingo" long before any of us were low on fuel. The Communists fell for this frequently enough to make it worth while, and we probably destroyed ten Migs with this gimmick.

Our planning group continually tried to figure out ways to solve the fuel problem. We decided to eliminate the engine run-up and emergency fuel check on the end of the runway prior to take-off. At first the pilots objected, considering it to be an unsafe practice contrary to the F-86 handbook of operating instructions. We pointed out that the check was all right for stateside practice, but that we could gain thirty gallons of fuel per aircraft at the start of each mission by doing it the new way. To my knowledge, no accident was ever caused because a pilot did not check his emergency fuel system.

We next decided that it was foolish to take off and circle over the field while all aircraft joined formation, because too much fuel was used prior to setting course for the combat zone. Accordingly we began to take off on a direct course, with no turning. After take-off the formation leader would slow down slightly until all others joined formation, then increase at best climbing speed to his desired altitude. Again many more gallons

45

of fuel were saved. Combat altitude was reached at a speed of over .8 mach number or higher, so that we would not be caught like sitting ducks when the Migs came barreling across the Yalu. The higher mach number enabled us to reach higher altitudes, and the higher the altitude the less fuel we consumed. Previously, combat with the enemy had been taking place at between 30,000 and 35,000 feet, but now we began to drive them higher and higher until most of the battles were being fought well above 40,000 feet. We also decided to make running take-offs instead of lining all aircraft up on the end of the runway and taking off two at a time. In the new manner we would taxi out of the parking area two at a time, down the perimeter strip to the end of the runway, around the horn and into the air. No more waiting, no delay and big savings in fuel.

During World War II our fighter forces had developed tactics involving large formations, and in peacetime operations prior to the Korean War it had become traditional to fly in the same large formations which had been so successful in the past. But now any substantial group of aircraft presented a perfect target for enemy radar, and after debating the topic for weeks I suggested that we take off for the combat zone in four ship flights with a 5-minute interval between flights. In this manner there would be an interval of 30 minutes between the time the first flight took off and the last flight released brakes, and in all probability the first flight would be in the combat zone before the last flight started out for the end of the runway. In this way we had friendly aircraft in the vicinity of the enemy airfields for a longer period of time, even though our forces were possibly weak at the beginning and end of a mission. If it appeared that the enemy was putting large numbers of his aircraft into the air to meet the early penetrators, we could always accelerate the take-off interval; conversely, if he started to put large numbers up just as our flights of four started home, we could always recall the whole force. Furthermore, a continuous stream of four ship flights heading into his area would give his radar operators fits.

All of these ideas worked for us and we began to catch the

46

enemy by surprise. The fighter director in Manchuria started having difficulty massing his forces advantageously to direct them into an attack on our F-86s. Of the original group of officers sent together for ninety-days duty in Korea, three of us—Bill Schaeffer, Van Chandler and I—were racing each other to see who would shoot down the most Migs before we had to return to the States. We were even-up at two Migs each. I nearly had a heart attack the day Bill came home with his second victory. He and his wing man had been cruising quietly along at altitude over the North Korean capital city of Pyongyang when they were attacked from above by two enemy aircraft. As soon as the Migs were in close enough Bill called for his wing man to "Break Right." A break in either direction is merely a turn a pilot makes as sharply as he can, usually in the direction of the attack, which he hopes will cause the enemy pilot to miss when he fires. As both Bill and his wing man broke into the attack the Mig leader and his wing man pulled into a tight turn to gain firing position on the two Sabres. When the Migs pulled in tight to increase their rate of turn, both aircraft stalled in flight and snapped over into uncontrollable spins. The two enemy pilots bailed out immediately. Bill recovered and flew back to take pictures of them descending in parachutes. When the combat film was developed Bill was given credit for the destruction of one Mig, and his wing man for the other.

I was having my share of luck in combat too. Gabby had finally decided to let me lead elements on my own, giving me a degree of latitude I hadn't had before. About the second time out I managed to jump a Mig at about 43,000 feet. The enemy pilot saw me coming and began to take violent, evasive action. Together we engaged in a regular Donnybrook which lasted some fifteen minutes. Although our dogfight started at high altitude, we chased each other around and around until we finally ended up about 100 feet above the ground. I found it easy to stay on the Mig's tail, although I could only get in a few shots because I couldn't pull in tight enough to hit him. As soon as the enemy pilot found he could go no lower without interfering with the ground he began to climb, and in our huge climbing and diving turns I found I could pull out more quickly and could close in on him every time he tried to gain altitude. By this time I was beginning to blow a few chips out of him with my machine guns, and when he had worked the fight up to about 25,000 feet I got him good. When I hit him with full force I was right behind in the jet wash of his engine and I could feel the burbled, rough air which was coming from his jet exhaust stop immediately. Naturally when his engine quit his jet stopped flying right there at 25,000 feet. I was going so fast that I overran him and passed about 20 feet from his right wing. His beautiful Mig was a shambles with pieces torn out all over the wings and fuselage. The aircraft was streaming fuel, oil and fire, and as I looked into the cockpit I could see the pilot slumped over against the instrument panel. I watched the Mig roll over into a dive, pull up once, roll over into a dive again and finally plunge into the ground. Now I knew I could lick the Migs if I could only catch them.

One night, after a particularly strenuous mission during which Gabby and I had both been shot at several times, we finished our critique early and went to bed. It had been weeks since we'd had a good night's rest; we were pooped and we both knew it. I had just fallen asleep soundly when the phone rang. Since I was nearest to it, I answered and found myself talking to the base switchboard operator. He said he had a call for either Colonel Gabreski or Colonel Mahurin and would we please stand by for a minute for the call to come through. I could hear Gabby moving around in bed in the next room, but I figured that he might just as well sleep. I'd take the call. All of a sudden a voice I recognized came on the wire: "Hey, Bud, we're having a party; you want to talk to the girls?" Throughout the years, I have been victimized by practical-joke telephone calls, but I just couldn't believe this one. It came from George Welch, who with Bill Wahl had just arrived in Japan and registered at the Imperial Hotel in Tokyo. One second later I found myself talking to a Pan American Airlines hostess who had put up with those two characters all the way across the Pacific. This gal

48

must have had the patience of Job, but here she was on the other end of the wire, wondering how things were in Korea.

It turned out that Bill and George had invited the whole Pan American stratocruiser crew to the hotel for a drink, and they couldn't resist calling us to give us a ribbing. They had convinced the command duty officer at Headquarters, Far Eastern Air Force that they were General George Welsh and General William Wahl and that it was imperative they talk to either Gabby or me immediately. The poor guy had worked out a call from Tokyo on the Island of Honshu to an airstrip in Kyushu called Tsuiki, to Pusan in Korea, to Seoul, Headquarters Fifth Air Force, to K-13 and finally to us. All of this just so we could talk to the girls. I could have killed both of them gladly for ruining a night's sleep, but all I did was yell over to the next room, "Gabby, this call is for you."

After I had flown about thirty missions a tragic thing happened—one I had been dreading for years. I had always taken great pride in the fact that I had never had a wing man shot down or injured while flying with me. It meant a lot to me. I had known many air leaders who flew with utter disregard for anyone flying in the same formation, people who were out to establish reputations and to hell with anyone who got in the way. The duty of a wing man is rather simple: he has to fly in close proximity to his leader, always keeping alert for the possibility of enemy attack from behind. He must try to keep watch both in front and behind so that his leader can concentrate on spotting a target ahead and getting into position to shoot it down. The leader must not have his attention diverted. The role of the wing man is a difficult one, since he does not get credit for victories that his leaders score. He takes solace in the fact that one day he will be a leader. I have always felt that I would rather not shoot down a single enemy aircraft than have some of my own people hurt, and I always took great care not to expose anyone in my formation to unnecessary risk.

By now I had finally made the grade with Colonel Jones, the group commander, and he had allowed me to lead the entire

25th Squadron into combat several times. This particular day we had completed our patrol along the Yalu and were on our way out of North Korea. Just as we passed over the city of Pyongyang we were attacked by over fifty enemy aircraft. All of the pilots in my flight of four F-86s were experienced, but it was going to be difficult to cope with a situation like this. My wing man, Lieutenant Jordan, had flown on several missions with me, and so had the element leader Captain Vernon Wright. Prior to the mission, I had briefed Vernon to the effect that should we become separated during a fight I would expect him to tell me that he could no longer see me, and after that make any attacks on his own as he saw fit. It was pointless, I said, to waste time attempting a rendezvous. In this fight, almost as soon as we had been attacked, Vernon called to let me know that he no longer had me in sight, so I told him to go on his way and shoot down what he could.

Both my wing man and I had been breaking left and right under attack for several minutes. We were unable to get into position to attack the Migs, but I was confident they would be similarly unable to get in a good firing shot at us. We had just staved off one attack which put us into a climbing left turn at about 20,000 feet when I looked back to see my wing man about 500 below, turning inside me to catch up. At the same time I could see a single enemy fighter approaching on a 90° angle to my wing man's line of flight. The odds of making a successful shot from a 90° angle are a thousand to one, because the deflection is so great, but I called Lieutenant Jordan to alert him to the Mig. "Watch it," I said. "There's a Mig coming in at a ninety-degree angle to your left. He can't possibly hit you." With that Jordan pressed his microphone button and shouted, "I've been hit, I've been hit!"

I immediately throttled back and dropped down to join in formation with him. In the meantime he had turned to a southwest heading and appeared to be on his way back to our home base. After his first broadcast he had failed to release the microphone button, and his labored breathing was being broadcast out into the air, overriding all other radio transmissions in the vicinity. As soon as he saw me flying alongside he said in a voice filled with deep concern, "Am I on fire? I've been hit personally." All of this accompanied by deep, labored breathing. I tried to indicate that all was well and that he should release the mike button, but I just couldn't get through to him. From all I could tell, his ship had been hit forward of the instrument panel, because I could see a small hole in that area. He had also been hit in the cockpit canopy, just aft of the armor plate behind the seat, and most of the canopy was gone, leaving him exposed to a rush of cold air. Otherwise he seemed to be intact, and since we had already cleared the combat zone, I thought he had a good chance of getting home.

I still couldn't get through to him to give him this information because of that damned depressed mike button. His breathing came faster and faster as he called once again with panic in his voice, "Tell me, am I on fire? Am I on fire?" By this time the only signal I could think of which might indicate to him that he was okay was the old Royal Air Force signal of the clenched fist with the thumb up. All over the world this indicated Keep Up the Old Fight. When I made this gesture I saw him look down inside the cockpit and then straighten back with his head against the headrest. The canopy, or rather what was left of it, shot off, and seconds later Jordan ejected from his cockpit. The ejection was successful, his parachute opened immediately, and he began to drift to the earth. I followed him down while making contact with the emergency rescue service, giving them a rough idea of our location. Within minutes Navy search aircraft were on the way to the scene. When Jordan passed through 10,000 feet on his way down I had to leave or run out of fuel. As soon as I had landed at K-13 I jumped in another F-86 in order to fly back to the scene. Together with the Navy aircraft, I searched the area for about an hour and a half, attempting to find my wing man, but I never saw him again. All of us were fired upon several times by antiaircraft guns until darkness fell and we were forced to call off the search and return to home base.

After the war I found out what had happened. One of the

shells from the attacking Mig had hit, just as I suspected, forward of the instrument panel. This shot had burst inside the cockpit, and shrapnel had hit Jordan in the legs. He didn't have any idea that he was pressing down on the mike button, but at the same time he was in a panic because he thought that his aircraft actually was on fire. When he saw me give the Thumbs-Up signal he thought I meant bail out. Bail out he did. His wounds were slight. He evaded capture for two days, and finally, suffering from cold and exposure, turned himself over to the Communists.*

While all this was happening Vernon Wright was in trouble. After he became separated from us he found himself in his own individual fight. He saw a Mig directly in front of him headed his way and decided to make a head-on pass. Evidently the Mig pilot planned the same tactic, for Vernon received a 37 mm. cannon shell smack in the nose of the F-86. His wing man reported later that the whole nose of the F-86 was encased in a ball of fire. Vernon immediately ejected, making it to the ground safely in his parachute.**

I found out about Vernon when I returned to base after my futile attempt to find Jordan. I was crushed because I hated to establish myself as a guy who had no concern for others in his flight, yet I couldn't bring either Jordan or Wright back now, no matter what I did. The war went on, and I went on with it.

---

* This story has a happy ending. Jordan came out of prison camp at the end of the war, alive and well.

** He, too, was released after the war. The last I heard he was flying the F-100 Super Sabre, sadder but wiser for his experience, I am sure.

4.

Associated Press, MONDAY MORNING, JANUARY 7, 1952 . . . Col. Walker M. Mahurin together with four other Fifth Air Force Sabrejet pilots were credited yesterday with blasting five Russian-built jets out of the skies and damaging ten others in four spectacular dogfights. The U. S. Sabrejets were said to be outnumbered two to one in the second day of furious air combat.

Altogether seventy-nine U. S. jets were opposed Sunday by one hundred ninety-six Migs. In one of the battles Sabres of the U.S. 51st Wing were outnumbered twenty-one to one hundred, but caught the Reds before the enemy planes could drop their cumbersome wing tanks.

The Fifth Air Force communiqué described the Red pilots Sunday as "very aggressive." Other pilots credited with shooting down the five Migs in two morning and afternoon engagements were: Maj. William T. Whisner, Shreveport, La., who now has three destroyed and four damaged; Maj. Van E. Chandler, Waxahachie, Tex., Capt. John M. Heard, Indianapolis, Ind., and Lt. Donald E. Little, Battle Creek, Michigan.

OUR new tactics were beginning to pay off in a big way, enough so that we could forsee even greater results in the future. We even began to be visited by dignitaries.

Many of them simply wanted to meet some of our new jet aces, but others were interested in knowing what tactics we were using, since we were claiming more victories than Colonel Harry Thyng's 4th Fighter Wing. Our tactics were closely held secrets. There was a constant influx of Indian-level pilots from the 4th, who tried to smoke out tactics from our junior pilots, but we were seldom visited by the 4th's chiefs. Brigadier General Jim Ferguson, Vice Commander of the 5th Air Force and

Colonel Gilbert Meyers, Deputy Chief of Staff for Operations, were among the first to arrive. They were visiting us, they claimed, to get away from the routine paper shuffling at headquarters, but when they started to ask probing questions it became evident they had come specifically to find out what we were doing. Now that our tactics were paying off in terms of enemy destroyed, they wanted to make the 4th Wing change over to our way of doing business.

Since my first day in the Air Force there has always been fierce competition between fighter units. During World War II the competition revolved around destroying the most enemy aircraft. During peacetime the competition involved the best accident rate, the most number of sorties flown, the best aerial gunnery scores, and so forth. Fighting the enemy with all we've got goes without saying. No one has to be told to do that. As far as helping the guy commanding some other wing to shoot down more enemy aircraft, the general attitude seems to be to let him think up his own ideas. If he wants to ask, we'll tell him, but we won't volunteer. If he thinks up a good idea and we find out about it, we'll use it if it will help us. This is the situation that existed in Korea and it explains why we weren't anxious to tell the 4th Fighter Wing what we were doing to improve our scoring ability.

In our enthusiasm to compete with the 4th, as well as to achieve satisfactory combat results, we found that our pilots were taking extremely hazardous risks. Whenever there was a chance of Migs taking off about the time we should be leaving the combat zone with minimum fuel, pilots would purposely forget to call out "Bingo." Thus began a rash of incidents in which pilots arriving over home base would call the control tower for emergency-landing instructions. Since all other ships in the landing pattern would be required to leave the area until the emergency case was safely on the ground, that one emergency would create a chain reaction of emergencies.

All of this led to some really hair-raising episodes during the landing phases of every mission. Although we always had adequate air-traffic control, the problem of recovering 20 to 30 high-speed fighters quickly wasn't an easy one. With an emergency or two thrown in, the landing problem became acute. Many times, several aircraft would be landing down the runway to the north and a few would be on the ground, slowing down, when a ship in emergency would ask for a straight-in approach to the south. The control tower would usually direct the emergency aircraft to enter the traffic pattern, but the pilot would reply: "I don't have enough fuel, I must make a straight-in approach." He would then land, hoping all aircraft on the runway would be on one side, leaving the other open to him. He would pass the others head-on at closing speeds of over 200 miles per hour with inches separating them. I never saw anyone hit, but it was a frightening experience each time. Often our pilots would touch ground safely only to run out of fuel before they could taxi off the active runway, and this would really jam us up because those remaining in the air could not land until the runway had been cleared.

There was one tragedy which was beyond anyone's control. A big battle had raged up and down the Yalu, and as usual, many of the pilots were returning extremely low on fuel. I was flying in a formation of twelve aircraft which landed uneventfully, and we were all taxiing back along the perimeter strip at the edge of the active runway in the opposite direction to landing traffic. Suddenly we noticed an F-86 on the final approach, about to land with his landing gear retracted.

The control tower immediately called: "Aircraft on final, pick it up and go around. You have no landing gear." At the same time the runway control officer stationed at the initial and of the active runway shot two red flares into the air to signal an unsafe landing gear condition. Then the pilot came on the radio with panic in his voice saying: "This is Maple Robin Four. Request closed pattern. I am showing zero fuel." Obviously he wanted to make a quick 360° turn, lower his landing gear and land without breaking out of the pattern and re-entering.

By this time every eye on the base was riveted to this ship. As the pilot flew downwind at about 1,000 feet we all saw the trail of black smoke stop abruptly, just before the pilot broadcasted: "I am flamed out." He tried desperately to make the final 180° turn to line up with the runway, but about 50 feet off the ground he stalled out and fell short. The wreckage was headed directly toward those of us who were taxiing back, and I distinctly remember yelling, "This is Mahurin. All you guys behind me pull off to the left immediately. The wreckage is coming at us." I especially remember someone else calling out on the radio, just before the F-86 hit the ground: "He's not going to make it."

When the aircraft hit in a slight bank the fuselage broke away from the wing section and rolled over and over along the ground. The first time it rolled on its back the entire top of the fuselage, including the top of the pilot's head, was sanded off by the rough ground. I helped pick up what was left of him, and it set me back for days.

Although there was no question that 5th Air Force was carrying the battle to the enemy, he tried to punch back once in awhile too. Occasionally we suffered from bombing attacks, North Korean style. There were foxholes all over K-13, but with the temperature ranging between 20° and 30° below zero it took more guts than I had to jump out of a nice warm bed into a wet, cold foxhole. The Communists were practicing a sneaky trick. They had stationed a few rickety, old two-seater biplanes called PO-2s in North Korea. These were made of wood and cloth, had a cruising speed of about 70 miles per hour and practically no radar reflective surface. They always flew at night, arriving at our air bases very low to the ground. The air alert usually began with sirens screaming all over the base, at which time we were supposed to leap out of bed and cower in a foxhole. Shortly after the sirens sounded we'd hear the *put-put-put* of the PO-2s bumbling along on their mission of death and destruction. When these enemy jokers flew over anything they thought was a target the lad in the back seat would grab a 50-pound bomb and heave it over the side. This kind of warfare could set aviation back fifty years. Once in awhile they'd manage

56

to hit something that would either go *Boom* or burn a bit, but usually they'd miss anything important by a mile.

It was absolutely no strain to outsmart them. Armed with a couple of bottles of booze, we managed to con several GI Army bulldozer drivers into helping us. They leveled off a long, rectangular patch of ground about half a mile away. When finished, it resembled our runway in size and shape. The next time one of the boys brought home a damaged F-86 we parked it on our new strip. From then on we kept putting old hulks all over the strip until we had a big junkyard of aircraft. When we were ready we would wait till the old PO-2s came over and then show a glimmer of light on several of our junkers, to make it look as if we were working at night to fix them. The Billy Mitchells of Pyongyang wasted more bombs trying to knock out 5th Air Force on our fake field. Someone had to spoil the fun, though. One smart aleck got the idea that we should surround our field with antiaircraft guns and nab a few PO-2s. After the first time the guns let go at them the enemy aircraft never came back.

The Communists used to make a big play in their papers and radio broadcasts about their very large air raids over South Korea. They reported that hundreds of bombers dropped tons of bombs on United Nations airfields every night. They even began to brag that the leading bomber pilot was a woman—I never did get her name. We all figured they had to have something to brag about, but we were equally certain that none of their expensive equipment ever came far enough south to do any damage.

Not only did the rank of our visitors improve, but also the caliber. Shortly after Christmas we had one to top them all: Cardinal Francis Spellman. We received notification that he intended to visit us the same day that he arrived, and there was little chance to lay on any special treatment. We met the Cardinal in front of our little chapel where he planned to be available to those officers and men who wished to talk to him. Gabby prevailed on him to say a special mass, and we sent out word all over the base. Prior to arriving at K-13, Cardinal Spellman had been visiting other bases, and we were sure that he was hungry, but he was willing to abstain until after mass. The mass was attended by several thousand men, and afterward we invited the Cardinal to have lunch in the officers' mess.

During lunch Gabby sat on one side of our guest and I on the other. We were both surprised that a man of his calling would know so much about the Air Force and about the activities of the F-86s in Korea. He possessed a warm and friendly personality which, coupled with an extremely intelligent mind, made him easy to talk with. After about five minutes we felt that we had known him for years and that he was an old friend.

After lunch the Cardinal did an amazing thing. We had arranged for a staff car to tour the base so that our airmen could see him in person. Everywhere we went he insisted that we stop to allow people to meet him face to face. He carried a sheaf of little forms on which he asked the men to fill in name, rank, unit and home address. By the time we finished the tour he must have collected thousands of these forms. The Cardinal used them to write to the families of everyone he had met in Korea. In his letters to families he would explain that he had met Sergeant So-and-So at K-13 and that the sergeant was alive and well. He would then add an item or two of local interest and close by wishing the family well. This was a tremendous gesture of good will and something unforgettable to me and to anyone else who received his thoughtful notes. This man has my vote.

There were still a few problems to iron out before we could consider ourselves an effective combat team, and one of them had become increasingly apparent. We were receiving a steadily building flow of information about enemy aircraft from both Dentist and Dentist Charlie, but much of it seemed to be in error. Although the broadcasts were usually accurate on the number of bandit flights rising to intercept us on each mission, they seemed to be inaccurate as to the enemy's position. If we heard from Dentist Charlie that Bandit Flight Number One was on a heading to Race Track, we immediately headed for that area. We seldom made an intercept. If we heard that they were circling Big City (Pyongyang), we made a determined effort to get there to attack, but seldom found them where our radar said they would be. Besides being a puzzle it was bad on the pilots' morale. In the bar at the officers' club after missions more and more adverse comment was heard about our radar capability. Most of the pilots felt it was no damn good. Many of them were so convinced that the information was always wrong that they refused to take any action on it.

Fifth Air Force had an important radar site just above K-14 which we thought was getting information on the enemy from all over North Korea. I knew quite a bit about our radar in the United States and was sure that our equipment was good enough to give us what we wanted in Korea. Still, something was wrong—it wasn't nearly as good as it should be. George Jones and I decided to visit the site for our own edification.

In war each side tries to monitor the radio communications of the other. During World War II we had what we called Y Service. Our side monitored all communications between the fighter aircraft of the *Luftwaffe* and the controllers on the ground as long as they were made within radio range. The Germans did the same to us. Y Service was extremely valuable to us because it plotted all the actions of enemy fighters: where they took off, what they did in the air, and above all the numbers of aircraft involved in any one action. This was primarily why radio silence was mandatory for friendly fighters not in actual combat.

Most of the time Y Service was a serious thing, but once in awhile it developed a humorous twist. In the Mediterranean area during World War II the Germans were staging their fighter aircraft out of a complex of airfields in the Foggia area near Rome. When our heavy bomber formations headed for targets in Italy the Germans put up a tremendous fighter blockade and in one such group—reputedly Herman Goering's pride and joy, whose pilots were noted throughout the war for their daring—there was a pilot named Mueller. When Mueller's group took off to make intercept, his flight leader, trying to maintain his equanimity under the most trying conditions, would manage to keep radio silence for a brief while. Then suddenly our Y Service would hear: "Mueller, get back into formation." A moment later the leader would say: "Mueller, you're too damn close. Move back out." Mueller would then start to talk: "Red One, this is Mueller. Do you hear me?" This running diatribe continued until Mueller's flight leader was in a screaming fit, shouting: "Damn you, Mueller. Stay off the air." It was perfect for us. Every time either Mueller or his flight leader opened his mouth we got a perfect fix on their positions and were able to vector our fighters so as to make perfect intercepts on the attacking fighters. The Germans never appeared to catch on. Standing orders were issued to our pilots to avoid shooting down any straggler behind German formations, because almost certainly it would be Mueller, and we needed his help. He lasted for several months, until one day there was an especially vicious air battle. Mueller must have snuggled close to his leader and looked to be a normal German wing man, because he was shot down. There were no cheers in the Air Force that night; the Mighty Mueller had struck out.

When George and I got to the control center at the radar site we made some fascinating discoveries, confirming our worst suspicions. Fifth Air Force was indeed operating a Y Service in Korea. This was good to know. The shocking aspect was that all of the enemy air-to-air and air-to-ground radio transmissions were in Russian. There was no doubt about it, we were fighting the Russian Air Force and in all probability pilots from all of the satellite nations. Instead of fighting Chinese and North Koreans, we were battling with Russians, Czechs, Poles, Rumanians, East Germans and all the rest. The Orientals were flying in very limited numbers. It was a startling revelation, and why the United Nations did not exploit it baffles me to this day.

Thinking about it now I can easily see the reason for Russian participation. When the Communists decided to bring the Mig-15 into the war they had to get pilots and get them quickly. The Chinese Communists probably had a few qualified people,

60

but most of the experienced Chinese pilots flew for the Nationalist Government on Formosa. Our intelligence briefings had revealed that there was a flying training school operated by the Russians at Fen-Chen, near Vladivostok, specifically for the purpose of training Orientals, but even so it is impossible to develop highly trained experienced combat pilots rapidly. It takes time and a lot of it.

We learned that the Russians were assigning complete units to bases in Manchuria. Hypothetically, let us say, it was decided to move the 204th Mig Fighter Interceptor Group stationed in Moscow to combat duty in Manchuria. All personnel of this unit would be moved into the combat zone, leaving their aircraft behind. They would take over aircraft already in place in Manchuria, and as soon as a necessary training familiarization period was over the group would begin combat as a fully integrated operational combat team. Because they had all flown and worked together in Moscow, they would have no adjusting pains. The pilots knew each other and each other's idiosyncracies; the unit leader would have evaluated his men and developed tactics suitable to his aircraft and the combat situation. All this made sense, and our intelligence revealed even more information. As soon as the Russian combat leaders decided that a unit had been in combat long enough to be considered experienced, it would be withdrawn and another sent to take its place in Manchuria. Thus the Russians gave all their jet combat units the very best training under actual combat conditions.

Since I had been in Korea we had noticed definite changes of pace by the enemy, but we had never been able to understand the reasons for them. Now they were obvious. When a new unit was assigned to Manchuria it flew north of the Yalu River in the sanctuary to familiarize the pilots with local geography. Then for several days the new unit penetrated North Korea for 100 miles or more to learn the territory over which it would fly in combat. Next, for a week or so, the pilots came close to us and looked us over in the air, but avoided actual contact. Finally they began to mix it up with us for several weeks, fighting whenever the opportunity arose. We liked this phase best.

61

Following periods of hard fighting there would be no enemy action at all; the units would have returned to Russia.

The United States, on the other hand, was sending small cadres of pilots to Korea. Pilots were assigned on an individual basis or in very small groups. Each time a pilot completed the required number of missions he was sent home and his billet filled by a new replacement. We were forced to operate training schools continuously within the group to give each newcomer the proper training before he went into combat. New people were taught the expected subjects of escape and survival; in addition, we had to acquaint each one with our particular way of flying. It was a cumbersome means of keeping the proper experience level, not to mention a most inefficient utilization of qualified officers as instructors. When our pilots returned to the States they often found themselves commanded by leaders lacking in experience in the very area in which the returnees were most qualified. It appeared that the Russian plan had merit.

George Jones and I spent a whole day at the radar site while two F-86 missions involving both the 4th and 51st Wings were conducted to the north. There was a separate communications center, off to one side of the main control center, where Russian-speaking officers listened to enemy combat communications during the air battles. When the Russian controllers gave instructions to the Russian Air Force pilots our listeners relayed the information to our controllers. They in turn radioed the enemy transmissions which would help us in the battle to the controller at Dentist Charlie.

When the Russian controller at Antung in Manchuria gave his first order to the first unit of Migs scrambling to intercept the F-86s—usually with instructions to climb to altitude over the city of Antung—we were given the message: "Bandit Flight Number One now in the Antung area." When he directed his airborne fighter leader to take up a heading for a given geographical location in North Korea we were told: "Bandit Flight Number One now on a heading to Race Track." The reason we were having trouble intercepting the Migs after receiving our information was that it usually took some time for them to perform the action they had been directed to take. It might take fifteen minutes for them to reach Race Track, while we would reach it almost immediately. We couldn't find them because they hadn't arrived. What was needed was a little interpretation of the information. There was no question but that it was the gospel truth.

As George and I listened it became quite obvious that the Russian controller on the ground had absolute authority over the battle, and when he gave his fighter leader instructions there was usually no argument. Once while we were listening the fighter leader did not like the instructions he had been given and began to argue with the controller. The controller immediately ordered the argument to cease and directed the fighter leader to report to him as soon as he landed.

The Russian method of control was in direct contrast to ours. We felt that the only way one can observe an air battle is to be up there in it. Of course it is possible to watch action on a radarscope, but the scope is small and there are many targets to follow. In the air, however, it is difficult to miss anything. We relied on the wisdom of our leaders, and we recognized that each individual pilot had the ability to think for himself.

After the first mission for the day was over, George and I shot the bull with our radar people to get supporting information for what we were seeing. It seemed that many times the Russian controller would overlook a few of our flights in his anxiety to vector his fighters into one specific unit of F-86s. When he did, the Migs would concentrate on targets in front and disregard other flights of Sabres close to them. Our pilots would get into them good and really give them a beating. One fighter leader had been shot all to pieces. Our controllers said that it was funny as hell to hear the fighter leader chewing big pieces out of the controller all the way back to Antung, where he was forced to crash land his Mig.

When the afternoon mission was in the air we again listened to the action. Toward the end of the fighting several of the Migs were damaged. Each time the Mig pilot who had suffered damage would call his leader in panic to say: "This is Ivan. I've been hit. What should I do?" Each time this happened the controller asked the pilot how badly damaged his Mig was, and when the pilot had relayed this information the controller either ordered him to abandon his aircraft or attempt a landing. The controller further specified on which airstrip the landing attempt was to be made. We later suspected that the controller could vector his fighters to any strip he wished. If a specific unit suffered heavy damage and many losses the controller—by skillful handling of the remaining aircraft—could divert a few here and a few there. When the pilots got together after a mission to discuss the activities and it turned out that Petrovitch was missing along with Feodor, Vladimir and Sacha, they could only surmise that these pilots had landed at another air base. It would never be said that they had been clobbered by the Sabres; thus the Indian-level pilots were ignorant of their own loss rate. This was about the only way the Russians could keep the morale of their pilots at a respectable level, for they were losing fourteen Migs to every F-86 they shot down.

Our own controller kept actual radar contact with us and knew where we were at all times. He was always alert to the possibility of the Russian controller vectoring enemy aircraft into a formation of our fighters, and he could tell when this was about to happen by listening to the orders given the Migs and looking at us on his radarscope. Several times had had been able to save lives by judicious use of his information. While we were watching, Gabby was leading a group of F-86s patrolling up and down the Yalu. He was being picked up by our radar, and the controller was keeping close watch on him and his flight. The Russians were also keeping close tabs on Gabby. Gabby was using his call sign, Maple Leaf, at the time, and the Russian controller was giving his fighter leader different headings which appeared to bring the Migs closer to the F-86s. By this our controller was repeating to Gabby everything he heard from the Russian side. Finally the Russian fighter leader informed his controller: "I have four Sabres in sight and I am ready for the attack." The controller then ordered: "You are cleared for an immediate attack on the Sabres." Upon hearing this our own controller immediately broadcast: "Maple Leaf, break left now."

Later I talked to Gabby about this mission. He had been puzzled by this instruction, but not enough to disregard the suggestion. He and his flight immediately broke to the left and looked behind. Coming down at him from above, in perfect position for attack, were eight Migs closing at great speed. After Gabby had turned through about 90° of his break the Migs disengaged and were last seen in a dive toward the Manchurian border.

The Russians also had a problem with the Orientals. The Chinese and North Korean pilots were lacking in skill, and this lack was aggravated by their inability to speak Russian. As the Orientals gradually worked into combat it became necessary to have a separate controller to speak North Korean and Chinese. When this happened there was no common communications link between all of the enemy aircraft in the air, and the Russian controller continually advised his pilots of the location of the Mig formations flown by the Orientals. When there were changes in course and altitude in the Oriental formations the word was passed along to the Russian fighter leader so that he would be aware of these activities. The Oriental group usually consisted of small numbers of Migs, and it seemed that this group was ordered into the air only when the Sabres were on the way out of the combat zone or when we were completely outnumbered by the Migs. I guess the controllers above the Yalu wanted to keep the Orientals out of trouble if they could.

This was just another situation that worked to our advantage. When our Y Service heard the Russian controller inform his flight leaders on the activities of the Orientals the information would be passed on to us as: "Jackpot Flight Number One is now in the Antung area." This had happened a few times before George and I had visited the radar site, and on each occasion our pilots had tangled with a small unit of Migs and enjoyed a huge measure of success. In fact the first time it happened we shot down seven Migs while suffering no losses. At the time none of us knew why specific formations of Migs were called Jackpot while most were called Bandits. Now we knew. Jackpot meant just what it said.

Our controllers told us of one incident in which the Russian controller had goofed so badly that he had probably had nightmares for weeks. The main force of Migs had been down in the combat zone, fighting with us, and we had been getting lots of information from our people. This meant that the Russian controllers were giving a lot of the same to their fighter leaders. Since the fighting was heavy, everyone was rather mixed up. Finally the Migs were instructed to return to home base above the Yalu. As the main force of enemy headed north across the river a small group of Migs swung down on them from out of the sun to make a high side attack. Three Migs burst into flames and plunged into the ground well into Manchuria. Somehow in the melee the Russian controller and the Oriental controller had become confused and Jackpot had done the ultimate and clobbered himself some bandits.

At the conclusion of our visit to the radar site George and I had a long chat with the commander. He didn't mind if we used what we had learned ourselves, but objected to our giving it to the other pilots indiscriminately. He was right. This stuff was valuable to us, and we didn't want any young pilot to get shot down and spill what he knew to the enemy under duress.

Accordingly I briefed the first mission the following day as follows: "Men, we know you have all had reservations concerning the information we have been receiving from both Dentist and Dentist Charlie. I feel it necessary to point out that you must put implicit faith in any transmissions you may hear. It is impossible for me to give you the details, but it is now known that the information you receive is accurate and true. If you heed the information, it may someday save your life, if you disregard it you may never shoot down a Mig and you may even endanger your own life. If you ever receive any calls stating that a Jackpot flight is in the air, try your best to get to it. If you do, it will be like shooting fish in a rain barrel. You can all become instant heroes. This is as much as I am able to tell you. Take heed, but don't press me for further information."

Now that we had additional information from the radar site, Gabby and I changed tactics once more. From that time on we decided to operate our flights of four aircraft independently from each other. Each flight leader could choose his flight route, heading and altitude, without regard to other flights and without instructions from the group leader. We called this Flight Leaders Discretion. The only time the group leader would issue commands to a flight would be when there was a battle or when enemy aircraft were sighted. With all of our flights patrolling up, and down, and around the combat zone willy-nilly, independent of each other, it would be impossible for the Russian controller to figure out what was going on at any given time. As a result of such frustrations there were some really bona-fide Donnybrooks between the Russian controllers and the Russian fighter leaders.

With us the new system worked almost perfectly. Our flights patrolling nearest the Yalu River would usually sight the Migs first as they climbed up to altitude above Antung in the sanctuary where they couldn't be touched. The first Sabre pilot sighting the Migs was under specific instructions to call out his sightings immediately. Usually the call would say: "All Maple flights, this is Wolf Red Two. I have thirty plus Migs sighted over Antung climbing through thirty thousand feet." Later the transmission would be: "The Migs are now turning south over the *mizu* at thirty-five thousand feet on a heading to Race Track, Wolf Flight is trailing." With that, Maple Leaf would direct: "All flights turn from present positions to an intercept heading." Each flight leader would then try to set a course that would take him to the main Mig formation as quickly as possible. By the time the Migs had worked their way south of the border they would be attracting as much attention as Jayne Mansfield at a USO dance. And by the time the Migs had reached a turning point, not only would there be several flights of Sabres chasing them, but there would also be Sabres all along the return trip, waiting to attack them as they tried to sneak back into Manchuria.

5.

THE 51st Wing had finally accumulated enough aerial victories to have many men eligible for decorations, and General Frank E. Everest, the commander of 5th Air Force, agreed to present the awards. The Distinguished Flying Cross was given to all the lads who had destroyed enemy aircraft, and the Air Medal to those who had flown ten combat missions. After the awards ceremony and the cocktail party at the officers' club we adjourned to our quarters where the General had agreed to spend the night with Gabby and me. We had been looking forward to shooting the bull with him for one reason in particular.

Back in our quarters, with a drink in hand, the General began to relax, and as the evening wore on and we became more congenial and less restrained, both Gabby and I felt that it was time to bring up the subject of the sanctity of the Manchurian border.

"My orders are to keep my aircraft from violating the border," he replied to our question. "These orders are from Washington, so I am duty bound to pass them on to you. However," he continued, "I do know the Joint Chiefs of Staff have approved what they call Hot Pursuit, but I haven't received this in writing, nor has General Weyland in Far Eastern Air Force. Until such time as I get instructions to the contrary I have to insist that none of our pilots fly north of the Yalu River." He indicated that he didn't like this idea any more than we did, and thought it tactically unsound if the United Nations wanted to win the air battle. These were personal opinions, though, and he couldn't make his comments official.

Here was a revelation. Everest wasn't in favor of the restriction, any more than we were. If the JCS had agreed to Hot Pursuit, they had come up with a good idea but hadn't gone far enough to give us adequate written instructions. To us, Hot Pursuit meant that if any of our pilots got close enough to a Mig to shoot it down, it was cricket to chase that Mig, regardless of where it went, until it was either destroyed or escaped completely. To hell with the border. Both Gab and I figured that maybe the old man would wink his eye if he heard anything from that point on about border violations.

The next day, after the General departed, Gab and I had a serious discussion on the subject. The air battles were becoming more difficult, since we were increasingly outnumbered by enemy aircraft. It was only because we had a fine plane, flown by exceptionally well-trained pilots, that we were able to do our job and destroy numbers of Migs. We had suffered combat losses time and again because the enemy could lurk on his side of the border, dart over to our side, shoot at an F-86 and return to his sanctuary at will. It was a distinctly unfair advantage and it was costing lives. If we adopted a policy of Hot Pursuit without proper written authorization, we were subject to court-martial if discovered; however, we would be much better off court-martialed and alive than dead in North Korea. The risks seemed worth the gamble.

But we couldn't do it on our own. We had to bring others into our confidence and ask them to cooperate with us on a trial basis to see if Hot Pursuit would give us a break. That same afternoon we discussed the matter with Colonels George Jones and Bill Schaeffer, Majors Bill Whisner and Van Chandler and Captains Jim Utterback and John Heard. All agreed to participate in our plan of action.

In addition to the normal support mission commitment the next day, we added eight aircraft in a special formation, with the call sign of Maple Special. Gabby led with me on his wing;

the other elements were led by Jones, Whisner and Heard. While the main body of aircraft headed as scheduled directly up to the Yalu we flew far out over the Yellow Sea, well above the Manchurian border. As soon as we heard Dentist Charlie calling out: "Bandit Flight Number One now in the Antung area," we turned toward land to penetrate about thirty miles north of the Manchurian border. This time we really achieved surprise because the Russian controller, although picking up the main force of F-86s on his radar, completely failed to spot us. When we got over Antung the Migs were climbing parallel to the border to gain an altitude advantage on the F-86s to the south. We dropped into perfect position for a tail chase and closed on them without difficulty. The minute the Migs were told to turn toward the F-86s we tangled with them and shot down three which fell to the ground in flames. The rest of the Mig pilots saw us and broke formation in wild disarray. So far our plan was a success, if we could only keep what we were doing quiet.

When we returned to K-13 we had to be debriefed by the wing intelligence officer as usual, and we mutually agreed to the following story: We had followed the enemy aircraft as they climbed for altitude, but kept well south of the border. When they came down into our territory we attacked, shooting down three while the rest escaped us by flying north. The three we destroyed fell to the ground on the Manchurian side of the border. This story satisfied our intelligence man, but I'll bet the Russian controller up north was having a hell of a time trying to figure out what had hit him.

When it was all over, the problem of tacitly violating the border gave us grave concern. We still felt—and I feel the same way today—that a nation should not handicap its fighting men so that their chances of survival in battle against the enemy are reduced substantially.

We ran several more Maple Special missions, although it became increasingly difficult to keep the other members of the wing from discovering what we were doing. Even the 4th Wing began to question us, especially when they saw several F-86s with our tail markings coming across the border from the north. We knew that sooner or later people would catch on, but for a time the few of us held tightly to what we were doing.

One of the first pilots to see the light was Captain Ivan C. Kincheloe. Kinch and I had both attended Purdue University before the Korean War when the Air Force sent me back to complete my undergraduate training. Kinch, who had been enrolled as a student in the Aeronautical Engineering School, was a brilliant fellow with a wonderful personality, and I was surprised to see him in Korea as an Air Force officer, because in college he had never expressed any ambition to join the Air Force. Kinch had no previous combat experience, so he sought all the information he could which would help him to shoot down Migs. He came to me from time to time to discuss air-to-air combat, hoping I could help him. Kinch saw us coming back from Manchuria one day, and when he connected what he had seen with the stories of destroyed Migs he wanted to get in on the action. I finally broke down and told him what was going on, telling Gabby later that Kinch now knew. We had to include him on the next mission. He managed to shoot at a Mig, but upon reviewing his camera film it was easy to see that he had been firing out of range. In a short time Kinch had damaged seven Migs, finally destroying one completely. He later became one of our leading jet aces.

The more we flew on the Manchurian side of the Yalu, the more trouble we had trying to conceal our combat film. One day I had a special kind of trouble. Lieutenant Bill Ginther, who was leading my element, was the squadron photographic officer in the 25th, and to date he hadn't been involved in our border violations. This day we managed to get into an air battle in which I took my flight deep across the border, only to lose Bill at the height of battle. Suddenly his voice came on the radio, laughing like an idiot, to say: "Wolf Leader, I've lost you. I'll meet you at Hey Rube." This was fine with me, but I couldn't understand why he was laughing. I called to him several times to see if he was in trouble, but no answer. Neither could I find him at the rendezvous point. When I landed back at K-13, Bill came running to my ship. "Hey, Colonel," he said, "we've got to do something about my combat film. Can you fix it so that all of the copies are given back to us when they are developed? We can't possibly let them get to higher headquarters."

I arranged to get the first rushes of his film, and when I saw it I realized what had worried Bill. He had attacked a Mig over the border, and in the battle the Mig pilot, trying desperately to escape, had made a vertical dive to the earth, pulling out just in time to pass down the runway at the Antung airstrip. Bill had followed him all the way down, leveling off about ten feet above the ground, shooting at the Mig the entire time. In the film one could see row after row of Migs lined up on either side of the runway, and it appeared that the F-86 was flying even below the tops of the Mig tails. Bill was so close that Russian crew members could be seen standing on the wings and around the fuselages of the Migs, watching the F-86 chase the Mig across the field. It couldn't have been more obvious on which side of the border the pictures were taken. At any rate, Bill got the Mig, and the Russians had a fine floor show put on at their expense. We burned Bill's film.

On the 14th of February we ran into a situation indicating that perhaps the Commies had finally caught on to our staggered flights-of-fours system. We were ordered on a combat patrol mission, taking off at 11:30 in the morning, and I was scheduled as Maple Leaf, group leader of the 51st. My classmate from flying school days, Ben Long, was my wing man, and John Heard was leading element. We took off first, followed in five-minute intervals by five flights of four aircraft each. The weather was clear over the target, and we were expecting activity from the enemy because the cycle of events indicatd he was through his training period and ready to fight with us.

As we reached altitude in the vicinity of Pyongyang, Heard had difficulties with his element and returned to base. Ben and I flew on, trying to maintain radio discipline, because we had no indication from either Dentist or Dentist Charlie that enemy aircraft were airborne. Suddenly Ben broke silence by calling:

"Watch it, Maple Leaf. There are twelve bogies at eleven-thirty high." Although I acknowledged the call I couldn't see a thing. A moment later Ben said: "Maple Leaf, those bogies are Migs and they are coming in." Just then I saw them. There was no question that they were in the attack phase, and I had to call Ben: "Break left! Now!" As we broke, the enemy also broke away from us.

We had hardly straightened out to set course before twelve more Migs bounced on us from above. This time we broke right, to evade attack, only to find that we were up to our necks in Migs. There had been plenty of bandits airborne, but Dentist hadn't bothered to call them out because our own radar hadn't picked out our flight on the screens. As soon as they heard Ben and me talking they began to advise of bandits here, there and everywhere, and all of them were zeroed in on us.

Every time a new group of the enemy would attack we'd be forced to break either left or right. When we took evasive action the enemy would dive out of the fight, and Ben and I would try to position ourselves above the retreating Migs. Just as I'd start down to attack, a new bunch of Migs would show up above us. Naturally, our conversations could be heard by all the flights following us, but we had carried some distance away from Pyongyang, and none of the other flight leaders could find us to offer help.

It was one hell of a fight—the worst I'd ever been in—because we couldn't attack as long as all the Migs seemed to be after us. One time, just after I had broken and straightened out, I saw a Mig climbing up directly to my left. He was firing his cannon as he climbed, but because of the angle I was sure that he couldn't hit either of us. I called to Ben to warn him, saying: "Ben, look at that silly bastard climbing at nine o'clock. Let's get him when he goes under us." Sure enough, the Mig went just below and in front of us, still climbing. It was a chance for a perfect shot. But just as we turned to get on his tail more Migs came in from above and behind, forcing us to break off once more.

We had been fighting for about forty minutes by this time,

talking like mad on the radio to keep from getting shot down. I'm sure that no one else in the air could get a word in edgewise. Both of us were running out of fuel when the last big gaggle of Migs dropped in on us. I yelled: "Break right and up, Ben." But Ben thought I said break left. When I broke he broke in the opposite direction. As soon as the Migs stopped the attack I called: "Ben, continue around the turn, and we'll head for home." Ben kept going around his 360° turn while I kept going around mine till suddenly we were face to face.

At these speeds it is impossible to tell one jet from another head-on, so I started firing immediately, taking no chance at all that it might be a Mig. As soon as Ben saw me pouring out 50-caliber ammunition he yelled: "Watch it, it's me." With that we joined up and headed for home.

On the way back I decided that the Migs had planned to intercept the first flight of four into the combat area with everything they had, hoping to bag some Sabres. If it hadn't been for the radio and for the fact that Ben and I had worked together so often, I'm sure that we would both have been destroyed. It was a funny thing that the Communists didn't try that same tactic again, even though it could have worked quite well.

When we got home George Jones was screaming mad because we had used the radio so much. Neither he nor anyone else had sighted Migs, and I think he was put out at that too. At any rate he grounded me for two days. Since I was a guest in his outfit, it was pointless to argue with him, and I'm sure he doubted the claims of numbers of Migs Ben and I had seen.

Later we got a call from Ben Preston, the commander of the 4th Fighter Group, wanting to know how Cousin Weak Eyes was getting along. He and his men had been listening to our battle from K-14, and they had heard me shoot at Ben. They attributed my shooting at him to my lack of good eyesight, because they knew I wore glasses when I flew. I couldn't have cared less about Cousin Weak Eyes, but Ben and I were both sore that we hadn't bagged at least one Mig.

When the 20th of February rolled around, those of us on

loan to the 51st Wing made our plans to go home. Our ninety-days temporary duty was over. Van Chandler and Bill Schaeffer had each destroyed 3 enemy aircraft, while I had destroyed 3 and shared another with my wing man for a total of 3½. Not too bad for part-time employees.

I was packing my bags the night of the 21st when Gab came into my room, wearing a suspicious look. "What the hell are you doing?" he asked, "If you're packing bags, you're just wasting time." With that he handed me a message from 5th Air Force Headquarters which read: "Current orders pertaining to Col. Walker M. Mahurin are hereby revoked. Subject officer is ordered to proceed as soon as possible to the 4th Fighter Interceptor Wing, K-14, to assume command of the 4th Fighter Interceptor Group. End. Signed, EVEREST." Wow! That did it. Not that I didn't want the job; I certainly did. I had wanted a command in Korea in the worst way, but what in the hell would I tell my wife?

I went to K-14 the next day to report to Colonel Harry Thyng, my new boss. When I saluted him Harry said, "Knock that off, Bud. I'm glad to see you here. I wish you had joined us in the first place. As far as I'm concerned, the Fourth Group is yours to run as you see fit. I will only take a hand in directing if you are doing things badly or wrong. If you need help let me know. In the meantime when can I get on the schedule?" I couldn't have asked for anything else. From that moment on I knew we'd see eye to eye and that our relationship would be of the very best.

Colonel Harry Thyng is one of the most delightful guys I've ever met. I hadn't known him until I got to Korea, but I knew of him and his activities from World War II. He had been stationed on Okinawa during the war as the commander of a group of long range P-47 Ns. He had sixteen aerial victories during World War II, and had added two Migs to his credit in Korea. He had a reputation of being an unassuming commander who go along beautifully with his people.

Harry was small in stature, but he more than made up for this in his eagerness to shoot down every enemy aircraft in the

sky over North Korea. His fighter pilot's spirit set a fine example
for his men, and he was a dashing example of what a combat
wing commander should be. I knew that he was married and had
children, but I didn't know much more about him. He spoke
with what I assumed to be a Boston accent, though he seldom
talked about his background. At any rate, he impressed me
when I reported in, and all the good things I'd heard about
him turned out to be understatements as far as I was concerned.

While I was in his office I asked Harry if I could go to Japan
and telephone my wife to tell her that I wouldn't be home as
planned. Permission granted, I went to the air base of Tsuiki
on the Island of Kyushu to put in my call. When Pat answered
the phone there was delight in her voice until I got up enough
nerve to say, "Honey, I'm not going to be home for awhile."
After that it was a one-way conversation until I had to hang up
for fear of breaking the Mahurin family bank. I did manage to
tell her that I would write her the details when I got back to
Korea. This is not the way to run a happy home, but when I
called her a week later the shock had worn off and she was on
speaking terms with me again.

Upon assuming command, I found that the 4th Fighter Group
had a terrible maintenance rate, with many aircraft not in flying
condition because of the lack of replacement engines. When the
normal operating life of an engine was over it was usually
removed from the aircraft and sent back to Japan for overhaul
and repair. Normally a replacement would be available for installation immediately. But this was not the case with the 4th.
I got the group maintenance officer, Major William Sands, to
give me a run-down on our problem. He said there were many
engines waiting to be shipped to the repair depot, but there
weren't enough engine dollies to mount them on, and the air
transport people wouldn't move them unless they were properly
mounted. In addition, we couldn't get a new engine if we didn't
turn in an old one. Altogether there were some 18 engines
sitting around on sandbags, waiting for dollies so that they
could be shipped. That meant there were 18 aircraft also sitting
on the ground, waiting for engines.

I spent the first afternoon of my new assignment walking around the air base, looking for engine dollies. I found 12 empty ones in back of buildings, stuck away in odd corners, covered with canvas and so on. To top the situation, I found 6 brand-new ones still in the packing crates in which they had been shipped from the United States. My boys hadn't been looking around. I went back to headquarters, mustered out the entire gang, marched them to each newly discovered engine dolly, made them put their hands on them in unison, then marched them back to an engine lying on the ground and had them put their hands on it. When they had finally marched back and forth across K-14 about eighteen times I asked them if there were any further questions. That night the sky was filled with the drone of transport aircraft arriving at K-14 to pick up F-86 engines for transport to the maintenance area. From then on maintenance worked out fine.

As soon as possible I tried to put all of the things we had been doing at the 51st into practice at the 4th. First I suggested that the pilots stop making emergency fuel checks on the end of the runway and just taxi out to the end and take off. My quarters were located near the take-off end of the runway at K-14, and the next morning when the first squadron took off for the early morning mission I was in the sack. The squadron taxied out to the runway, lined up, ran up the engines, burned gallons of fuel while checking systems and finally took off. When they came back I was waiting for them in the briefing room. "Maybe I didn't express myself too clearly," I said. "I'm going to tell you one more time, stop running up those goddamn engines on the end of the runway." We had no more problem with that.

As soon as I could, I had the 4th Group's F-86s painted. When I arrived at K-14, each F-86 was decorated with a large white band around each wing with a black border on either side. There were four black bands around the fuselage, each band separated by white. I had the aircraft painted exactly like the 51st Sabres, except that we added a yellow band with black border on the verticle stabilizer, to set up apart from Gabby's boys. The aircraft looked sharp in their new colors.

Within a few days we were flying exactly like the 51st, although we had one more squadron. Things were working out well enough, but as a professional soldier I now wanted to beat Gabby and the 51st Wing in everything they did. Shooting down more Migs was one way, but there were others. We were going to fly more sorties, higher, longer, farther and better than they did, or go down in the attempt. I had to have more aircraft in commission to accomplish this.

Many of our aircraft were continually out of flying condition because we didn't have certain parts on hand in our base supply and it took time to get them from Japan. I found we had a highly experienced master sergeant in the technical supply field, working in fighter group headquarters. I pulled this man away from his job and sent him on temporary duty full time to FEAMCOM, Far Eastern Air Material Command, the major supply depot for the Orient. This full-time temporary duty stuff is strictly against regulations, but what the hell. I had our man occupy a desk alongside the man who was in charge of all supply requisitions from Korea. When our man saw a parts requisition coming from the 4th in Korea he would personally assume responsibility to track down the parts. If they were not in the stock bins he would find substitute items and send them to us by airmail. When a requisition asking for a part showed up from the 51st Wing our man would put it on the bottom of the In basket. We got fat in a hurry.

We pulled another one on Gabby which worked fairly well. K-14 was about thirty miles closer to the front lines than K-13, so pilots returning home in badly shot-up F-86s would try to land at our base rather then take the risk of going on to K-13. This looked like a parts bonanza, so we set up a special moonlight requisition unit under my group maintenance officer, a man with the improbable name of Pinky Lavender. Pinky had several highly trained enlisted men—the best we could find in the maintenance and repair field—standing by at all times, waiting for a damaged F-86 from the 51st Wing to arrive. Occasionally one of Gabby's pilots came wobbling in to K-14, shot all to pieces and just plain lucky to get home. Before Gabby could send his maintenance people up from K-13 to examine the aircraft for repair possibilities, Pinky and his gang would remove everything useful and substitute all the unusuable parts we had lying around. If we had an aircraft with a damaged right wing, and an F-86 landed at our base with a good right wing, we switched them as quickly as we could. I heard Gab remark time and again: "For Christ's Sake, I don't see how that aircraft could stay in the air long enough to fly all the way back home. The thing is a wreck." I couldn't have agreed more. We had a big supply building just full of Gabby's wonderful parts.

I finally stumbled onto an idea as good if not better than all the rest. By this time 5th Air Force was sending both wings of F-86s into combat in 4 ship flights with a 3-minute interval between each flight. If Gab sent off 24 Sabres, it would require 18 minutes before his entire unit was airborne. We usually put up 36 Sabres because we had one more squadron than he did, and we'd usually take off from K-14 exactly 3 minutes after the last of Gabby's squadron had passed over our air base. Jointly our wings could cover the combat area for the normal endurance time of the aircraft, plus the 45 minutes elapsed time between the first flight and the last in the combat zone. As soon as I could get enough aircraft in commission to meet my commitment of 36 aircraft for each mission, plus an additional 8, I began to bootleg my own pilots into Gabby's formations. We would wait until several flights of the 51st Wing had passed over K-14 on the way to the combat zone and then launch a flight of our own. We'd wait till a couple more flights of the 51st had passed by, then stick in 4 more of our own. We could usually count on having from 8 to 12 of our fighters mixed up in Gab's formations. Each of our flight leaders tuned in to the radio frequency of the 51st Wing and waited for further developments.

As the stream of fighters flew up to the combat zone our people would switch frequencies to a private channel we had in our operations shack to keep us advised of the events transpiring up north. If any of Gabby's boys had anything unusual to say, our people relayed it to us immediately. If they resorted to any unusual tricks or formations, our lads passed it on to us immediately. When Dentist Charlie, well beyond the reach of our radio set on the ground, called Maple Group to advise of enemy action we got the word practically at the same time. If the 51st got into a fight with the enemy, our boys were right in the middle, trying to do them out of a Mig or two. It worked perfectly. When we got word there was an unusual number of Mig flights airborne we'd fudge a little and launch our scheduled fighters before we were supposed to. We usually managed to get into the fun with, or a little ahead of, the pilots from the 51st.

This business of intense competition with Gabby may seem a little obtuse in view of the fact that there was an actual war going on, but at the time it didn't seem strange at all. I knew Gabby was aware of our efforts to outdo him. After all, I expected the same from him, and I suppose that his boys played little tricks on us that I never did find out about. Naturally I would have given my eye teeth to shoot down all the Migs in China—especially if it contributed to bringing the war to a close. At the same time I would almost have given my right arm to beat Gabby in every way possible. I guess it was just that there were several ways of doing an excellent job, and if it didn't cost lives or cause inconvenience, it was fair game to do almost anything.

Of course I heard about this from Gabby from time to time. On returning to K-13, his pilots would sometimes report that they had seen several Migs destroyed on a particular mission, and then would try to find someone to congratulate. When no one would put in a claim of destruction, Gab went crazy trying to figure what had happened. Once in awhile his pilots spotted some of our aircraft at the wrong place at the wrong time, so Gabby would call us up and howl like hell. Harry was a good listener, and we'd always thank Gabby for his call, then try to think up other ways to get into his business.

Upon assuming command of the 4th Group, I also acquired the call sign of Honest John. Fifth Air Force had assigned this call sign to the group leader of the 4th, and it applied to whoever was the group commander. I inherited the name from Ben Preston, the commanding officer I replaced. I have an irritating, high-pitched, squeaky voice on the radio, and I'm sure anyone within earshot could tell who I was, even without a call sign. Nevertheless I had to use Honest John. I got so I rather liked the name. We had a talented squadron commander, Major Felix Asla, who was a very fine artist. I had him drawn a caricature of a disreputable, dissolute, awful-looking bum which I had painted on the side of my aircraft so people would know who was coming. The pilots never stopped riding me about my name, although I claimed it was most fitting.

When I first took over the group I had a meeting of all pilots to acquaint them with my command philosophy. I told them that I made it a point not to stand on rank. As long as Uncle Sam paid my salary I was happy; I didn't need to browbeat anyone to get enjoyment from rank. Any officer could feel free to discuss any topic with me at any time, because I refused to erect a rank barrier to keep others from speaking their minds. However, it was a different story in the air. I would be the boss, and there was to be no question about it. If I gave an order in the air, all pilots were to hop to it. If they didn't like my instructions, they'd do what I told them to do and wait until they were back on the ground to discuss it. We'd hash it all out then, but not while there was danger of any of us getting shot down by Migs because we were holding an airborne seminar on the Manchurian border. I demanded that all pilots acknowledge that they understood exactly what I had said. Since there were no questions, I assumed we had reached an understanding. Shortly thereafter, though, I wasn't so sure I had been understood.

This time we had a rather large show going and had managed to put 44 F-86s into the air for our usual trip north. We had maintained complete radio silence all the way to the border and had started our routine patrols. With all flights operating independently, I could only see about 12 Sabres flying in my general vicinity, although I knew the rest were reasonably nearby.

There were several bandit flights airborne, but none had crossed the Yalu. Suddenly one of my men, whose voice I didn't recognize, said on the radio, "Hey, I think I see something." The normal procedure in a case like this is to identify oneself as well as the man being addressed. The call should have been; "Eagle Red Leader, this is Eagle Red Four. I think I have something spotted at twelve o'clock high." That way everyone knows what is going on. Not this guy. His leader apparently knew who he was, because he said, "Well, watch it and let me know what happens." There were a few moments of silence, and then the first voice said, "I can see what it is now. Eight Migs." This is exactly like giving everyone in the air a hot foot. Immediately forty-four pairs of eyes started to whirl in every direction, trying to spot Migs. The addressee replied, "Okay, watch them. If they start to attack, give me a call." Pretty cool. Almost immediately the first voice screeched, "They are attacking us right now! You'd better break left immediately." There was a moment of silence, then the second voice yelled, "One of them is on my tail! Get him off." This was accompanied by considerable heavy breathing, as if our reporter was out of breath. With this I couldn't stand it any longer. I got on the air to say: "This is Honest John. Tell me where you are, and I will come over to help you out." No answer. Next, voice Number One came out in panic with: "You'd better pull in tighter. He's shooting mighty near you." Voice Number Two yelled back, "For Christ's sake, get him off my tail." Obviously there was a hell of a fight going on somewhere, so I got on the air for the second time. "This is Honest John. Tell me where the fight is so I can help out." Just then one of these jokers pushed down on his machine-gun trigger and the microphone button at the same time, and all that could be heard on the radio was the terrific clatter of six heavy machine guns being fired. Voice Number One broke in to say: "I think I got one. Are there any on my tail?" I couldn't stand it any more. "Listen, you bastards, this is Honest John. If you guys want help, tell me where the fight is and tell me now." Another moment of long silence, and then a sober voice came back to me: "To hell with you, Colonel. Find your own damn Migs."

I had now been with the 4th Group long enough to go into the problem of border violations, since the pilots of the 4th Wing were seeing F-86s from the 51st crossing the Manchurian border. This time I explained the situation to all the pilots, mentioning briefly what General Everest had told Gabby and me. I explained that there was no question about our violating direct orders when we flew across the Yalu, and obviously I couldn't order anyone to cross over into the sanctuary. "We are now operating at flight leaders' discretion in choice of altitude and direction," I said. "It is up to you flight leaders to discuss this situation with your flights. If any of us are caught crossing the border, I will most certainly tell General Everest I did not tell you to do so. However, I will defend your action with all my power." I went on to say, "I can tell you what I have been doing and what I am going to continue to do. If I can get anywhere near a Mig, I intend to get him if I have to chase him all the way to Peiping. I want this war to end and I want to go home just as much as you do, but the peace negotiations seem to be getting nowhere. If the Migs get in among our slower aircraft, a lot of Americans will be hurt. I don't want that to happen. I think we can force the Communists to come to terms more rapidly if we whip them at every chance, especially in the air. That is all I can tell you. The rest is up to you."

The reaction to my little talk was good. Only one man didn't want to have anything to do with crossing the border. I told him I thought he was a fine officer who was absolutely right in following his orders to the letter. After that we made sure that he only went on flights we knew would stay south of the border, and I think both he and I were happy. With the border restrictions off, our pilots began to gain in victories over the 51st. We had to kill a lot of combat-film footage, and for the benefit of the intelligence officer we still had to shoot them down on our side of the Yalu and watch them crash on the other side, but the concensus among ourselves was that what we were doing was working out fine.

As in the 51st Wing, we were forced to set up a screening process for all of our combat film before it went on to higher headquarters. Usually copies went to Headquarters Air Materiel Command, Headquarters Far Eastern Air Force, and Headquarters 5th Air Force. One copy stayed with the wing and one was given to the pilot. We just couldn't let anything incriminating get away from our base. Our pilots were coming back from missions with some of the damndest pictures. Migs with wheels, flaps and dive brakes extended in preparation for landings; Migs just breaking ground after take-off; Migs upside down, sideways, in formation, out of formation and so on—with most of the pictures taken just around the enemy-held air bases. We shot them down in the landing pattern, we shot them down on local test hops, we shot them down on training flights, and we shot them down anywhere we could find them. Some of the film even showed the runways ahead of the Migs just before they blew up or caught fire. We considered it slightly dirty pool to shoot them down just as they were trying to land, but each victory added up. Still that film had to be screened because— to anyone who asked—we had shot them down on our side of the Yalu and they had crashed on the other.

The Communists obviously knew what was going on; they had to. They were picking up pieces of Migs all over Manchuria. We were sure they were in a panic, because they came up to fight us in smaller and smaller numbers. For some reason, though, they never did gripe in front of the United Nations on this score, perhaps figuring that as long as we didn't strafe their aircraft as they sat on the ground they had it pretty good. They knew as well as we did that at any given moment we could have wiped out their entire compliment of aircraft by strafing their airfields. They must have also known how much we wanted to do it.

Both of our wings had to submit combat reports at the end of each day's activities, for intelligence reporting purposes. We could usually find out what each wing had accompanied by reading these reports. One day I ran across a lulu. The 51st had claimed 37 aircraft of various types destroyed on the ground, and the report even mentioned the name of the airfield on which the action had taken place. When I asked my intelligence officer where this particular airstrip was located he looked at every map he had, but couldn't find it. I decided to call Gabby to get further information, but when I did he would just barely talk to me. He did say, however, that the report was accurate; the 51st had really made an accurate claim. The next day I cornered one of Gabby's pilots to get the full story. It seemed that some eager-beaver pilot had been flying north of the Yalu on patrol. He was a bit farther north than he thought. As he looked down at the ground he spotted a dirt landing field on which 37 aircraft were parked. On the way down with his flight he had planned to keep the whole thing quiet so that he could shoot all 37 himself, but as soon as the first few started to burn they were so visible that every pilot in the air jumped into the fray. When the pilots of the 51st came back to home base they couldn't find the name on any map, so they dreamed up a name. No wonder we couldn't find it. The next day I noticed an amendment to Gabby's mission summary: "The 51st Wing deletes that portion of the previous mission summary pertaining to the claims of aircraft destroyed on the ground. There are no claims for the day." Gabby simply couldn't figure out how to shoot up 37 aircraft on the ground in Manchuria and then transport them into North Korea so that they would constitute a legitimate claim.

One of my squadron commanders was a delightful guy named Zane Amel. On the ground, the members of Zane's unit were perhaps the raunchiest looking bunch of guys I had ever seen. I had a big campaign going to paint and spruce up all the squadron areas, but I just couldn't light a fire under the 335th Squadron. Maintenancewise and flyingwise it was a different story. Zane's pilots had the best aircraft-in-commission rate, the most kills, the most aces and the biggest stories to tell. These boys were good and Zane knew it. One day we were patrolling on the Yalu and the standard number of Mig flights were airborne. However, none of them would venture across the Yalu; they just kept circling around on the opposite side, looking us over. I could hear Zane talking to his flight about the Migs and how the Sabres were in a good position to attack from up-sun and so on, when all of a sudden the Migs made an attack on Zane. I called to him to find out where the fighting was going on, in order to help if any of our pilots were in real trouble. "I can't tell you where we are," Zane said, "but we've got about fourteen of them cornered, and we can't figure out how to let them go." I kept on asking Zane for his position and he kept answering that he couldn't tell me where he was. Finally, in desperation, I said: "Goddom it, Zane, I want to know where you are." His answer was: "Honest John, I am in deep center field." We didn't have a code name even similar to that, but I checked my map just to make sure. "Where the hell is that?" I asked him. "I can't find it." "I know you can't find it," he replied. "I'll tell you where it is, if and when I get home." I could hear the fighting for several more minutes until Zane came back on the air to tell me he was clear of the hornet's nest and on his way home.

Back home again, I waited for Zane and his flight to land. Altogether they had destroyed three Migs and damaged two others. When I had called to ask where the fight was taking place Zane was about 40 miles north of the Yalu, above the city of Antung. Naturally we didn't have a code name for anything above the Manchurian border, and he was afraid to tell me exactly where he was for fear that General Everest, who usually watched and listened to the combat missions in his control center in 5th Air Force Headquarters, would hear and get us for violating instructions. Zane said he had to think of something fast and the only thing that came to mind was "Deep Center Field." He'd hoped I'd get the message, but like a dope I hadn't. Once again, for the benefit of the intelligence officers, Zane's boys shot the Migs down on our side of the river, and they crashed 40 miles north.

While I was still talking to Zane about Deep Center Field, Major Boots Blesse came running up completely out of breath. "Guess what happened, Colonel," he said. "I got first Mig. But wait till I tell you the circumstances." It seemed that Boots had finally lined up an enemy aircraft during the same battle Zane had been fighting. Boots had hit the Mig time and again with machine-gun fire until it was severely damaged. The Mig pilot elected to bail out of his burning aircraft at about 14,000 feet. To substantiate his claim for one enemy aircraft destroyed, Boots decided to take pictures of the enemy pilot floating to earth in his parachute. Boots made several passes on the parachute while taking gun-camera moving pictures. Each time he came as close as he could to the enemy pilot, in order to take a good look. As he did he was able to see that the Mig pilot had lost his helmet but still retained the rest of his flying gear. Much to Boot's amazement, the enemy pilot was a white man with bright red hair and a long red beard. On each pass of the Sabre the enemy pilot shook his fist violently at Boots. To even matters, Boots shook right back at him. If our pilots had not been good sports, that Mig jockey would never have reached the ground in one piece.

Harry Thyng pulled a sneaky one on us one day too. While we were all patrolling up and down the border as usual, Harry took his flight up to 46,000 feet and throttled away back to conserve fuel. The rest of us, flying at a lower altitude, burned fuel at the normal rate while Harry sat in his high-altitude foxhole, quiet as a church mouse. After the rest of us had run out of gas and headed for home the Communist controller apparently missed Harry while following us on his radarscope, because he finally considered the air clear of Sabres above the Manchurian border. And while Harry was watching the airfield at Antung the Russian controller dispatched two Migs on a ferry flight to Mukden, about 200 miles north of the border. Harry immediately dropped down behind these two and gave chase. The rest was a bit brutal. Harry had both speed and surprise, so he sneaked right up the tail pipe of the Mig leader, about 100 miles north of the border—far enough north so that the Mig pilot was sure there were no F-86s within miles. After Harry clobbered this man he shifted over and clobbered the wing man, who couldn't have had time to figure out what was happening. With that, Harry picked himself up and returned to home base. Harry's wing man, Squadron Leader Paddy Harbison, a Royal Air Force exchange officer who had been flying with us, was really bitter about Harry's being so greedy. Paddy claimed that Harry should have shot the first Mig down and turned the other one over to him, sharing the wealth, so to speak. Harry couldn't see it, because those two victories made him a jet ace. Naturally the Migs were hit south of the Yalu and crashed just north of the border.

Something I had been dreading for a long time finally happened; we received an emergency wire from 5th Air Force Headquarters directing all group commanders in Korea to attend a meeting at 0900 the following day. Because of the unusual nature of an emergency wire, I was sure something serious was afoot—something like the subject of border violations. When all of us were assembled we were ordered to attention and General Everest stormed into the room. I had never seen him so angry. He had, he said, become aware that our pilots were violating the Manchurian border, an action he could neither tolerate nor condone. He went on to say he had been in the 5th Air Force control center the previous day, watching a strike mission on the plotting board, when he saw a track being plotted on a single F-86 which had taken off from K-13. On each F-86 there is a small device called an IFF set. IFF stands for Identification, Friend or Foe. When this set is turned on it transmits a distinctive signal which can be picked up by friendly radar sets. Any aircraft with the IFF set turned on is obviously friendly, while all others are not. In the case General Everest watched the pilot had turned on the IFF set as he departed K-13, so he was being followed by our radar throughout his entire flight. As General Everest watched with mounting anger the track went to the Manchurian border, crossed it, and kept north toward Mukden. The General almost had apoplexy as the radar pilot circled the city of Mukden twice, then headed south, and finally stopped at K-13. The General couldn't believe this gross violation of orders, and since there was no change in his instructions from Washington, we group commanders were to do as we damn well had been told. When he asked if any of us had questions he was so red from rage we didn't dare open our mouths. "All right, gentlemen," he said, "that will be all." We all popped to attention as he started for the door. As he reached the door and started to pass through he turned around and said, "And furthermore, if you are going to violate the Manchurian border, for God's sake turn off the damn IFF set."

One day my Group Armament Officer, Captain Marion Benefield, came to me with a gripe. It seemed that one of the officers in the 334th Squadron returned from each mission with all of his ammunition expended and all six gun barrels burned out. Benny said that he was having trouble keeping Captain Jack Owens' aircraft in tiptop shape and his men were having trouble finding enough gun barrels to keep the group supplied. Benny went on to say that he had checked Captain Owens' combat reports and the captain had yet to put in a claim for anything destroyed. This seemed like a mighty queer situation.

It turned out that Owens hadn't been having too much luck running into Migs. In thinking about the situation, he had decided it didn't make sense lugging 1,500 rounds of ammunition all the way up to the combat zone only to turn around and lug it home again. Up near the Manchurian border he had noticed that the Communists were driving trucks, tanks and rolling equipment on the highways, even though we were in the vicinity. They obviously didn't think the F-86s would drop down for strafing attacks. Owens was paying them back for their disrespect. When he heard the code word Bingo, Owens would drop down to the deck to shoot anything he could find moving until he ran out of ammunition; then he would come home just like the rest of us. Owens hadn't mentioned his exploits because he wasn't sure whether it was considered cricket for us to be strafing. However, he had bagged a rather good score of Communist equipment and hoped I didn't mind. "Mind, hell," I told him, "I'm all for it. Just put your claims in the daily mission summary." On the way back to group headquarters I thought, If that guy can do it, I can do it too. Further than that, if I can do it so can everyone else. Off we went. We made a practice of beating up and down the roadways about ten miles south of the enemy airstrip at Antung, hoping we'd stir up some fighter reaction. Within sight of the Mig bases I began to shoot up ten or twelve trucks, not to mention an occasional tank or gun emplacement, on every flight.

When the 5th Air Force found out what we were doing they asked us to send a four-ship flight into North Korea at low altitude daily to reconnoiter the major railroads—in hopes of finding repair gangs at work correcting the damage wrought by our attacks the previous night. Since the prerequisite for leadership is to know in which direction to lead, I had to take the first of any new type of missions just to show that the old man could do it. We had been flying at low altitude, so it appeared this mission would be a snap. On the first flight I dropped down to about 50 feet above a railroad, just north of Pyongyang, while the rest of the 4th Group was on patrol at high altitude farther north. About halfway up the peninsula I ran smack dab into a big railroad train. It shook me so much that I almost didn't know what to do. However, I started working the train over, climbing to about 15,000 feet on each strafing attack, and diving down to ground level at high speed, shooting as I went. I got going so fast on each pass that my bullets were spraying all over North Korea, but eventually the train blew up with a bang. On each pass I noticed that the enemy antiaircraft fire was more intense, until it became unbearable. I headed home with good combat films of the train, but an aircraft full of holes. I should have been forewarned by this action, but to hell with it, I thought, they'd never hit me again. When I got back to home base my crew chief met me with a can of red paint, and from then on I was the only F-86 pilot in Korea who had a picture of a train painted on the side of his fuselage along with three and a half red stars.

May 1st was coming up now, and we began to fear what would happen, because for Communist societies the world over, May 1st has a special significance. At night in our quarters we could hear the rumble of the heavy field artillery on the front lines, some distance to the north of K-14, and since the tempo of fire seemed to be increasing, the rumors we had heard of the possibility of a heavy Communist offensive appeared plausible.

A few days before May 1st a local Korean boy was found making his way into K-14 illegally. A houseboy in one of the officers billets, he had not been seen for days. When captured he had a pistol in his possession. The South Korean police are rather direct fellows, and they wanted the youth to tell them what he was up to when captured. By using the latest police methods of integration—beating him about the head and shoulders with a baseball bat—they found out that he was part of a Communist plot to kill all of the wing and group commanders in South Korea. Sometime before, many houseboys faithful to the Communist cause had made their way across the Han River, just outside Seoul, into the Communist lines at a predetermined place. They had received training, had subsequently worked their way back into good graces as houseboys, and then, on May 1st, were to kill as many high-ranking Air Force officers as possible. Fortunately we were able to break up this action before it actually came off, and did so by closing all air bases to indigenous personnel a day before and a day after May 1st.

Needless to say, most of the senior officers in Korea were rather keyed up by this news. I began to hear all sorts of noises at night—noises that sounded like hordes of sneaky North Koreans about to ambush my quarters. But one night topped them all. I had issued instructions that all of our aircraft were to have periodic gun-firing tests to make sure that all machine guns were pointing in the right direction. This was to be done on the basis of one firing per aircraft per month on a regular schedule. We didn't have an adequate place to shoot the guns, so the construction crews had built a huge revetment—right in front of my quarters—into which the guns could be fired. An F-86 would be placed on a small concrete pad about 500 feet from the revetment, and the armament crews would fire about five rounds of ammunition into the revetment simultaneously from all six guns. Just after the Korean houseboy had been captured my men managed to get the first F-86 ready for gun tests in the new revetment. They shot off the first rounds about three o'clock in the morning on the last day of April. Coming on the heels of the arrests, right in the middle of the May Day

91

scare, in the dark of night and just outside my window, I thought the world had come to an end. Along with every other officer in the quarters, those guns lifted me four feet straight up into the air. It took me the rest of the night to get my heart slowed down to the point where I could again hear noises outside. For about a week after that I was the only guy in Korea who would step outside his quarters in the middle of the night and go to the john with a gun in each hand.

Although we continued to receive reports of pilots who suffered death at the hands of the local populace once they had been shot down in North Korea, I didn't give the prospect too much thought because I figured they'd never shoot me down in the first place. It was frightening to think of the chances of survival up north, but war was war and we all had to take our chances.

Then one day a true-to-life story from pilots who were eye-witnesses really shook us all up. For many months the United Nations had wanted to lay hands on a real, live Mig pilot, because in all probability he would be a white man. Many times when a Mig had been shot down in North Korea the pilot had managed to parachute to the ground safely. In such cases we always put a top cover of F-86s over the enemy pilot when he hit the ground, in an effort to keep him out of contact with his fellows and to keep other people on the ground from reaching him while we sent a helicopter to pick him up. We tried to pick up enemy pilots time and again, but they always managed to run to safety before our helicopter crews could get there to grab them. However, during one of our largest air battles a Mig was hit out over the Yellow Sea, and the pilot who had bailed out landed in open water several miles offshore. This was a natural for us. We immediately put a top cover of F-86s over him while Dentist Charlie, on Cho-Do Island, dispatched a helicopter to pick him up. When our helicopter reached a point about fifty miles from the downed Russian pilot, the Russian controller at Antung dispatched four separate bandit flights into the area. The enemy aircraft jumped into the middle of our F-86 top cover, forcing them away from the pilot in the water. When the F-86s had drawn sufficiently far away a flight of four Migs strafed the poor devil in the water. By the time our helicopter reached the scene there was no trace of the Mig pilot.

It was obvious that the Russians were desperate to keep the identity of those who flew the Migs a secret, and certainly gave us who flew F-86s a grim insight into the minds of the people who were trying to foist their glorious Communist philosophy on the rest of the world.

6.

AFTER the first of May we found the enemy markedly reluctant to challenge us in the sky as we patrolled up and down the Yalu. Part of this inaction could be attributed to transfers of Russian fighter units in and out of Manchuria, but it appeared that we had caused the enemy so many losses that he had decided against coming up to meet us. We could still see the same number of Migs on the ground on each of the enemy airfields, but calls about airborne bandit flights were few and far between. This concerned us because the enemy inactivity was adversely affecting our combat scores. We were still not allowed to shoot an enemy aircraft on the ground in Manchuria, so we had to figure out someway to get them into the air where they'd be fair game.

The F-86 had originally been constructed to carry bomb shackles and various combinations of bombs, but, because of tremendous fuel consumption, we needed external fuel tanks in place of bombs. One day during a briefing I talked the situation over with the pilots, explaining that if we exploited our bombing capabilities we could add to the bombing effort in the north and still defend ourselves in case of attack. We all agreed that a few bombs dropped in the vicinity of the enemy airfields in Manchuria might force the Russians to send Migs up to drive us away, because they would have no real assurance from mission to mission that we wouldn't bomb their airfields, even though they were in the sanctuary. Although few of us had experience in dive bombing, I instructed Captain Benefield to find the necessary equipment to carry bombs on at least one squadron of F-86s. Benney had a great deal of trouble locating the bomb shackles and allied equipment, mostly because there had been no previous call for them, but he finally found what he needed in a depot in Japan. Eventually we were able to put twenty-five dive-bombing F-86s into the air.

Meanwhile I began to soften up the people in 5th Air Force Headquarters to gain their blessing for our plans. I talked the situation over with Colonel Joe Mason, an old friend from World War II days who was director of operations for 5th. Joe had a few reservations, not about our being capable of doing this type of work, but about reducing the number of escort aircraft required to perform the daily missions. I explained that our daily mission commitment involved 12 aircraft per squadron, but that we had been putting up at least 16 per squadron per mission. I added that we would bomb on an experimental basis only, while 5th Air Force would advise us on target selections. Joe finally agreed to ask General Everest for permission, stating that we would know when we had approval by the instructions issued in the daily operations order from headquarters. I asked Joe if he would omit details in the operations order because I didn't want the men from the 51st Wing to get an inkling of what we were about to do.

Once we had approval, we began to pick targets. Fifth Air Force, never having considered using F-86s for this form of attack, was unable to help us, but if we wanted to taunt the Migs into rising to meet us, I was certain that it would be to our advantage to bomb areas along the Yalu just in front of the enemy-held airstrips. If we couldn't get them into the air that way, they just weren't going to fight—no matter what we did. The 67th Tactical Reconnaissance Wing, commanded by Colonel Edwin Chickering, was located just across the field from us, so from them we got pictures of the various targets we could attack. Included were some very fine low-level shots of the city of Sinuiju, just across the Yalu from Antung, which we decided would be our first target. Sinuiju was roughly 200 miles from K-14, right in the middle of the Mig's home territory. We couldn't get there without external fuel and still fight our way back out if attacked; we'd have to carry a bomb on one side of each F-86 and a fuel tank on the other. We planned to use 12 bombing aircraft equipped with 500-pound bombs set to burst at 75 feet above the ground, while the rest of the group performed the patrol mission. On the 8th of May the mission directive from 5th Air Force stated that 4th Group would carry out a special effort as planned. No mention of detail. If Gab and his boys could figure out anything from these words they were psychic. The daily mission was briefed as usual, only this time we added dive bombing. Again I felt I should lead, considering the fact that I had set the whole business in motion.

We arrived over the target area uneventfully, without one bandit flight coming up to greet us. Once over Sinuiju, I gave orders to drop the external fuel tank, then rolled over vertically to drop my bomb from 18,000 feet. After release I circled the target to watch the others bomb, while determining the location of each bomb burst. Actually we threw bombs all over North Korea, although several hit rather near the center of town. One bomb burst caused a large secondary explosion in a group of buildings which, we had been told by intelligence, housed a training school for North Korean officers. When we had delivered our bombs I announced to the Communists, who I knew would be listening on our frequency: "This is Honest John. All right, you bastards, the next time we are going to bomb the airfield at Antung." Still no Migs in the air. Maybe we'd have better luck next time.

Upon reaching the pilots' shack back at K-14 after the mission I got a call from General Everest. He had been watching from his control room, but wanted first-hand information on the attack. He gave me seven kinds of hell for using the radio to taunt the enemy, saying we should reserve our air time for more important broadcasts. I couldn't help but agree with him, although I secretly hoped we'd get some Migs the next time because of what I had said. I didn't mention the dive-bombing attacks in our mission summary, because I still wanted to keep the information from Gabby and the 51st Wing if I could.

The next day we received authority to conduct another dive-bombing mission—this time with 1,000-pound bombs. The concept was beginning to catch on at higher headquarters. If it could be shown that the F-86 had dual-mission capability, perhaps all the other wings equipped with obsolescent aircraft could be re-equipped with F-86s and do their job twice as well. After all, the F-86s didn't need protection from the Migs; they ate Migs up. If such were the case, it might be well for us to attempt to demonstrate accuracy by doing our bombing at a lower altitude and against targets with more military significance.

For the next mission I selected a series of very heavy anti-aircraft gun emplacements near the airfield at Uiju, just inside the North Korean border. There were about eight separate emplacements of eight guns each grouped around the field, and intelligence information revealed that these guns, manned by Russian soldiers, were directed by radar. I led the attack again, and as I rolled over to dive on the target from 12,000 feet I noticed several bright flashes on the ground. Moments later my aircraft was surrounded by puffs of heavy black smoke indicating that we were all being subjected to fire from 88mm. cannon similar to those used by the Germans during World War II. Although these Russian gunners were accurate, they were having difficulty hitting us because we moved too fast. At least we were beginning to worry the Communists this time. Once again we began to hear the familiar broadcasts of: "Bandit Flights now in the Antung area." Our efforts were starting to pay off.

As I pulled out of my dive-bombing run I was surprised to notice that I had plenty of fuel remaining, so I called to my wing man to follow me while I picked up targets on the ground.

We both spotted a large convoy of trucks on the ground, not too far from the Uiju airstrip, and immediately went in to make attacks. Shortly after, we had twelve trucks burning fiercely. During our strafing attacks my wing man began to complain about his aircraft, stating that it was flying slowly and didn't climb as well as it should. As we continued to shoot at targets on the ground I found myself in back of him, and much to my horror saw that his 1,000-pound bomb was still clinging to the wing of his aircraft. Here we were, over 200 miles from home base, down on the deck, using fuel rapidly, and he still had that apple under his wing. It looked as if the only way he'd ever get back home would be to walk. I began to talk him into trying various manuevers to shake his trouble. We did everything we could think of except step outside to give it a kick when he finally made a diving, rolling pull-out, releasing the bomb. When we got home he shut down his engine at K-14 with 15 gallons of fuel remaining. This in an aircraft that can use over 900 gallons an hour.

For the next several days the group weather officer indicated that the weather would be unfit for flying, so I decided to take one of the less seriously damaged combat aircraft back to the major repair depot in Japan for reconstruction. This was not done because of any special devotion to duty on my part; the depot was located just outside of Tokyo, and I wanted to spend a couple of days there to stock up on provisions. By provisions I meant the makings of Martinis—anyone can get food. Finding the makings for a proper Martini wasn't an easy order in Japan, because one just couldn't walk into a liquor store and order gin. It took special effort to find the gin and even greater effort to talk the owner into selling it. This, however, wasn't the worst part. It was impossible to find olives and onions. I happened to remember that the Pan American crew which had brought George Welch and Bill Wahl to Japan many months before had offered to help us anytime we wanted something special. I called the Haneda Airport in Yokohama on the off-chance that this crew might be in town. The only member I could find was leaving for Hong Kong almost immediately, but promised to put me in contact with the purser of a stratocruiser just arriving. I talked my way into enough olives and onions to last us for at least another month, and much to my surprise I was also able to find a whole case of gin. My aircraft was ready to go back to Korea on the 12th of May, but late that evening I was back home, equipped for almost any eventuality, in time to read that the 4th Group was scheduled for two more dive-bombing missions on the 13th.

On the first scheduled mission we were to use a squadron of F-86s to bomb the airfield at Uiju again with the same loadings as before; on the second we were to use only four aircraft, equipped with 2,000-pound bombs and no external fuel tanks, to bomb a small rail center near the town of Kunuri, about 150 miles from K-14. We were to use only four aircraft on the second mission because 5th Air Force wasn't sure we'd have enough fuel to do the job and still get home safely. We didn't want to lose any aircraft by fuel starvation while we were just experimenting.

On the first mission several bandit flights rose into the air while we were bombing, but none ventured across the river to engage us in action. I again took my flight down to the deck for strafing action, but about the only thing the wing could claim for the morning was a number of trucks and tanks destroyed on the ground.

On the next flight, just before noon, I scheduled three pilots with well above normal talents to accompany me, in case we encountered fuel shortages. Major Ted Coberly, who had been my group adjutant at George Air Force Base, was to fly my wing. Ted had been in Korea only a short time and he was already credited with the destruction of two enemy aircraft. Major Clyde Skeen, my element leader, was a National Guard pilot who had been called back to active duty at the beginning of the Korean War. He had been flying F-84s on ground-attack missions, and having completed his tour of duty in Korea, had asked to stay on for an additional tour, providing he could fly

F-86s. This was the spirit we were looking for, and we were glad to have Clyde working with us. The fourth man in the flight, Major Dan Sharp, also had dive-bombing experience although he was new to Korea.

We departed for Kunuri behind all other flights of Sabres bound for the combat zone. Over the target I was the first to roll over for the attack, from about 12,000 feet. As soon as I had released my bombs at 6,000 feet I broke to the right and began to climb while the Communist artillery shot at me with everything they had. After calling to the others to break left, thus avoiding antiaircraft fire, I circled the target to observe where our bombs fell. The 1,000-pound bombs made a considerable explosion, and to my satisfaction I noticed that almost all of our eight bombs fell within the target area. We had destroyed many railroad cars along with hundreds of feet of railroad track. We appeared to be learning. While we were bombing it sounded like the rest of the group were in one hell of a fight up north. Many bandit flights were airborne, and some had even crossed the Yalu to mix it up with the Sabres. When I heard a couple of the pilots shout excitedly "I got one, I got one," I knew our plans were beginning to bear fruit. It turned out that the Communists didn't like to have us dropping bombs so near them, after all. Our four ship flights returned to K-14 uneventfully, although on the way home my flight members complained over the radio that the other pilots were getting all the glory while we did all the work.

After we had shut down our engines I asked the line chief to load the same four aircraft with two 1,000-pound bombs again, because I intended to ask 5th Air Force for permission to go after Kunuri one more time that day. The other pilots agreed we had been successful, but all thought we had enough fuel left to make our bombing runs at an even lower altitude, thus improving our accuracy.

I had to call Colonel Harry Doriss, Chief of the Joint Operations Center, for permission to go, which he gave over the phone. Next I had to find Harry Thyng at the mess hall to tell him. Harry had planned to go on the third mission that day, having heard that two enemy aircraft were destroyed on the second. I told him that this would be my last time as leader of the dive-bombing flights and from now on I'd turn the job over to others while I resumed escort. Harry said that he was glad to hear I intended to lay off for awhile, because he didn't want me to get shot down dive bombing. He had just talked to General Everest about our work and had good news for me. In four days I would be receiving orders transferring me to the 51st Wing as wing commander. Gabby was returning to the United States, and I was to get his job. Colonel Al Schinz, who had been deputy wing commander of the 51st, had been shot down in a big air battle about a week before, so I was about the only full colonel who could assume Gab's job with little or no indoctrination. I was tickled pink. There were few wing commander positions open in the Air Force to men of my rank, and it would mean a great deal to me to have a big command such as the 51st.

I asked Harry what had happened to Al. It seemed the 51st, led by Schinz, had been patrolling as usual in the combat zone. Al's wing man, another full colonel named Al Kelly, had noticed a great number of Migs in position for an attack on the lead flight, and called to Schinz several times to break right. Just as Schinz finally heard him and called back "Who do you mean, me?" one of the Migs let him have it with all guns. By the time the sky had cleared, Schinz was nowhere to be seen. Much later I learned that, although Al's aircraft had been heavily damaged, he had been able to fly southwest toward Cho-Do Island until he was out over open water in the Yellow Sea. Just as he had cleared land the aircraft had become uncontrollable, and he was forced to eject, landing in the water a short distance from a small island. Al had made his way to shore and set up house-keeping, hoping to be rescued immediately by friendly forces. He actually spent one month on the island before low-flying friendly aircraft spotted a large HELP sign he had scratched out in the underbrush. He existed by eating vegetation and whatever small animals he managed to kill, and for relaxation chased a small cat which seemed to be the island commander. He never caught the cat, so he never found out the nutritional value of cat food, but he certainly tried. Al's unique story was printed in detail in *Life* Magazine when he returned to the United States. The boys remaining in Korea officially named the island Schinz-Do.

On the way down to the briefing room from the mess hall Harry explained to me that he was sorry to see me go back to the 51st, but he felt we'd do well competing with each other. I explained a plan which I had been generating for several days —a plan to put the 4th Wing on top of all others in Korea. Shortly before, the 8th Wing, under the leadership of Colonel Levi Chase, had established an all-time record for combat sorties in a twenty-four-hour period by flying 256 individual dive-bombing flights near the front lines. I intended to beat his record by scheduling 275 sorties beginning at dawn and ending at dusk. On the 12th of May my group had flown 196 sorties, so we were sure we could make the additional effort. This would take some doing because there were only 75 F-86s assigned to the group, of which only 54 would be in flying condition at any given time. We would have to refuel and rearm all of our flyable aircraft five and one half times in order to accomplish our goal, but our enlisted men were willing to do the additional work to outperform everyone else. Two hundred and seventy-five individual aircraft over North Korea, plus whatever number the 51st put up, should completely confuse the Communists. I asked if Harry would carry out my plan even though I was to leave the wing, and he agreed. Once this was settled we turned our attention to the mission ahead.

This briefing was much the same as the last. For the first time in many a month I listened to our intelligence officer give his portion of the briefing. He began with the usual escape-and-survival information, followed by the reading of a message from 5th Air Force outlawing border violations. Next came a short discussion of the current battle situation on the front lines, followed by the latest news from the peace negotiations at Panmunjom. The intelligence officer closed his remarks by saying, "Gentlemen, if you are shot down I cannot tell you

101

what to do. You will have to do what you see fit to meet the situation. If possible, give only name, rank, and serial number. If you can get away with it, don't talk at all. If the going gets rough, tell anything they want to know since none of you know enough to effect the future of the war. Remember one thing, though, do not divulge any information that will in any way cause injury or death to your fellow United Nations soldiers. That's all I have." My sentiments exactly. I wound up the briefing by wishing everyone good luck, and off we went again.

While the initial flights of Sabres were on the way up to the border the Migs began to rise in droves. This could be the best day of combat yet. I had briefed that we would begin our bombing run from 6,000 feet, so I let down to that altitude, and upon reaching the target rolled over into attack. I remembered that on the last mission I had received intense ground fire from the right, and elected to make a rolling pull-out to the left. But ground fire seemed to be directed at me, no matter what I did. Once again I called the flight, appraising them of the situation, and began circling the target to observe hits. To my amazement I noticed a truck heading for the town from the north—a very improvident thing for any truck driver to do during an air attack. I decided to line up for a strafing attack on the truck, followed by a pass on the railyards to see the bomb damage close at hand, thinking I would have a fine story to tell the boys when we gathered around the bar that night. I figured I'd be able to determine exactly how much damage we could do with the amount of fuel we were carrying. But I forgot to think of a couple of things.

It has always been accepted as gospel that the most dangerous thing a pilot can do on a ground-attack mission is to fly back over the target. All the antiaircraft gunners who were asleep in the sack on the first pass have had time to run out to their guns for the second. Also, those who missed the target on the first shots will have improved their accuracy on the second. It really is a silly, stupid thing to do. But I was carried away. I just knew they couldn't lay a gun on me. After all, hadn't I been doing this very maneuver for weeks without being hit very hard? Besides, I had been through my share of bad luck over the years and I was now living a charmed life. So what the hell, let's get the truck.

I pulled back on the throttle, popped the speed brakes to slow down, and lined up on the truck just in time to see him turn off the highway into a small clump of trees, leaving me with an impossible shot. At this I shoved on the throttle and pulled in the speed brakes when suddenly—*thud*. Good God! I'd been hit. Immediately the cockpit filled so completely with smoke that I couldn't see a thing. And I panicked. This can't be happening to a nice guy like me, I thought. What the hell am I going to do? I called to Ted Coberly, "Hey, Ted, I've been hit. I think I'm on fire. Can you see me?" Of course he couldn't. I hadn't even thought to tell him what I was going to do, and by this time he was probably halfway back to the officers' club. He did hear me, though. "Honest John, switch to emergency channel while I set up air-sea rescue." This I tried to do. To say that I was rattled would put it mildly. Although I had opened the canopy partially, to clear away the smoke, I still didn't know whether my ship was on fire, and I was much too low to give my parachute a chance to open if I bailed out. The indicator on my instrument panel showed that the tail pipe was way overheated, requiring that I reduce the throttle setting to about 70 percent of power to keep from burning off the tail end of my aircraft. I didn't know what else to do. A million thoughts flashed through my mind. If I did go in, what could I expect from the natives? By any chance could I possibly nurse this crippled machine back 100 miles to home base? Whatever the alternatives, I had to keep flying as long as I could.

At Ted's suggestion I switched channels, only to find that I had lost communication with the rest of the world. My battery was dead. I took stock and it was shocking. All the instruments had failed except engine revolutions, tail-pipe temperature and rate-of-climb indicator. I couldn't even tell how high I was, although I could see mountains well above my level on either side. I found that I was flying down the bed of the Chong-Chong

River, headed for the Yellow Sea, some 60 miles away. If only I could reach the mouth of the river, there would be salt beds in a location where we had previously rescued downed pilots. I had no idea how the F-86 would ditch, but I really had no other choice. With the tail-pipe temperature as high as it was, all I could do was to pray my ship would hold together long enough for me to reach the Yellow Sea.

En route I had to pass an obstacle I had completely forgotten: two of the most heavily defended cities in all of North Korea, Anju and Sinanju. By this time I surmised I had been hit by 40mm. antiaircraft fire somewhere aft of the cockpit, with the shell exploding into the intake duct of the aircraft. The explosion must have destroyed the generator, parts of metal had probably been ingested by the engine compressor, and part of the intake duct must have been blocked off, disrupting the flow of air to the engine. By now the engine must have been smoking badly in flight, making my aircraft plainly visible to anyone on the ground.

Flying is usually rather dull, so it is hard to realize the anxiety occasioned by the malfunction of an aircraft in flight. Realizing danger ahead and knowing nothing can be done to avert it, is the most unnerving experience imaginable. Practically my whole life passed before me during those few moments after I had been hit. Just as I flew up to the city of Anju I glanced out of the cockpit to determine my position, and a terrifying sight met my eyes. The Communists were shooting at me with everything they had. Tracer bullets converged on my aircraft from all directions. I saw so many tracers flying through the air that for a moment I was convinced that the turbine wheel in my engine had finally disintegrated and that I was looking at the pieces. Much of the heavy fire was so close that I could hear the explosions as the shots burst in the air. I felt four more *thuds*, indicating that I had been hit again and again. I think the only thing that saved me from destruction was that I was only flying about 150 miles an hour, and since the aircraft had an extremely high noseup angle of attack, the gunners were inaccurate. It appeared that most of the fire was directed in front and above me. Just then I noticed the forward engine compartment fire-warning light come on brightly, indicating an overheat condition in the front end of the engine. At the same time the emergency hydraulic flight-control light informed me that there was damage to the flight controls and that perhaps a major portion of the hydraulic fluid had been lost. As I passed the town the ground fire slackened, only to start up again as I approached Sinanju. I was in trouble all over again. As I tried to dive, climb and turn, in an effort to evade the ground fire, I heard two more loud *thumps* as the Communists scored hits. Shortly the aft section fire-warning light came on, forcing me to reduce throttle setting to 50-percent power—not enough to keep the aircraft in the air. I knew I was going in.

As my aircraft sank lower and lower I gradually pulled back on the control stick, hoping to stay in the air longer. All the while the nose of the machine was rising higher and higher until I could no longer see in front of me. I knew I would have to hit the ground, but had no idea what the terrain would be like when I finally hit. I could feel the control column tightening, indicating that it would be just a few more moments before I lost control completely. When it appeared I was about ten feet above the ground I heard a *thump* and felt the aircraft shudder in flight. I pulled back on the throttle, cutting off the fuel supply to the engine, and we stopped flying all at once. The Sabre slammed to the ground with a terrific impact, and from then on things happened so fast that I hardly knew what was going on. The impact I felt just before hitting the ground was a telephone pole which had buried itself in my right wing. When we hit, the wings—covered with mud—stopped forward direction immediately, while the gyroscopic action of the rotating part of the engine caused the fuselage to separate from the wings and roll over and over in the direction it had been traveling.

As the fuselage rolled into an inverted position the entire top part of the aircraft was sanded off like bumps on a small log, and as we rolled over and over I was conscious of thinking,

My God, I'll scrape the top of my head off if we keep this up!
But I was lucky. I had crashed in a rice field covered with mud
and water, and this cushioned my head from abrasive action.
However, each time we went over, the cockpit scooped up water.
I was sure I would be drowned if the fuselage stopped in an
inverted position. Finally, after the fuselage had made two
complete revolutions while reversing direction, we came to a
stop about 100 feet past the point of original impact. Although
I had had to use my parachute on three previous occasions, this
was the first time I had crashed. I didn't like it a bit.

I found myself still strapped into the cockpit, covered from
head to toes with a thick layer of mud and slime. Around me
there was nothing but silence. The fuselage was resting on its
back with the cockpit down, and all I had to do to fall out into
the mud was release my safety belt with my right hand. As soon
as I could get my legs under me I stood up and tried to release
my parachute harness, so as to begin to run unencumbered
toward the coast, about one mile distant. To my consternation
I found that my left wrist was broken. At that time two hands
were required to release a parachute harness—one to hold and
one to twist. Try as I could, I couldn't manage to do it with
only one arm. In addition to the parachute I was weighted down
with some 75 pounds of escape-and-survival-gear which included
a one-man life raft, several guns, an escape kit, and a portable
emergency radio. I knew I must run toward the ocean if I
wanted to escape, but the combination of the parachute and that
sticky, oozy, Yellow Sea delta mud was just too much for me.
For every step I took forward I slid back two. The jig was up
and I knew it. I had been through a lot of similar experiences
during World War II, but I was certain that this would be
like none of them.

And I was right.

Part 2: The Big War

1.

THE author of almost every flyer's book tells of wanting to fly from his earliest days. As for me, I took my first flight with my dad in Fort Wayne, Indiana, when I was twelve years old. Red McVey, one of dad's more swashbuckling friends, took us up in a Stinson Gull Winged Reliant, a rather hot ship for its day. I can remember almost all the details even now, because I was mighty impressed at the time. But though I liked the sensation of flight, I also wanted to be a fireman or a railroad engineer, or even—strange as it may sound—a businessman.

I didn't forget that airplane ride, though, especially when I discovered that Howie Miller, the boy who delivered groceries to our house, actually owned a JN-4, an old World War I student-trainer. He was trading it for a newer Waco Taper Wing, and he allowed as how he might take me up in the new machine, providing I got permission from my mother.

Now, a little thing like permission from Mom is never going to stand between a boy of twelve and an airplane ride, so one

Sunday morning I hopped on my bicycle and headed for the Guy Means Airport, some twelve miles from home. Howie was busy taking up paying passengers when I arrived. I hung around looking obvious for what seemed to be hours and hours. Finally, just before dark, the paying-customer line had thinned out and Howie let me hop into the forward cockpit with the last passenger. We took a five-minute flight and it was a wonderful experience.

These were Depression days, and my family was having its troubles. Though Dad might have been one of the best architects in the Middle West, new construction jobs were few and far between. Then, too, Dad's heavy stock-market investments had been virtually wiped out in the crash. As a result, there just wasn't money for frivolous things like airplane rides.

My dad's health deteriorated during the early thirties and he finally suffered a nervous breakdown. Mother tried to keep ends together by conducting tours to the World's Fair in Chicago, and one summer I managed to get a job as dishwasher at the local Y.M.C.A. boys' camp at Blackman Lake, Indiana.

In school I was an undistinguished, skinny little runt who couldn't afford to buy season tickets to the football games and social events that loom so large in a teen-ager's eyes. I went out for football, only to find that I couldn't even hold down the fourth-string quarterback position. Everyone else on the field weighed more than my 123 pounds. Then I tried track, baseball, swimming, and everything else but the tiddlywinks team, until I concluded I was not and never would be an athlete. As a last resort, I tried out for and made the cheer-leader squad—small consolation for a boy anxious to take his place with the "men" in the school, but at least I got into the athletic and social events free.

During the summer of my sixteenth year I was promoted to the position of assistant cook at the boys' camp. Not much of a raise in salary, but a great increase in prestige, and by careful saving I was able to buy my first car—a 1917 Model T Ford touring car with bucket seats. I paid fifteen dollars for it, and from then on every cent I made went for repairs. The first day

110

I drove it I was stopped by a policeman. It turned out that he didn't want to see my license, nor had I broken any regulations; he just wanted to know how old the car was.

During my senior year two things happened that had rather profound effects on my life. My dad was now suffering from what was called softening of the brain, and he began to behave as a child. While my mother sold real estate I spent a large part of my time caring for him, and I learned to iron a white shirt in fifteen minutes, to can grapes and tomatoes, and to cook.

One Sunday while Mom, Dad, my sister and I, were eating dinner, and I was impatiently trying to help Dad, Mom blurted out, "Bud, if you and Margaret were our own children instead of being adopted you'd understand your father better." Margaret, who was four years older than I, had apparently known she was adopted for some time, but I hadn't even suspected. I was stunned. For the first time in my life I felt alone. I had to find someone to take into my confidence, and I called one of my closest friends, John Miller, whom I had known since we were each four years old.

When I had given him the big song and dance about being adopted John turned to me and said, "Bud, I've known that ever since I've known you. It doesn't make any difference to me or to anyone else you know." There were twenty-two boys my age living in the same neighborhood, and I had known them all almost like brothers. None of them had ever hinted at or even mentioned my being adopted. Obviously it couldn't be the bad thing I had imagined. In fact, now that I thought about it a little, it seemed rather wonderful. Here were two people who couldn't have children of their own, who were willing to take a chance on someone else's child. They had given me a wonderful life—which I had taken for granted. Gradually I began to feel an obligation to amount to something in order to repay them for all they had done.

Naturally I was curious about my real parents. I thought it would be interesting to know who they were—interesting, but not important. I never asked.

The father who adopted me died in 1941, but my foster

111

mother is still living, and this will be the first time she'll know how I felt when I learned I was adopted. I only hope she has realized all this time that she has been the best mother a son could ever want.

I graduated from high school and wanted to go to Purdue University and become an engineer, but this ambition would take big money. I worked in a parking lot for fifteen dollars a week, but couldn't save enough for school. Even working full time at college wouldn't swing it for me; I'd have to work for a year, go to school for a year, work for a year, and so on. I resigned myself to the fact that it would take me eight years to get a degree.

It was 1937 and Hitler was preparing his attack on Poland. China and Japan were at war. The nation's periodicals were full of stories concerning the international situation, and the United States Air Corps had stepped up the campaign to recruit aviation cadets for Randolph Field. In addition, our government had started a civilian pilot-training program. This appeared to be the solution to my educational problem. If I could get in one year of college, I could take civilian pilot training, and if I could manage another year of college, or pass an equivalent mental examination, I could join the United States Army Air Corps and graduate within a year as a second lieutenant. After three years of active duty I could resign and fly for an airline.

My first year at college was an eye opener. I went to Purdue with $75 in my pocket—$3 more than the registration fee. I had no job, no assurance of one, and no place to stay. But I was invited to stay at a fraternity house for a week or so while I made up my mind whether I would join, and I used this time to advantage. I found a job, working in a rooming house as handy man and general cook and bottle washer. I decided against joining the fraternity for financial reasons, but the members gave me a job for several hours each Sunday for the magnificent sum of $1.25.

Carrying a normal curriculum and working on the outside for about fifty hours a week just didn't work. The first semester

I passed 12 out of 17½ hours, and the second semester only 10. This put me on probation for the forthcoming year. College was supposed to be a rewarding experience, but I hated it.

In the summer of 1939 I worked as a secretary-clerk in the City Light Power plan at Fort Wayne, took university extension courses at night to make up for my various failures at Purdue, and began to learn to fly in the civilian pilot-training program. By the end of the summer I had become a pilot with a student pilot's license, had made up all of my college credits, and had taken the mental entrance examination for the Army Air Corps—which I failed. I had also saved up enough money to go back to Purdue.

This time I lived in a dormitory and worked at waiting on table and washing dishes in the dining hall. I managed to do all right in my studies the first semester, but by the second I was on probation again, and my mother received a letter from the president of the University suggesting that I stay out of school a year because of academic deficiencies. I had passed only 3 of 17½ hours, but I made up 12 by taking make-up final examinations. Back to Fort Wayne, back to City Light, and back to night school.

By fall of 1941 the draft was in full swing. The Battle of Britain had focused world attention on the gallant Royal Air Force fighter pilots who were fighting against great odds in a tremendous effort to stave off German attacks. As for me, I was aware of the war in Europe and in China, but was so concerned with my own problems that I found it difficult to worry over the world. Still, I had submitted another application to the Army Air Corps.

Meanwhile I had been dating a lovely girl. Patricia Sweet, the daughter of a Midwest celery grower, was four years younger than I. We had known the same group of young people in Fort Wayne even before we met, and our parents had known each other casually for years. We liked each other very much, but marriage was out of the question, not only because of money, but because Pat planned to go to college. And then, regardless of our hopes for the future, the Air Corps intervened.

In September 1941, I received instructions to report to the Primary Flying School at Wilson-Bonfils Field, Chickasha, Oklahoma. After a few preliminary examinations in Fort Wayne I said good-bye to Mom and Pat and boarded a bus headed for Fort Benjamin Harrison in Indianapolis and a completely new life. My class was the first at Wilson-Bonfils, and it was composed of men from the universities of Kentucky, Tennessee, Indiana, Princeton, Mississippi, and Purdue. The base was new and incomplete, but out on the ramp were rows of Fairchild PT-19s. I had never seen one before, and after the cubs I had been flying they looked big and powerful to me.

Late on the evening on December 7, while we were studying in our barracks, we were routed out by the station fire-alarm signals. The standard procedure was to grab all the fire-extinguishing equipment handy and rush to the headquarters building. Our commandant, Captain Johnson, was standing on the steps of the building with his entire staff. "Men," he said, "the Japanese have just attacked Pearl Harbor, and a state of war exists between our two countries. There is a giant Japanese aircraft carrier fleet steaming up the Gulf of Mexico to attack us. Until we can evacuate the aircraft you must stand guard around the airfield."

Captain Johnson and his men had already been to town and rounded up all the guns and ammunition they could get their hands on—everything from ancient shotguns to worn-out pistols —which they now proceeded to divide among us cadets. Each of us was assigned a post along the perimeter fence, which we were to protect until relieved by civilian guards the following day, and as they say in regulations, ". . . to walk my post in a military manner, keeping always on the alert."

It was a night to remember. None of us had been allowed to listen to a radio, so we only knew what we had been told. For all I knew there was a Japanese fleet within easy attacking range of Chickasha, Oklahoma. At any moment all night long I expected to see hordes of Japanese paratroopers descend on my post. Fortunately the panic wore off, and the next morning we went back to the routine of learning to fly.

After two and a half months at primary school we were transferred to Randolph Field, San Antonio, Texas. Though Randolph was supposed to be the best there was, and though it was called the West Point of the Air, I hated the place. The base was beautiful, our uniforms were unique, and we flew the best training aircraft in the world—the BT-14—built by North American Aviation; yet the hazing of cadets, the rigorous schedule, and the deadly routine, made Randolph a three-months nightmare. In basic training we were given the opportunity to indicate which type of flying we wanted to pursue—fighters, bombers or transports. I chose fighter training, and my instructor, Lieutenant R. G. Alexander, backed up my choice. I was sent to bombers.

It seemed that Boeing Flying Fortresses, the B-17s, had begun operations in England. United States bomber formations were being sent over German installations in daylight raids in France and in the Low Countries, and after the first few successful attacks, were being clobbered by German fighter pilots. One famous *gruppe* stationed in Abbeville, France—and dubbed the Abbeville Kids by our pilots—was taking the highest toll of our aircraft. The noses of their Messerschmidts were painted yellow in a very distinctive fashion. As a result of the Abbeville Kids and other *Luftwaffe* units, our losses were much higher than anticipated, and back home it didn't make much difference to the authorities what the individual wanted, he was needed in bombers, and to bombers he would go.

I was sent to advanced school at Ellington Field, Houston, Texas, a base equipped with AT-17s, the twin engined Cessna Bobcat; the AT-9, a twin-engined machine built by Curtiss-Wright; and the AT-6, a North American single-engined trainer much advanced over the BT-14 I had been flying. Though cadet activities were less rigorous because we were soon to become officers, nothing could make up for my disappointment in flying bombers. I simply didn't like being a bomber pilot. It seemed that all we did was fly around the sky in a big gaggle of aircraft, following our instructor leaders while they made their way to and from simulated targets. Since every pilot in the formation had to keep his eyes on everyone else at all times, only the leader knew where we were at any given moment. I always felt that if ever I had to pull out of formation I wouldn't even know how the hell to get back to home base. At Ellington most of us were exposed to instrument flying, link trainers, night flying, cross-country flying, and best of all—Rat Racing, in which the instructor placed his men in a line astern, then proceeded to go through all sorts of intricate maneuvers to shake off the planes behind him.

On graduation day we all had to brace for our first assignment as officers. Some, we knew, would be instructors, others sent to replacement crew-training centers to begin training on either B-17s or B-24s, and still others would be sent directly to combat units and then overseas. I didn't know what I wanted to do most, but I knew for sure I didn't want to fly bombers. I wasn't too keen to go into combat and get shot at, yet I wasn't much interested in the training command either. The day before graduation we all lined up for duty assignments. It turned out that all cadets 5'10" tall or over would be sent to bombardment training, and those under that height would be sent to fighters. I was 5'9½". Fighters after all!

As a brand-new second lieutenant, I was assigned to the 56th Fighter Group at Mitchell Field on Long Island. The 56th was one of the old-time fighter units organized during World War I, and its 61st, 62nd and 63rd squadrons were equipped with the P-38, the Lockheed Lightning, a twin-engined single-seat fighter equipped with four 50-caliber machine guns and one 20-caliber cannon. But rumor had it that the group would soon be re-equipped with the Republic P-47, the Thunderbolt, the nation's newest and most powerful single-engined flying machine. Before they let us fly in the newest equipment we had to check out in the Curtiss P-40, the Warhawk, which at that time was being used extensively in combat in Africa and China and in the Pacific.

Checking out in a single-seat fighter is at best a rather haphazard affair. Since there is only one seat, no skilled pilot can go along with the novice to give advice. And since it is not possible to explain all that is going to happen—not to say all that can happen—the new sport must find out for himself. In those days check-out consisted of becoming familiar with the cockpit, then cranking up and taking off. I knew that the jump from 450 horsepower to 1,100 would be a big one, but I didn't realize how big.

When my turn came I taxied out to the end of the runway with two other P-40s ahead of me to wait my turn to take off. My feet fairly danced on the rudder pedals with anxiety. To put it mildly I was scared to death. The first of our trio applied the throttle to his machine and ran right into a mechanic's stand, hopelessly ruining his engine and bending the propeller all out of shape. The pilot next to me applied his throttle and started down the runway, only to ground-loop into the center of the field, spinning like a top. Then it was my turn. I managed to get airborne, and once in the air all I could think was, My God, how will I ever get this monster back on the ground? That entire first flight the aircraft was easily ten miles ahead of me, a horrible experience. The P-40 cruised at about 240 miles an hour, and in those days that was speed to burn. I was used to flying at 160, and so it seemed to me that I was really boiling around in the sky. That first flight convinced me that I wasn't fooling around with toys, that I'd better get to work and really learn my profession. Thus, while the other guys talked about buzzing New York City, flying low over beaches and golf courses and taking airborne sight-seeing trips all over New York State, I stayed close to home and worked hard at my flight technique.

When I thought about the prospect of combat I never visualized myself as being any great shakes as a fighter pilot. I knew there were going to be aces, even though our nation hadn't produced any up to that time, but I never dreamed of becoming one. All I wanted was to be acquainted with a few of them personally. Some of the more experienced men in my group were exceptional flyers, and I felt that they would be

117

aces for sure, even though none of us—including the leaders—had any idea of what combat would be like. One thing was sure. We wouldn't find out flying up and down Long Island Sound.

2.

THE 56th Group, having received orders to ship to England, left the port of New York on the Cunard liner *Queen Elizabeth* on January 6, 1943. We weren't ready to go, by a long shot, but I suppose no unit is ever completely prepared for war, no matter how good its training. It had managed to accumulate 250 hours in the P-47—time enough to discover many things about the aircraft. For one thing, I flew it wide open on the deck to find out how fast it would go. It had been touted as a 450-mile-an-hour fighter, and I was extremely disappointed to find that it would only do 320 about fifty feet above the ground. Of course, I hadn't taken into consideration that an aircraft will perform faster in higher, thinner air. I mulled over my new knowledge for days before I told anyone, and then found that I was the only guy in the squadron who had ever flown a P-47 that fast. Another thing bothered me. All of us had been practicing aerial gunnery time and again, and I found that I couldn't hit the broadside of a barn. For that matter, neither could anyone else. We ought to be just great in combat.

Although we had spent hours practicing formation flying, navigation, night flying, and everything else our commanders could think of, and although we had been visited from time to time by experienced Royal Air Force fighter pilots, we still didn't have the foggiest idea what we would encounter once we met the Germans. We knew that we were to be the first

118

group to go into action with the P-47, but how would the aircraft compare with the ME-109 and the FW-190 we had been hearing so much about? No one knew the answers.

Just before we left for the embarkation point my flight leader was killed in an accident, right before the eyes of our whole squadron. Bobby Noel was one of the first captains created in the 63rd Squadron. An excellent pilot in every respect, he had been in the Air Force for several years prior to the war. We had been having trouble with the wooden radio antenna mast on the P-47 because the masts had been breaking off at high speeds. Republic Aircraft had redesigned the antenna, and it was put on Bobby's aircraft for testing. When Bob took off he told us that he would fly over the field at 15,000 feet and go directly into a dive. "Boys," he said, "I'll really show you some speed." True to his word, he came over the field and rolled over on his back into a vertical dive. He never pulled out. His aircraft hit about 500 feet off the end of our only runway at a speed we estimated to be in excess of 650 miles per hour. It was a hideous sight as the engine screamed louder and louder, climaxed by the thump of the machine burying itself in the ground with an accompanying puff of black smoke. At the site of the crash there was only a hole in the ground, about 30 feet in diameter and 20-feet deep. The aircraft had disintegrated. It was the first fatal accident I had witnessed.

Our first station in England, Wittering near Stamford in Norfolk, had been an old Royal Air Force training base. Its grass airfield was shaped like a dumbbell, with a three-mile runway used to recover crippled aircraft returning from missions over Germany. RAF Spitfires and Mosquitoes operated from the field, and it was our first opportunity to see what the British were flying. Compared to the P-47, both of these aircraft were like toys, particularly the Spitfire. It appeared to be light and tiny, but its history clearly demonstrated its excellent performance. The Mosquito, a twin-engined machine made of plywood, also had a very high performance rating, and compared to the P-47, it was small even though it carried two men.

Shortly after our arrival we moved again, this time closer to the Channel to Norwich, again in Norfolk, where the RAF had established a permanent base called Horsham St. Faith. We were ready for combat now, and all that remained to be done before we started the entire group into battle on its own was to send our leaders to operational units for one or two missions.

During the Battle of Britain the RAF had included a unit called the Eagle Squadron, composed of American airmen who had joined the British prior to our entry into the war. The Eagle Squadron had been in combat for several years, and just before our arrival had been incorporated into the United States Army Air Corps and redesignated the 4th Fighter Group. It, too, was being re-equipped with the P-47s, having previously flown Spitfires, and twelve of us were sent to Debden—the home of the Eagles—for our first combat mission, on April 13, 1943. I was next to the lowest-ranking man in the team and therefore entitled to the dubious honor of playing "tail-end Charlie" for the mission.

We flew just over the English Channel into France, then back out again as quickly as possible—the whole episode lasting two hours from take-off to landing. We saw neither Germans nor antiaircraft, nor—for that matter—anything but ourselves. Nonetheless, the powers that be felt that we were now sufficiently experienced to take our group over Europe on our own.

Back at Horsham St. Faith, we were added to the regular operation orders emanating from 8th Fighter Command. Our commitment was generally for twelve aircraft per squadron to fly fighter sweeps over enemy territory. The third time out, on April 29, 1943, the group ran into Germans. I wasn't along, but back on the ground we listened to the mission on the radio and there was plenty of excitement. Several of our pilots were shot up; two, Captain J. C. McClure and Lieutenant Winston S. Garth (a classmate of mine), were lost. Our crews didn't fire a shot. At that moment it looked bad for us and bad for the P-47. It didn't occur to us that we weren't using the right tactics, and it especially didn't occur to us that we were eventually going to catch on.

120

Colonel Zemke, in order to meet the exact take-off time specified on the operations order, usually held briefing two hours ahead. We were required to be in the cockpit one hour before take-off, and that one hour of waiting would just about do me in. I've heard lots of talk about bravery under various conditions, and I'm convinced that people who are just naturally unafraid have something I don't have. As I sat in that cockpit, waiting to take off into the unknown, waiting to go against a foe who I was sure was more skillful and flew a better aircraft, I was petrified. In fact I would reach a point where I would almost jump from the cockpit and refuse to fly, and all that kept me from doing just that, as I recall, was fear of my fellow pilots' criticism. I wanted to be one of them and I wanted them to like me, yet I didn't want to be killed and I didn't know what I would be up against once I ran into Germans.

On May 4 the 8th Fighter Command ran the very first fighter escort mission for a formation of B-17s. The operations order called for fighters of the 4th, 78th and 56th groups to join the bomber formation over Antwerp and provide withdrawal support across the Channel. There were 54 heavy bombers in the formation, and somehow we found out that Clark Gable—then assigned to Bassingborn, a B-17 base—was to be riding along in the bomber formation as a tail gunner.

Since we hadn't the slightest idea of how to provide bomber escort, our leaders decided we would fly in flights of four aircraft with each flight, separated by a five-mile interval. We would thus have a steady stream of fighter aircraft which would circle behind the bombers, fly over the top in the direction of the bomber stream, then return to home base. If attacking German aircraft were sighted, we were to make intercept if possible.

The mission came off as Colonel Zemke had briefed. I led my flight behind the bombers, flabbergasted by the size of the formation which appeared to cover the whole sky. As we passed over I looked down to see at least fifteen enemy aircraft going around and around in a giant circle while shooting head-on at the lowest bomber in the formation. Off to one side, perhaps

121

fifteen other Germans were lined up, waiting for an opening. When one would fire all his ammunition he would leave the circle to return to base and another would take his place. There appeared to be German fighters everywhere.

I called my sighting to Colonel Phil Tukey, my squadron commander, but Phil was having trouble with his radio and couldn't hear me. Since our orders were not to deviate from the plan of action without the permission of the squadron commander, I decided not to attack unless given an okay; meantime my flight passed over the bombers headed for England. About five miles ahead of the bomber formation I looked down to see four German fighters some 5,000 feet below, flying at right angles to my flight path while chasing an RAF Spitfire.

This time I ignored any contact with Phil Tukey and called to my flight to follow, because I intended to make an attack. Then I did everything wrong. I was so excited and frightened that I rolled over on my back and gave the Thunderbolt full throttle straight for the ground, completely forgetting how fast the machine would accelerate in a dive. When I tride to pull out to get on the tail of the last aircraft in the German formation my P-47 was going so fast it would not respond to the controls. On pull-out I wound up some 500 feet below the Germans, headed in the same direction with about 200 miles an hour closing rate. I knew that I would go by them in a perfect position for all of them to shoot at me, but I couldn't do a thing to prevent it. I slipped my aircraft a bit as I went by, hoping to throw off their aim, although I was still in a vertical bank which allowed them to turn slightly and start shooting. When I was well out in front of them a 20mm. cannon shell hit the ammunition bay in my right wing, causing the ammo door to flip open, blowing a hole in the bottom of the wing, and flipping my aircraft upside down into another dive. It all happened so fast I couldn't even think. I managed to pull out of the lopsided dive at 15,000 feet and limp for home while calling in a weak voice; "Postgate Blue Flight, this is Blue Leader. I've been hit and am heading for home." We changed the wing that night, but you can't win a war that way. At least the Spitfire managed to escape.*

On the 18th of July, our group having been grounded for several days because of bad weather, it became mandatory to fly all aircraft at least once, in order to work out any mechanical difficulties. While circling over our base in my P-47 I noticed a B-24 bomber flying slowly along at low altitude, and I decided to fly alongside in close formation to give the bomber crew a thrill. For several moments I kept the wing of my fighter tucked in closely, about one foot from the bomber fuselage, while the crew waved and laughed and motioned for me to come closer; then I decided to break formation. As I dropped down slightly and pulled ahead of the bomber I felt the tail of my machine being drawn inexorably into the bomber propellers. Suddenly I felt the propellers cut into my tail. Simultaneously the controls went limp and I knew I would have to bail out. I opened the canopy and jumped immediately from about 500 feet, landing on the ground about 2 feet away from the crater created when my P-47 hit the ground and exploded. The B-24 crew feathered both starboard propellers and landed at an air base several miles from the accident.

I was close to a farmhouse and hurried over to call Colonel Zemke to tell him what had happened. When I came back to what was left of my aircraft I found an ambulance and a flight surgeon, Major George Green, who was poking around in the molten metal looking for the body of the pilot. George took me back to base in the Meat Wagon and the next day I was fined under the provisions of the 104th Article of War for: ". . . use

---

* Early in 1961 I paid a visit to Germany as a guest of the German Fighter Pilots' Association. While there I met a German who recalled the incident of the first time he saw a Thunderbolt in combat—an aircraft which he claimed to have destroyed. I had a chance to check his logbook on the date of his claim, and found it to be May 4. In the discussion that followed I became convinced that he had potted me. After talking to him I was no longer disturbed about being hit, because he was ultimately officially credited with 101 aerial victories—49 of them B-17s. Georg Eder is now one of Germany's most highly decorated pilots—a man who fought for his homeland with utmost valor.

of government equipment prejudicial to the best interests of the United States." The accident cost me $100—a small price to pay for a P-47—and made me ineligible for promotion for one year. Since I had recently been promoted to captain, the ineligibility didn't bother me too much, but I did feel like a chump for destroying the aircraft.

Finally, on the 17th of August, after I had failed in combat and fouled up in practice, 8th Air Force went out on what was to be a historic mission, a raid on the German aircraft factories at Schweinfurt and Regensburg. During this great air battle our air force lost a total of 60 heavy bombers out of an attacking force of 360, one of the most severe losses of the entire war. However, the 56th Fighter Group came into its own by destroying 17 enemy aircraft, probably destroying another, and damaging 9. And I contributed by shooting down 2 FW-190s.

For several weeks I had been reading combat intelligence reports detailing individual descriptions of enemy aircraft engaged. The first American ace, Captain Charles London, had shot down his fifth enemy aircraft on the 30th of July. Several more had since broken into this select group, and Lieutenant Colonel Gene Roberts of the 78th had shot down six. In his combat intelligence reports I read that Gene found the enemy about fifteen miles to the side of the bomber formations. From his reports it appeared that the enemy would fly parallel to the bomber stream at some distance on either side. When well in front, the enemy pilots would turn into the bombers to make head-on passes while flying through the formations. There appeared to be a regular queue at either side as each successive group of enemy fighters made its attack.

At the height of the battle on the 17th I went to the spot where Gene Roberts reported having found his Jerries. I found some of my own, but I had to pass over the bomber formation to do so. As I crossed over I looked down to see German fighter after German fighter flying through the bombers with cannons blazing. I could see hits on the bombers and several in trouble going down. The scene served to make me mad as hell. My only thought was: By God! They're hurting our boys. When I got to

Gene's magic spot I saw a single FW-190 about to make a right turn into the bombers. After alerting my wing man, Lieutenant George Hall, I headed down to make a pass on the enemy. Obviously the Jerry didn't see me, because I came to within 500 yards dead astern before opening fire. When the ammunition from my eight machine guns hit the German he sparkled like fireflies, from the impact of explosive shells. His aircraft immediately flipped over on its back and bobbled erratically upside down. Then it gradually began an inverted dive, trailing fire and smoke. George, like me, had never seen such a thing happen before, and yelled over the radio, "Nice shooting, Bud! You got him!"

As I pulled up I looked to my right just in time to see another FW-190 flying along in the identical position to the first, so I merely made a descending 180° turn and found myself on his tail. Again closing to about 500 yards, I fired. As before, the FW sparkled all over, spewing large blobs of oil which came back to cover my windshield. The FW yawed to left and then right, finally ending up belching fire and smoke in a wild spin. George, probably as excited as I was, yelled, "You got that one too! You got him!" I was almost out of ammunition, so I called George to head toward England and home. But then we spotted an ME 109 at a lower altitude. Both George and I opened fire at what seemed to be an impossible shot. But we hit. How badly we hit I couldn't tell, though it seemed enough to bring the enemy aircraft down. We didn't see it burn or hit the ground or explode so we had to call it Probably Destroyed.

On the way home I was so excited that the thought of having killed two human beings didn't enter my mind. In the first place, I had been spurred to action out of anger; in the second place, the planes I had just shot down were objects, not people; and third, I had paid my country back for the P-47 I had destroyed. Finally, judging from the sounds of combat, others in the group had been shooting too. From a yell on the radio— "Look at him go! You blew him up, Jerry!"—I knew that Jerry Johnson had brought down at least one German. At last we

125

were functioning as a team, and at last all that training had paid off.

It turned out that Jerry, a classmate of mine from flying-school days, had shot down three enemy aircraft, putting him well on his way to becoming an ace. In fact, two days later he shot down his fifth aricraft, to become the first member of the 56th to enter the charmed circle.

On the 4th of October the 56th provided escort to heavy bombers attacking the town of Frankfurt in the Ruhr Valley. Dave Schilling led the group, while flying with my squadron, and during the engagement 15 enemy aircraft were destroyed. I got 3, my wing man got 1, my element leader got 3.

While flying in large S turns over the bomber formations I noticed what appeared to be a small box of bombers at a lower altitude, trailing the main formation. These aircraft were in essentially the same formation as their big friends, but somehow they didn't look right. I decided to drop down to investigate, and found to my surprise that there were from 40 to 60 twin-engine aircraft closing in on the friendlies. After calling Schilling, I went down, taking my entire flight with me. We came boiling up behind the enemy aircraft, which turned out to be ME-110s—the twin-engined fighters the Germans had used with little success during the Battle of Britain.

I let go at the first one I saw. With terrific closing speed, I was within 500 feet of the enemy when my shots ripped him to pieces. Many large parts flew from the wings and tail, and both engines caught fire almost immediately, causing him to dive out of control. Simultaneously others in the squadron had started to fire, and the German formation was splitting up in every direction. As I broke away from my attack I pulled up in time to see several enemy aircraft above and in front of me. I was so confused and excited that I started to take snapshots at every enemy aircraft I could see, even though I didn't have a chance of hitting them. Suddenly I realized that I would squirt away all my ammunition if I didn't manage to get into a good firing position behind just one of the enemy, so I pulled out of the fight to find a German in the proper position for attack. Off to my right I saw a single ME-110 letting down underneath the B-17s, obviously on his way back for landing. Diving behind him, I opened fire at close range and at great closing speed. There were many sparks as the bullets struck home, causing large pieces to fall away from the aircraft, and then something happened that I had not really wanted to see. Passing by the enemy about 50 feet off his right wing, I saw the pilot slumped over the instrument panel. The canopy had blown away, and in the rear cockpit the aerial gunner had apparently become stuck while trying to bail out. He was held to the seat by one foot, with the rest of his body sprawled back along the top of the fuselage. His arms were flapping wildly in the airstream. He was caught tight, going down in a burning aircraft.

It was one hell of a shock. I didn't know how others felt about killing, because it was scarcely a topic of general discussion at the officers' club bar. Marines and Army infantrymen are trained to kill, and perhaps psychologically prepared for it, and yet I would think the memory of a killing would burn in a man's mind like a torch. Maybe some can forget about it; I've never been able to. I hadn't been trained for face-to-face combat. My training had told me to get on the tail of an object in the sky and shoot it down. Yet at that moment I knew I had just killed two men—two human beings who had been alive a few moments before. It shook me badly, but the sky was so full of enemy aircraft that I had to keep from getting killed myself.

I broke away, only to spot another ME-110 heading 90° from the friendlies in a gradual dive toward Frankfurt. With full throttle, I closed astern and let loose. As soon as the shots began to pepper him he rolled over on his back, performing a split S maneuver so as to head for the ground vertically. I didn't want to let him get away, and split S'd with him, firing down vertically until I could observe many hits all over his machine which by this time had begun to disintegrate. My overtake speed in the dive caused me to pass over him, and I pulled back into level flight position.

The bomber stream had progressed many miles ahead of my position, and I found that I was alone. I could still hear sounds of fighting ahead, and at full throttle I sought to catch up with the rest of the fight. For the last time I saw one more German heading in the opposite direction, going back into Germany. It was a simple thing to make a 180° turn into position for attack. I really clobbered this guy until I ran out of ammunition. Many pieces had fallen away from the ME, and its right engine was on fire when I saw the enemy pilot leap over the side and a few moments later pull his parachute rip cord. Then, without ammunition and alone in the sky, I had to get home.

All the way back my engine groaned, popped and wheezed, after running at full throttle for over forty-five minutes. But what the hell—if I could get it home, one engine was a cheap price to pay for four enemy aircraft. When I realized I had finally broken into the ace circle myself, mutilating that P-47 didn't seem to matter too much. Still, I had to prove what I had done. We could make claims for enemy aircraft destroyed, by detailed written statements of the combat action. Wing men were required to make supporting statements of any combat to substantiate claims of leaders. Gun-camera film, if good, would also support claims. If the enemy aircraft was seen to be definitely on fire or if it hit the ground, a claim of destroyed would be accepted. All documentation was sent to Headquarters, 8th Fighter Command, to be studied by a claims board.

For the October 4th mission the claims board awarded me three enemy aircraft destroyed and one probably destroyed. After I lost my wing man I was without a supporting witness. My gun-camera film clearly showed the last two aircraft I attacked, but many of the hits made on the ME in the vertical dive didn't appear on the gun-camera film. When I had to pull away because I was overrunning, the camera had no chance to record the last of the bullets striking the enemy aircraft. My camera film corroborated the claims I had made on the other aircraft. At any rate, I now had five destroyed, and the "shoot-em-down bug" had really bitten me.

The business of claims is a funny one. Although our methods

of establishing claims were rather stringent, pilots would often imagine that they had seen things that had actually not happened at all. When the war ended and the German archives became available to us we had a chance to compare actual German losses for a given day against our claims of German aircraft destroyed. We often had claimed twice as many as they had lost. They also had the same trouble. Heat of combat, excitement, fear and anxiety, all help the imagination along. I shot down three aircraft on one mission three different times. Each time, when I returned to base, I had trouble remembering exactly what had happened. Often it was a matter of hours before I could describe the action accurately. I know of one pilot who shot down seven Japanese on one mission in the space of about ten minutes. How the hell he ever remembered what had happened or how he even managed to count the aircraft as they went down baffles me. Not that I doubt his claim, because I don't. A German pilot, Colonel Erick Hartman, the highest ranking ace in the world, credited with 352 aerial victories, once shot down seventeen enemy aircraft in one day. Christ! On a day like that I'd even have trouble filling out the Form 5.

3.

BY the end of 1943, fighter group after fighter was arriving in England to join either 8th or 9th Air Forces, and with the steady influx of new pilots it was virtually impossible for all the newcomers to make combat flights with more experienced units. Thus General William Kepner, Commander of 8th Fighter Command, sent out a letter to leading aces in the theatre, asking us to put our philosophy of combat in writing. He intended to publish all comments in a classified booklet which would be used as a combat manual by all pilots of the command. I replied in part as follows:

> ... Most of us have some sort of an idea formed in our heads when we finally get into a Combat Theatre. We like to think that the battle will assume proportions equal to those of the movies. You know how it is—one pilot sees the other, they both grit their teeth to beat hell, and finally the deadly combat begins with violent maneuvering by both parties. This field of thought is entirely erroneous. The combat usually takes place at a hell of a speed; the enemy plane is only seen for a few seconds. In nine cases out of ten the victor never sees his victim crash. As a result of the wrong idea, the new pilot who first sees a Jerry ship, goes into attack hell bent for election, and winds up feeling futile as the dickens because he didn't even succeed in frightening the Hun. I know, because I've done it myself many times. In fact, I've blown some darned good chances by just that sort of an attack.
>
> The conclusion I draw from this is that no combat is worth while unless the pilot does his work in a very cool and calculating way. I don't do it that way myself, but I think that if I have got things pretty well figured out before I make a bounce, I stand a much better chance of bagging that guy I'm going down after. The cardinal points in an attack are first: be sure of your own position. See that there are no Jerries around to make an attack on you. Secondly, make sure that you know what the Hun is doing. Try to figure out what you would do if you were in his position. Third, try to get up-sun on him. This is extremely important, because once the element of surprise is lost, the Jerry is about ten times as difficult to bring down. Even if he is not surprised, he still can't see into the sun—so the chances of getting to him before he can make a turn are pretty darned good. Last, close right up his old rudder and let go. Then he'll be a dead Hun. ...
>
> In regard to looking behind and around, I realize that it is a subject that has been harped on by every guy who has ever spent one measly hour on a combat operation. It is an absolute

130

necessity. The result is most obvious. The Hun will never bag an American fighter if the Yank sees him coming in time to take proper evasive action. It is still a bad thing to spend all one's time looking behind. The idea behind fighter aircraft is that they will seek out the enemy and destroy him. A pilot will never accomplish this aim by looking behind all of the time. He must divide all his time to where it will do him the most good. If he knows that there are Huns above him, then, sure, look above and behind, but if he thinks the Hun is below him, then for God's sake look in front and down. When you spot the Jerry go down and get him. . . .

The last thing that I can stress is training. I think that my group probably does more training than any other in the ETO. At least, it seems that way to me. I've been training ever since I got to the group and I imagine I'll continue to do so till the war is over. It really pays . . . Aerial camera gunnery is absolutely the most valuable training a man can get. Almost exactly like the real thing, only played with our own ships. Next in importance comes formation—both tactical and close. A good formation flyer will almost manufacture gasoline—something of which we don't have enough as it is. Third comes acrobatics, because a guy who knows what his airplane will do won't have to worry about how to make it do it when he could use the time shooting down a Hun. Fourth, anyone knows just how good a red-hot outfit looks when they take off and land. They really look good. This is all done by practice, and don't think they don't feel proud of themselves when they do make good landings and take-offs. I know, because I'm in one of those red-hot outfits, and it makes me feel good as hell. The same old axiom applies: "Whatever is worth doing at all, is worth doing well."

Besides aerial camera work, I don't know of a thing that closely parallels shooting in combat. I certainly wish I did. My shooting is probably the worst in the whole Air Force. I know that most of us feel the same. Jerry Johnson is probably the best shot in the Air Force, but he won't tell me how he does it. I have to get close enough to the Hun to reach out and club him before I can hit him. Usually even that won't work. But, boy, if I knew how to practice shooting I would spend all my waking hours at it. If we—and I speak of the Air Forces as a whole— could only shoot perfectly, we would double our score with no effort at all. When the man does come forth who has invented a way of simulating combat, complete with shooting down the target, then we will win the air war hands down. . . .

On November 26, 1943, 8th Bomber Command ran its largest combat operation to date, with 633 heavy bombers attacking targets at Bremen, Germany, and Paris, France. Seven combat wings of B-17s and 2 of B-24s attacked Bremen, and our group rendezvoused with the lead bomber force just after it left the target area. Once again we spotted 50 to 60 enemy aircraft attacking astern the bomber formations, although this time the twin-engined aircraft were being escorted by single-engined fighters flying above. Almost our entire group attacked the enemy fighter formations simultaneously, and we bagged a total of 23 enemy aircraft destroyed (8 of which were twin engined), 3 probably destroyed, and 9 damaged. I managed to down 3 enemy aircraft, thus becoming the first pilot in the European Theatre of Operations to score 10 victories.

From then on my competition got tough. The 353rd Fighter Group was stationed eight miles away from us at a base called Metfield. Although this outfit was somewhat newer to England, we had a friendly rivalry because some of our senior people had been transferred to help whip the 353rd into shape. Pilots of the 353rd started to score victories, and one man especially was going like a house afire. Major Walter C. Beckam was their hottest shooter, and I worried about him in a competitive way because he reached 15 enemy aircraft destroyed just before I did. There were several men in my own group who were in the running too. Lieutenant Colonel Francis Gabreski had 10, Captain Robert Johnson had 14; Lieutenant Colonel Dave Schilling and Colonel Hub Zemke were also double aces. But the natural desire to excel was to have dangerous consequences before many months had passed.

By this time I had begun to draw a few interviews from newspaper people who were not only interested in the Zemke Outfit but in aces in general. One of them was reporter Collie Small from International News Service. I had a deputy flight leader, Joe Egan, who was my best friend as well as my assistant. Joe, the son of the president of Western Union, was a Dartmouth graduate and a New York City boy who had aspirations of becoming an advertising man when the war ended. He and Collie Small took to each other like bees to honey. Apparently Collie couldn't find much copy in me, so one night he was griping to Joe at the bar in the officers' club. Joe, who had probably had one or two more than usual, formed an idea that makes me wince every time I think about it.

The acknowledged leader of the German fighter pilots was a major general whose name was Adolph Galland. This man was credited with 101 aerial victories during the war and was probably the most respected officer in the *Luftwaffe*. His name was mentioned repeatedly whenever our fighter pilots got together, and the RAF knew him, too, from the Battle of Britain days. I had read a good deal about him in intelligence reports and had even seen pictures of him examining the wreckage left from the ill-fated Dieppe invasion. He was hot as a pistol and we all knew it. Occasionally he would be interviewed over the German radio system which was beamed to England. We used to listen to him talk about his aerial successes for this day or that day, and we were sure that this was one guy who did not boast in vain.

Collie and Joe cooked up a big article about an interview which never took place. They said that I had vowed to destroy General Galland in aerial combat and that I flew daily over Europe in an effort to seek him out. They went on to say that I claimed that if I ever saw Galland in the air I would instruct my fellow pilots to stand aside while I brought him down. Altogether this story was probably the biggest amalgam of baloney ever conceived, but worst of all INS carried it. It came out all over England and in the United States too.

I didn't find out about it until one of my boys rushed into the barracks and said, "Good boy, Walker. I want to be there to see

133

this." He had to show me the article before I'd believe what it said. My God! I no more wanted to tackle that tiger than fly to the moon. He'd been up against the big boys. Believe me, I looked all over that base for Collie Small, but he had left the afternoon the article came out. For days I flew in somebody else's aircraft because I was positive after reading that damn article that Galland would be looking for me.

On February 3, 1944, our group provided escort for the withdrawal of bombers from targets in Wilhelmshaven. I led a flight with Adam J. Whisnewski as my wing man and Butch O'Connor as element leader. Butch's wing man had to quit, but Butch decided to stay on with us. On the way to rendezvous I spotted four Lockheed Lightnings being closely followed by a German ME-109. I called to Colonel Zemke to tell him of the situation and to advise him that I intended to make an attack, but apparently he didn't hear me. I went down to the ME-109, finally destroying it after several passes, but in so doing became lost from the major portion of my own group formation. Butch O'Connor had managed to squeeze in a shot or two at the ME in between my passes, and when the enemy burst into flames he followed it down into the overcast, leaving Whisky and me alone in the sky. Although I called time and again on the radio, I could not make contact and so decided to continue on the flight as planned, hoping to meet more friendly aircraft. I eventually came upon a large formation of B-24 bombers on the way home, and to my great surprise found that they were under attack from an ME-110 which was busy lobbing large rockets into the formation. I managed to sneak in behind the ME-110 without being seen, and shot it all to pieces. Then, seeing there was little else I could do, I told my wing man we would return to home base.

When I got back I found the entire group assembled in the briefing hut while Colonel Zemke gave them all holy hell for not having completed the mission. When he found out that mine had been the only flight to make contact with the bombers he became really angry. And when he heard me say I had destroyed two enemy aircraft he blew his stack. I had left the group formation and this was a cardinal sin. He was not going to put up with this sort of thing and he intended to court-martial me this time, for sure.

The following day he flew down to Headquarters of 8th Fighter Command to explain his intentions to General Kepner. When Zemke had finished the explanation Kepner looked him in the eye and said, "Hub, you go right ahead and court-martial Mahurin if you think you ought to. In the meantime I am going to award him the Distinguished Service Cross." I didn't learn this until a long time after the war when General Kepner visited my home and explained what had been done. About a year later Hub also visited me and repeated the story. Since we had become fast friends, we both enjoyed a big laugh about it. But at the time Hub was dead serious and I was scared to death.

One day Walt Beckam shot down his eighteenth aircraft but didn't come back. He had gone down with his squadron to strafe a German airfield, and the Jerries shot him down. His squadron mates were sure that he was alive, but it was certain that he wouldn't be home till after the war. Then my leading contender became Captain Bob Johnson of the 61st Squadron in our group. One day he'd be one behind me, the next he'd be even. It seemed that there weren't enough Germans to go around. And in order to keep ahead I began to do some foolish things. Later, in reading the copies of my combat action reports, I noticed the following remarks made at the time I destroyed two JU-88s and went after a third:

> By this time there were several more Thunderbolts in the fracas and my memory of the following incidents is rather garbled. I started after another enemy aircraft and began to fire at him. I am not sure whether or not I hit him, but during this time I ran out of ammunition. At the time I was within fifty feet of him. I tried several times to ram him, but each time I would get into his prop wash and miss him. He finally

135

straightened out and headed for the cloud layer. As I tried to ram him for the final time he rolled and disappeared into the clouds.

On the 8th of March I again became the leading ace in the ETO by scoring three more victories, but my time was running out and I didn't even realize it. This was one of the missions on which I got credit for the destruction of an enemy aircraft that I'm not really sure I shot down. Our group provided top cover for the bombers penetrating to the VKF Ball Bearing Works in Berlin. Four hundred and eleven Fortresses and 209 Liberators had reached an area between Dummer and Steinhuder lakes, en route to the target, when we arrived to escort. Our squadron was positioned on the left of the lead box of bombers, the 61st stationed in front and the 62nd stationed on the right. Just as we got into position I saw about 150 enemy fighters in close formation, heading for the lead box of B-17s. The 61st was in an excellent position to attack, turning into the enemy as they approached, but 12 fighters are no match for 150. The enemy drove right into the middle of the bombers, and within seconds I saw 12 heavy bombers either burning, spinning or falling apart in the sky. A few moments later the sky was clear of enemy aircraft as the 61st Squadron chased them toward the ground.

I kept looking below to see if another attack could be forming when I spotted an ME-110 on the deck, headed toward an airdrome near Hanover. I called my flight to follow and headed down from 30,000 feet to attack, only again—like a fool—picking up so much speed that by the time I had reached the ME's altitude I couldn't fire accurately. I had to pull up to avoid a collision, but my element leader, Lieutenant Barney Smith, who had more patience, came in behind the enemy at reduced speed to shoot him down. As we were joining up I looked out to the right just in time to see an FW-190 taking off from the Wunsdorf airdrome. This one was a breeze as I turned in behind to pepper him soundly. Heavily hit, he rolled over on his back and plunged into a forest to explode.

Just as I yelled "Let's get the hell out of here" to my flight

I saw another aircraft take off from Wunsdorf, this time a JU-88. I couldn't believe that we could be wandering around a German airdrome, without drawing heavy ground fire, and above all I couldn't believe that the Jerries would let their pilots take off with enemy aircraft in the vicinity. There was an answer, though; this mission was directed at Berlin. We were farther into Germany than we had ever been before. They just didn't expect us. A fast turn brought me around to the tail of the JU-88 as it reached an altitude of about 100 feet. I fired at a very high closing rate, noticing many pieces falling from the aircraft and an explosion resulting in a fire in the right engine. I had to bank and go past its right wing about 30 feet away and 30 feet above, and in so doing saw three men in the cockpit, dressed in brown leather jackets and leather flying helmets. They were not wearing oxygen masks, and I could see their faces looking up at me as I went by. A moment later they attempted to land straight ahead into what looked like a plowed field. When they did, the JU-88 blew up.

Once again we started for home. Once again I saw an FW-190 heading for Wunsdorf in an apparent landing attempt. But this guy must have gotten the word from the tower, because he picked up speed, dropped to the deck, and headed east. I began to chase him as fast as I could, but we were going back into Germany instead of the way I wanted to go. Moreover, he was skimming along only a few feet above the treetops. I couldn't seem to get the nose of my aircraft down low enough to shoot at him without running into the trees. I could pull up a bit, then dive down and shoot, but each time I did I seemed to loose distance on him. I kept firing, though, until I ran out of ammunition, then called the flight to break off and head for home. Just then I heard Russ Westfall, the Number Four man, yell, "Hey, Walker, you missed it. He just went in."

Smitty's ME-110 showed up clearly in the gun-camera film. So did the FW-190 and the JU-88. But that last FW really surprised me. My film showed him out in front, sparkling from time to time as I hit him. In one sequence we both passed over giant high-tension lines, and the cables looked as if they had passed about three feet under my wing. At the time I didn't even see them. The final sequence showed the enemy smoking very badly just above the trees. Russ said later that he had rolled over on his back and dived into the trees just after I broke off the attack. I got credit for the victory, but somehow I still doubt that one. Nevertheless, that brought my score to 20. But damn it! On the 15th of March on a mission I missed, Bob Johnson—who had 18—shot down 3 more, which put him 1 ahead.

4.

ON March 23 I received a fine surprise; orders came promoting me to the rank of major. Exactly one year before, to the day, I had been given the 104th Article of War for running into the B-24. The orders couldn't have been timed better, because I had just submitted papers asking for an extension of missions. In England 100 missions were required to be flown before transfer. I had flown about 80 and my time was getting close. I had adopted the same practice many others were using: I didn't log combat missions unless I had seen a German aircraft over enemy territory. Still, the missions were mounting faster than I wanted them to. I didn't want to go home, and above all I didn't want to stop flying combat to let someone else become leading ace in my stead. With the rank of major I was also given the job of squadron operations officer, while my friend and classmate Jerry Johnson, also a major, became squadron commander. Jerry had been the second person in the Air Corps to become an ace and he too was shooting the Germans down with regularity.

By this time the 56th Group was head and shoulders above all other groups in England in terms of number of enemy aircraft destroyed. We had been given enough aircraft and pilots to make what we called double groups. The normal complement of fighter aircraft per group is 75, and usually there are about 150 pilots assigned. Because we had been doing so well, we had about 125 P-47s and about 150 extra pilots. Hub put 2 groups in the air for every mission instead of the 1 normally called for in the mission summary. We were usually able to put about 36 aircraft per group into the air for any given mission.

On March 27 the mission summary directed us to provide escort for the heavy bombers in a bombing raid on Tours, about 150 kilometers southwest of Paris. The bombers were to bomb a German airfield and factory just outside the city, and they planned to be over the target at noon on the 27th. The 56th Group was to provide target support for the bombers with both A and B groups, and after the bombers had departed the target, were directed to find targets of opportunity on the way back to England. It looked like a pretty good show. At the briefing I found I was to lead the A squadron of the 63rd Fighter Squadron, while Jerry Johnson would be leading B squadron.

We took off as planned and made our way into France without difficulty. When the heavy bombers approached the target we were in position to observe the action. Although they were considered in bad taste, there were several smart remarks about the ability of the heavies to hit the target, and I took several bets to the effect that they would miss by a mile. But the bombing was surprisingly good, with little or no enemy reaction, so Dave Schilling, who was leading A group, elected to leave the bomber stream to work his way toward Paris.

As we headed northeast I spotted an enemy light bomber, flying at low altitude some distance away from us. I kept my mouth shut until I could work my way over near it, then called out, "Dave, this is Bud. I have one sighted and I'm going in to get it." "Go ahead," Dave replied. "I'll cover you."

With an altitude advantage of about 15,000 feet I found I was really boiling along when I started to close on the bomber. Although I had recognized the type of aircraft and was well

139

aware that it contained a tail gunner, I was unconcerned. I surmised that once the tail gunner had seen me he would immediately recognize that his 4 little 50-caliber machine guns would be no match for my 8 and he would quickly leave the aircraft. I forgot that he would have to crawl over the pilot to do so, and in this case the pilot must have been pretty loyal to Adolph Hitler. As I closed range, firing wildly in every direction, I saw bright flashes indicating that the tail gunner was firing back at me with all he had. I finally got close enough to see strikes of my bullets all over the wings of the enemy aircraft, but I also noticed that a big glob of oil had appeared on my windshield.

I closed on the bomber, firing all the way until I was about to overrun it, then pulled up to slow down. After calling to the other members of the flight to lay off, I settled down behind it once again and gave it all I had. As large pieces began to fall away I noticed an escape hatch separate from the aircraft, and shortly thereafter four parachutes blossomed as the crew made a desperate effort to bail out. However, they were much to low, and when the unmanned aircraft struck the ground and exploded, the crew appeared to be caught in the blast.

When I broke away from the attack I called to Dave, "I think I've been hit, but everything seems to be all right. Cover me, and I'll climb up to you." But as I started to climb I happened to look over the side of my ship and was horrified by what I saw. It was high noon and the shadow of my aircraft, with a long, black trail of smoke, was silhouetted on the ground. I seemed to be in more trouble than I had thought. When I reached about 800 feet I heard a loud explosion and saw a sheet of flame spewing from the engine cowl. As I threw open the canopy and jumped I heard Dave Schilling say, "Watch it, boy, your aircraft is on fire!"

I had enough altitude to watch my fighter explode before I hit the ground in my parachute. Once on foot and alone, I became frantic. To begin with, I couldn't get rid of that swarm of P-47s circling directly over my head. There is nothing noiser than 36 fighter aircraft circling at once, and I was sure I would be spotted immediately. German soldiers had to be lurking behind every bush and stone, and those damn pals of mine were trying to decide who was going to land and pick me up. There was a small road near the wreckage of my aircraft, and they obviously intended to make a landing on it. Once on the ground, the pilot who landed would throw his parachute out of the cockpit and I would sit on his lap to fly the aircraft back to England. My wing man, Captain George Hall, was determined to make an effort, but Dave Schilling, with a cooler head, was equally determined to examine all the possibilities before anyone took a chance. Much to my relief, they evidently decided that the road was too narrow, for after flying by me several times as close as they could, they headed away toward the Channel.

Alone and in enemy territory, I cut off all insignias and ripped my clothing to shreds. Then I rolled in the dirt. About a mile away I could see a small forest, and started to run for it, but when I got there, all out of breath, I was completely dismayed to find that few of its trees were over six feet high. I ran among the trees, dug a hole in which to bury my .45, then ran out on the other side, hoping I could find something to hide under.

I found a stack of faggots piled neatly like cordwood, on the other side of the woods, a very convenient place for a guy in my circumstances to hide. I crawled into the pile and lay as quietly as I could. Whenever I heard the sounds of birds I adjusted my position, but when all was quiet I remained still. I heard people in the background, and though I could also hear motorcycles, I was sure no official person had arrived at my aircraft. As night drew near I decided to head south for the border between France and Spain, because our intelligence briefings had indicated that many airmen had returned to England by reaching Gibraltar. When all was quiet I began running in a direction I knew, by watching the stars, to be southwest of Paris.

As I ran through the French countryside I was often confronted by main highways and hid in ditches until I was sure the coast was clear. Toward daybreak I was pooped from running all night. Silhouetted against the approaching dawn, I saw

141

in the distance a small village with several tall buildings, and while avoiding it, spotted a smaller village where I found a very large haystack. I crawled to the top and burrowed down deep inside, determined to spend the day in hiding.

Deep in my burrow, I listened to the sounds from the community around me. Until noon there were only peasant voices, barking dogs and crowing roosters.

About midafternoon I heard the roar of many heavy bombers approaching. Though I dared not stick my head out, I had the pleasure of hearing approximately 60 B-17s plaster a German airfield at Chartres, about fifteen miles away. Now I was fairly certain that the heat would be off me, because the Germans would be busy trying to repair the damage to the airfield.

But the shock of bailing out in enemy territory, together with running all night without food and water, forced me to take action. About four o'clock in the afternoon I peeked from the top of the haystack to see a quiet little village with very few people. Several blocks away I saw a man dressed in peasant clothes, working alone in a vegetable garden behind his house. I decided to take a chance on him.

I jumped down from the haystack, ran over to the small house, and whispered *"Psst, Psst"* to the Frenchman. He was probably more frightened than I when he saw me, but he came close as I whispered, *"Je suis* American aviator." Nothing. I tried again, still nothing. In desperation I took off my wristwatch, my dog tags, my flying-school class ring and a handful of English coins, and gave them to him. *"Ah, oui, oui,"* he said, motioning me to follow him around the corner of his house. *"Cache ici."* He then had another thought. *"Manger, manger?"* I hadn't the foggiest notion of what he had said, but by this time I was answering Yes to everything. He disappeared momentarily and returned with a bottle of red wine, a loaf of French bread and a boiled pig's nose. I knew then what *manger* meant.

The Frenchman set off on a dead run down the street. Shortly thereafter he returned with the mayor of the village. With my meager French and the help of a paper and pencil I explained my circumstances. I told the two men that I wanted help in

142

reaching the French-Spanish border, so I could return to England. Interspersed with rapid-fire French, I could occasionally hear the words *oui* and *bon* as they discussed my situation.

To my relief the mayor motioned me to follow him home. There I was introduced to Mrs. Mayor, who began rummaging in the cupboards for food which turned out to be a cut of pig's nose. Just after dark a car drove up and a man entered, dressed in a tan raincoat with a brown felt hat pulled down over his eyes. He was greeted with respect by the mayor, but he scared the hell out of me. His thin mustache coupled to a hawklike nose made him look naturally sinister; he habitually had a cigarette in his mouth, and he spoke in whispers. This man, Jean Baptiste Le Curer, was head of the local underground organization, a member of the French Forces of the Interior and a leading grain merchant in the community. He did business with the Germans yet at the same time ran the underground organization. The Germans needed his grain, so he was able to travel extensively and was given substantial gasoline and food rations.

Jean Baptiste informed me that action would be taken to assist me to return to England at some future date, but that I was not to expect too much because there were many hundreds of downed airmen in the organization who were also waiting for help. Movement depended largely upon rank, with the highest ranks moved first. I felt that a major should be high enough in rank to be assured a front-running position in the escape system, and I told him so. He was visibly unimpressed. At the conclusion of our conversation another man came into the house. Pierre was the manager of a community-owned threshing machine. He, with ten other men, visited farms in the area to thresh grain. A bachelor, he owned a very small house, and I could stay with him without generating comment from other Frenchmen.

At daybreak the next morning Pierre woke me, saying, "*Travailler.*" I was delighted, because I was starting out for Spain just one day after I had been shot down. But *travailler* means work, not travel, and off we went to the threshing machine. I had been given some French clothing including a beret so

143

I would be inconspicuous, and apparently I was accepted immediately by the crew, because I was put to work wrapping wire around the bales of straw emerging from the machine.

As the day went on I learned something about the people working around me. One man was a Polish officer who had escaped a German concentration camp by killing a German guard. Another had been ordered to Germany to work in munitions factories, but had disobeyed and was now hiding out. Pierre himself was a saboteur who had killed several German soldiers in different localities throughout France. He, too, was wanted by the Germans.

On the next Sunday a woman came from Paris to serve as an interpreter and to give me instructions, since the underground did not want to take the chance that I might not understand. She explained why I was working by saying that the underground could not risk having a German pilot parachute over France and work his way into the underground only to expose those he contacted. The underground must check the identity of everyone. I had been assigned to the threshing-machine crew to keep me out of mischief, and had I been a German pilot there were enough people on the crew to dispatch me easily. Confirmation from the Air Ministry in London had been received the previous day. It was time to move me to another place.

I should wait at the mayor's house until a young boy arrived with two bicycles, then follow him at a discreet distance until he motioned arrival at our destination. Not long after, I was pedaling furiously down dirt roads, trying to keep up with a young Frenchman who must have felt like the devil himself was on his tail. Whenever I neared him he began to pedal faster and faster to keep away from me, apparently wanting to be well in the clear if we were stopped by the Germans. After an estimated fifteen miles I was about to collapse from sheer exhaustion when the lad pulled up in front of a small, two-story brick building at the side of a single railroad track.

Two people came out to greet me fondly—two people whom I came to know almost as well as my own family. Papa Chaurin was the stationmaster in the small town of Voves in Eure-et-Loire. Mama Chaurin maintained the brick home owned by the railroad, and her job was to open and close the gates over the tracks each time a train came by. Papa and Mama had two children, Jacques, sixteen, and Monique, eleven. They were the most loyal and wonderful people I have ever had the pleasure of knowing, and to this day I love them dearly.

Papa and Mama had previously sheltered nine members of a downed Air Force B-24 crew who were now on the way to Spain. They liked Americans and missed the previous tenants. Papa gave me a French-English dictionary and a blackboard which I found useful, and within several days I could understand a bit of what was being said and even try to say a few things myself. The second night, Papa brought home a radio—a crime punishable by death if discovered—so that I could listen to news broadcasts from England.

Soon I had settled into a routine of waiting until my name came to the top of the list and I could start for home. Each night Papa and Mama took me to meet some new family whose feelings, Papa assured me, would be hurt if I did not come to visit. During the day I had almost nothing to do because I was confined to my quarters upstairs in the brick house. Many times I saw German soldiers walking down the road, but they didn't bother us and I felt relatively safe.

Shortly after Easter, Jean Baptiste went to Paris to arrange with the underground headquarters for my trip south, and the following night he came roaring into the Chaurin's kitchen, so excited he could barely talk. Believe me, for a Frenchman this is excitement.

The night he reached Paris there had been a heavy British bomber raid over the city. No damage had been done to non-military objectives, but the rail stations and surrounding railyards had been heavily damaged. At the same time, the British bombers had dropped propaganda leaflets which were in French, and carried a picture of me and Walter Beckam. Jean Baptiste pulled one out of his pocket and gleefully showed it to Mama and Papa. The captain told of a heavy bomber attack on Berlin

145

on March 7 in which many German fighters had been destroyed. The leaflets were now apparently all over France. Jean Baptiste was absolutely hopping with excitement.

"Why didn't you tell us?" he kept saying. "This would have put you at the head of the list."

"I tried to," I replied, "but you couldn't understand my French."

"I have taken action to arrange for your escape from France," Jean said. "We have devised three plans."

The first was to dress me as a gendarme, escort me to Chartres, and place me on a train for Paris. In Paris I would go alone to the underground headquarters. Imagine! What if a French citizen asked me for directions to the men's room? The next plan was to escort me to a village called Pithiviers on the main rail line between Paris and Marseilles. I would climb into the coal tender of a steam engine to go to Marseilles, then make my way over the Pyrénées into Spain. The third plan was the worst of all. They were going to fly me out.

It was beyond my comprehension that the French could expect an airplane to land in the middle of hundreds of thousands of Germans, pick up one Walker M. Mahurin, and fly back to England. I explained to Jean Baptiste that he didn't need to use any of his fancy methods to get me back to England; just a plain little old plan would be plenty good enough. But no, by God, they had an important man on their hands, and he just wasn't going home any old way. He would soon give me the date and time, so I might just as well count on Plan Three.

The wait was intolerable, and while I waited an underground agent arrived who wanted me to do a favor for France. This man lived in the city of Châteaudun, about twenty miles from Voves. He had been able to draw a complete set of plans of the German airbase at Châteaudun, including all the antiaircraft gun emplacements, locations of buildings, ammunition and supply dumps, together with a complete listing of all personnel on the base. He had this information in a large envelope which he handed me with great pride. The envelope was sealed with a large red blob of sealing wax stamped TRÈS SECRET.

146

That envelope looked like a ton of dynamite to me. Here I was, an American airman in France, wearing French clothes, with no identification, and this guy wanted me to accept something that would label me a spy in any court in the world. I tried to explain that I wasn't a spy, but he didn't hear. "You just take that back for us," he said, "and we'll appreciate it very much." He was so damn sure of himself and I was so damn unsure of myself we reached an impasse. Mama finally said that she'd take the envelope and hold it, in case I changed my mind.

Early the next afternoon the owner of the local pub drove up in a small French car. Mama told me I was to go along in the car because I would be flying back to England that night. She had the presence of mind to slip that *"très-secret"* envelope into my coat pocket just before we drove off, saying she knew I wouldn't mind taking it to England with me.

We drove about twenty miles through several towns to a large farmhouse. I was led behind the house into a kitchen where some people were seated. I inferred that they were members of the underground and were waiting for an important news broadcast to come over the British Broadcasting System at six o'clock that night.

As we waited for six o'clock I was absolutely amazed to learn that two of the men in the room were actually French spies who intended to go back to England with me. These men, trained in England, had parachuted into France months before. They had been active for some time and were scheduled for a vacation in England. Unlike me, they were obviously happy, laughing and talking as if they were about to take a trip to the next village instead of flying in an unarmed aircraft over enemy held territory, without parachutes, at night.

At the end of every news broadcast the British gave instructions to underground groups under the guise of "personal messages." A message might read: "Suzie meet David on the corner of 7th and Vine." Or perhaps: "The grass is green today." Our message, which I didn't understand, came through in the affirmative.

The plan called for four of us to bicycle to another farmhouse to meet two more men that night. At midnight a small aircraft was to appear over a clover field, about five miles away, to pick us up. The pilot would be watching for a signal when he passed over, and when he had identified us he would land between the two men who would each be holding a flashlight at ends of the field. He was to stop before he reached us, whereupon the two French spies and I would hop into the aft cockpit. After that, England. It all sounded so simple.

A rising full moon lit the sky much more than I thought advisable for such a mission. At the beginning of the ride the leader of the group, a man called Philip, and the others had checked their guns to make sure they were in perfect order, because they had once before encountered a German patrol. Philip called my attention to a small bicycle trailer being drawn behind. It contained four suitcases of information that was extremely important to the British. Among other things there was a complete production background for an aircraft engine factory just outside of Paris, as well as many details of the German fortifications on the French Coast. The more I learned, the more frightened I became at the prospect of being caught.

Arriving at our field, we heard a steady drone in the distance and realized that we were on the flight path of a tremendous British heavy-bomber raid. The sky was soon filled with the roar of four-engined bombers, and, to complicate matters, the Germans had put up an extremely heavy concentration of night fighters. Junkers JU-88s were flying low to the ground along with Messerschmidt ME-109s. Four times we heard the loud, tearing noise of 20mm. cannons fired at the big bombers by German fighter pilots. Four times we saw the flashes followed by small glows as the bombers caught fire. In the moonlight we saw a long trail of smoke as each bomber plunged to earth. Each giant aircraft carried thousands of pounds of bombs which exploded on impact with the ground, a truely awesome sight.

We didn't know when to signal. Several times we thought we saw our aircraft, only to find it was an ME-109 or perhaps a JU-88. The noise was so great and there was so much confusion that we had to give up and wait for the sky to clear. One engine

noise seemed to circle us, then head off to the east of our location. As we strained to get a glimpse we saw sheets of gunfire
rise from the ground about ten miles away. The Germans were
shooting at something, and the glow of incendiary bullets
seemed to converge in one spot—a spot which began to glow.
The glow brightened into a ball of flame which plunged into
the ground with a loud explosion.

Our plane never came.

Later that afternoon Philip returned. Sure enough, our aircraft had crashed in flames and the body of the pilot had been
all but consumed in the fire. The Germans had found pieces of
French money strewn about and concluded that the pilot had
been dropping money to the underground. We would have to
go to Orléans while Philip made contact with the Air Ministry
in England to set up another rendezvous. He anticipated a
week's wait.

We bicycled into the nearest small railroad station and
boarded an electric train which would take us into Orléans.
Riding tourist class in a compartment with about ten other
Frenchmen, I felt that every eye in the train was directed at me.
At one point a lady sitting next to me asked if I would help her
lift her bundles down from a rack above as we reached her
destination. I didn't understand a word she had said, but thank
God, Philip performed the service with dispatch.

The train station in Orléans was filled with over 15,000 German soldiers, members of a Panzer tank unit being transferred
to Holland. There were several trainloads of tanks in the railyards, and thousands of black-booted soldiers milled around.
Many came parading through our car. Fortunately, this was
probably the last place the Germans would look for a downed
American airman, and we got away with it.

Some days later our pick-up was finally arranged the second
time, and we boarded the train to take us close to our rendezvous point. Members of the gang would bring us six bicycles
to reach the airfield. While we were waiting in the small station
the others brought out some sandwiches and bottles of wine.
Though there were several German soldiers in the station with

149

us, when one of the Frenchmen offered me some food and wine I was much too scared to think of food, and could only say, "*Non, merci.*" With that the whole group blanched. My French had English written all over it. Even the Germans began to stare at me. Philip rushed me outside and said, "Goddam it, don't ever try to speak French again. That was terrible."

We took our appointed positions at our pasture just before midnight. There was still a full moon and the countryside was quiet save for the distant barking of dogs. At midnight we heard the sound of an approaching aircraft and the pilot saw our signals. I watched him make his final approach to the field and began to pray he'd make a safe landing. Within several feet of the ground he elected to go around and make another attempt. There is nothing as loud as an aircraft engine, and this one was louder than most. As the pilot lined up for the second time I found myself on my knees, praying aloud that he'd make it this time. Once again he pulled up and went around. By the third try I was screaming, "Make it boy, make it! Cut the damn throttle. You've got it made, but for God's sake don't go around again." At last, thank the Lord, he touched down and taxied up to us.

The aircraft was a Westland Lysander, a single-engined, two-passenger plane with fixed landing gear and a high gull wing. Built years before the war, it had been used for everything from a fighter to an observation plane. At best it would probably cruise at about 100 miles an hour, but this one had a very large external fuel tank welded to the side under the fuselage. It couldn't have flown over 90 miles an hour straight down. Under the circumstances, however, I didn't feel I should wait for the first-class flight.

That flight was the damnedest I have ever made or hope to make. It took four and one half hours to fly back to England. Those crazy Frenchmen drank from a bottle of wine and sang wild French songs all the way. They didn't have a worry in the world. As for me, I was sure we'd be shot down. At ninety miles an hour we were absolute dead ducks. The pilot varied his altitude from sea level to about 12,000 feet to throw off interception. At sea level the back seat of the aircraft was so hot we nearly suffocated, and at altitude we nearly froze. I prayed all the way back.

Fortunately the Royal Air Force had been bombing a target about 100 miles north of us and most of the German night fighters had been drawn into that area. We came through unscathed. Back in England, I was delighted to hear the voices of the control-tower operators all over the Midlands, directing landing traffic returning from heavy-bomber missions. We landed at a base near Cambridge, and the pilot parked the aircraft over to one side of the normal location on the field. When the engine stopped I climbed down the ladder to make my way to thank the pilot, and felt giant hands on either of my shoulders. Then I heard someone say in a clipped, British accent, "Where do you think you are going?"

"For Christ's sake," I replied, "unhand me. I'm one of you. I'm just going to thank the pilot."

"We'll just have a look," the voice said. "No offense intended." After close scrutiny I was allowed to thank the pilot, then was hustled off to a well-guarded room. After all those days of hiding from the Germans and after that God-awful ride in a crate I wouldn't go up in again on a bet, I found myself under arrest back in England.

5.

THE next day I was driven to the Air Ministry, accompanied by two quiet and uninformative escorts who took me into the Office of Intelligence. After investigation and interrogation I would be released to rejoin my combat unit. Not only was it necessary to see if a returnee could give any significant information, but steps had to be taken to prevent a German from entering England as an escaped Allied pilot. When I discovered that the British were interested in intelligence I gave them the envelope with the data on Châteaudun. They appeared pleased to have it, although they said nothing about putting it to use.*

I was then taken to a builidng on Downing Street which served as an Air Corps reception center—and, thank God, I was home. The reception center, completely equipped to handle cases such as mine, gave me a uniform sans rank, and the colonel in charge cautioned me not to talk to anyone until he gave me permission. I was not to leave the building unless escorted, and especially not to call outside to any of my friends. He explained that this was necessary because he knew who I was—or at least who I said I was—and that I was a "Hot Potato." The Air Corps wanted a proper press release regarding my return, so that other airmen still on the continent would be protected. A member of my group had made a visit to London the day I was shot down, to send a wire to my mother saying that I had been sent on a trip and would return home shortly. The wire was meant to let my mother know that I had been alive when last seen. Unfortunately, the Western Union office in my home town had called the Fort Wayne *News-Sentinel,* which published the story with headlines. My own group withheld mention of the incident to higher headquarters because Jerry Johnson, my squadron commander, had been shot down the same day, about 100 miles away from me. Jerry was last seen running from the crash, and the group thought he might reach safety. It had appeared that we would both have more of a chance if the Germans did not know we were on the ground. Since we were fairly high-ranking officers with more aerial victories than others, the Germans might double their efforts to locate us. As it was, Jerry was captured shortly after he hit the ground. In my case the story originating from Fort Wayne had reached the British press before it reached Headquarters, 8th Fighter Command. There

* Sometime later the BBC announced that an RAF attack on German installations near Châteaudun had achieved great success.

had been some unhappiness about the security breach. The Germans had actually increased their efforts to locate me when they found out, via our newspapers, that I was among them, and now the Air Corps wanted to protect others.

It seemed that I was the twelfth Allied airman to fly back to England after having been shot down over the continent. I was to keep this information confidential, on the pain of court-martial. If word ever spread that pilots could be flown out, all airmen who went down subsequently would demand to return to England by air, or would think that I had been given prefer-ential treatment. Mum was the word.

When the interrogation was completed, five days later, the center commander asked our group intelligence officer to come to London. Major David W. Robinson, one of my most re-spected friends, appeared in complete ignorance. When he walked into the center to make positive identification he stood there nonplussed. For a moment all he could do was stammer, "But you're still in France." On the way back to base I think I really hurt Dave's feelings because I wouldn't tell him how I escaped. But orders were orders.

Dave and I reached the air base at dinnertime. As we walked into the officers' mess every eye in the place turned to us in disbelief. Hub Zemke insisted we join him at the head table, and exerted real pressure on me to tell how I had worked my way out of the continent so rapidly. But I couldn't. I did tell about making contact with the French underground, hoping the information would be of value to anyone finding himself in the same position. No doubt most of the guys pressured me because there was a good chance they, too, might be shot down. I hated to withhold information, but I didn't want to spend time in Leavenworth, either.

Hub invited me to stay in his headquarters, because many of his senior officers were leaving England for the United States and he wanted me to remain with the group. He thought I would not be allowed to fly over the continent immediately, but figured I'd be cleared for combat after the invasion. He planned to give me one of the squadrons and promote me to lieutenant colonel as soon as possible. While I was gone, Bob Johnson had become the leading ace in Europe with a total of 27 victories, followed closely by Gabby, Dave Schilling, Hub and many others. Because the invasion was imminent, there was heavy aerial activity, with many German aircraft destroyed per mission. Maybe if I stayed on I could get back into the business again.

About ten days after my return I got a call from Headquarters, 8th Air Force, saying General Carl A. "Tooey" Spaatz wanted me to visit him. He was interested in conditions in France and wanted a first-hand briefing. General Spaatz lived in a delightful English manor outside London. At dinner I sat down at a table surrounded by generals whose names I did not know, and after the first minutes of embarrassment found myself jabbering with the best of them. When General Spaatz asked me to tell him of my escape I figured he was the man running the show and I'd better tell all I knew. It took four hours to satisfy him, especially on questions involving the state of preparedness of France. It was easy to see that we were close to invasion. After dinner he told me he could not let me go back into action against the Germans. If I was shot down again I could be treated as a spy. He was going to send me home.

One week later I left England for Washington, D. C. I didn't tell my family I was coming home, because I wanted to get a feel of the situation in the States before I did anything. As soon as I arrived I called Joe Egan, who was visiting his parents in New York while home on thirty-days leave. Joe invited me to stay with him before I left for Fort Wayne, and after a few days with the Egan family I asked my mother to come to New York for a couple of days and to bring Pat. Mom, Pat and I spent a wonderful few days seeing the sights. Then I left for Fort Wayne on a train which arrived at four in the morning, the day of the invasion. I figured I could escape any welcoming team by coming in at this hour, but when we pulled into the station at Fort Wayne there stood the mayor, the chief of police and several other civic dignitaries. I was only going to stay in town for a few days before proceeding to Miami Beach for thirty-days leave, but the mayor informed me that I was to be the honored guest in a parade that afternoon!

The parade was a horrible experience. Thousands of people lined the streets of Fort Wayne, and I had to make a speech. The following day instructions came from the United States Treasury Department, telling me to participate in a War Bond drive in Indianapolis. I was requested to make a speech before about 18,000 people at the State Fair Grounds! Fortunately, however, with Paul Whitman's orchestra playing and William Holden and Ingrid Bergman as featured attractions, the crowd paid little attention to me.

After the bond-drive program I decided it was time Pat and I were engaged, and we then decided to take a short vacation at Gatlinburg, Tennessee, before I went to Washington and Miami. Mom agreed to go with us, and we spent several delightful days away from the terrible swirl of war. Yet, news of the invasion forces kept pouring in. I didn't like to be loafing while other guys were fighting; it just wasn't right.

In Washington I learned that two of my friends were recruiting pilots for new units scheduled to leave shortly for the Pacific theatre. Colonel Phil Cochran—the Colonel Flip Corkin of the comic strip "Terry and the Pirates"—and Colonel John Alison were organizing two new air commando groups. Both men, as leaders of the 1st Air Commando Group, operating with British soldiers under the command of General Orde Wingate, had distinguished themselves in the China-Burma-India theatre. I contacted John to see if my services could be used in either of these two new units. Although there was a regulation preventing combat pilots who had been sent back to the United States from returning to combat duty until one year had elapsed, John could get a waiver for me if I wanted it, and would also try to find me a job.

On the date specified in my orders I reported to one of the plush hotels on Miami Beach to begin my thirty-days rest leave. Guy Means, a long-time friend from Fort Wayne, had loaned me his car, and I had all the comforts of a millionaire, but

I wasn't very happy, knowing a war was going on. Nor were my feelings helped when I received instructions directing me to Atlantic City, New Jersey, for a war-bond drive.

The airplane I was flying when shot down in France had been called The Spirit of Atlantic City, N. J. The people of that city had contributed enough money in war bonds to pay for it, and I had elected to leave the name on the side of the ship when it was assigned to me. The leaders of the community now wanted to raise a similar amount of money to pay for another P-47, and I was assigned to help them.

I flew to Philadelphia and took the train to Atlantic City the following morning. As the train pulled into the station I saw a tremendous crowd of people jamming the station while several marching bands played at fortissimo, and I wondered what all the excitement was about. After all the passengers had left I stumbled out of the train and found that they were waiting for me. The city owned a tremendous open touring car which it used for parades, and I had to climb in the back seat and drive all over town on display. Combat in it's worst form was ten times better.

The next few days were reasonably enjoyable because the people were very kind. We managed to raise enough money via the war-bond route to buy several P-47s, but I just wasn't cut out to be a celebrity. After all the bond drives and celebrations I was so glad to get back to my hotel room in Miami Beach that I couldn't stand it. Besides, a telegram which was waiting for me read: POSITION OPEN FOR YOU AS SQUADRON COMMANDER, THIRD FIGHTER SQUADRON, THIRD AIR COMMANDO GROUP, LAKE-LAND, FLORIDA. REQUEST YOU WAIVER PROVISIONS OF REGULATION 36-24 PERTAINING TO OVERSEAS ASSIGNMENT. SIGNED ARNOLD, WASHINGTON. The waiver went out by wire within five minutes.

At last I was back in the saddle.

6.

THE group was commanded by Colonel Arvid E. "Oley" Olson, who had been a member of the American volunteer group under General Chennault in China. Long before, he had crashed in a glider 150 miles behind enemy lines in China, then made his way back to friendly hands through hordes of Japanese soldiers. Oley, Phil Cochran and John Alison were old friends, and he was bringing the 3rd Group into combat readiness. Our mission was to seize territory behind enemy lines, then conduct harassing operations. There were eleven squadrons in the group, consisting of fighter aircraft P-51s, cargo aircraft (C-47s), liaison aircraft (L-5s), light transports (Norden Norsemen) and gliders.

The pilots in both the 3rd and 4th Fighter Squadrons had more fighter experience than almost any unit in the war, although most of their time had been accumulated in the United States. To a man, they had read and heard so much about the war that they were champing at the bit for some kind of action.

As for me, there was another problem. I was engaged to be married. The longer I thought about it the more I didn't like it. Not that I didn't love Pat; I just didn't like the idea of getting married and then leaving almost immediately for combat, perhaps never to return. It didn't seem fair to her. I talked the situation over with my closest friends in the squadron, some of whom were married, others who were not, and we all concluded that marriage was out of the question.

But I hadn't reckoned with Pat. I began to notice that her letters were full of plans for a wedding dress, reception, invitations and all such things. Since I had planned a two-weeks leave, I would lay all my cards on the table. After a decision was reached (my way, of course) we would agree to wait until after

157

the war to marry. I was so sure that I was right that I made many positive statements to this effect at a party the guys gave me at the officers' club before I went home. "I'm going to be firm," I told them. "I strongly feel that postponement is the right thing."

Two weeks later I was back in the same club with the same guys. "Well," someone questioned, "how was the vacation?" "Fine," I replied, "I had a good time." "How about Pat?" they asked. "Did you tell her off?" "I sure did," I said. "In fact, she'll be along in a minute. We were married three days ago."

Pat has always resented my telling this story, but I'm glad things worked as they did. When I got home I found the wedding date had been set and invitations sent out. We had a wonderful wedding—something we'll both remember always— and I've been proud of her ever since.

The war in the Pacific was totally different from that in Europe. Since the 3rd Air Commando Group was a relatively inexperienced combat organization in the southwest Pacific, we didn't get good combat assignments. In December of 1944, the air battle was concentrated around a small island called Biak, off the northern tip of New Guinea, but by the time we were transferred to Biak the fight had moved on to Moratai on Halmahera Island in the Moluccas. Then the war moved on to Leyte, and finally we got into action.

Shortly after we landed in Leyte the surface vessels carrying our ground-support echelons arrived offshore a mile or so from the airstrip. All in all, our boys made a glorious landing.

Just before leaving the States we had chipped in to buy band instruments for the more musically talented. Several thousand dollars had purchased enough equipment for a small marching and dance band. This equipment was carefully packed and loaded with our military gear. As the landing vessels approached the shore the bow doors opened, with our lads poised and ready to wade ashore, musical instruments in hand, to do battle with the Japanese. When the vessel had anchored, orders came over the ship's intercom: "Prepare to disembark"; then "Disembark."

With that the leading troops stepped off into thirty feet of water. Fortunately we got the men back but the music was long gone. To make this story short, the Navy folded the bow doors till night, and then, in the cover of darkness, moved closer to land so that our men could wade ashore.

A week later our people, bivouacked in tents on the beach, created another incident which reflected great credit upon the Commandos. At the southern end of our camping area the Army had constructed a huge ordnance supply dump containing 50-gallon drums of aviation gas and 250-, 500- and 1,000-pound bombs. This area was casually guarded but the dump was not fenced in. Late one evening one of our mechanics, having run out of fluid for his cigarette lighter, spied the drums of aviation gasoline and decided to help himself. I have always supposed that it would be difficult to pour fuel out of a 50-gallon drum into a cigarette lighter, and such was the case. But some of the gas must have gone into the lighter, so the GI decided to see if it would work. It did. It worked so well the whole gas dump went up in flames.

After the first few drums exploded, quite a few people gathered to put out the blaze. It was dark and Japanese bombers could be heard overhead, attempting to bomb on the bright light as the fire spread closer to the rows upon rows of high-explosive bombs.

An Army three-star general came rushing to lend his talents as a fire fighter. As he barked out useless orders to all within earshot his glance fell on Captain Charles James Russhon, the photographic officer of our group, who was standing by, watching the fireworks. "Captain," he shouted, "are those bombs hot?" Rush, who didn't know that "hot bombs" meant those that were active and could be used for combat, replied, "I don't know, sir, but I'll sure find out." With that he ran over to the nearest row of bombs, felt one, then ran back to report, "General, they don't seem too hot to me." Two days later Rush was awarded the Soldier's Medal for gallantry, but the Commandos weren't too popular for several weeks after the night of the great fire.

159

For several weeks we dropped bombs up and down the Philippine Islands in support of ground actions, seeing enemy aircraft in the air only at night when they were dropping bombs on us. A few of us managed to shoot down enemy aircraft, but the pickings were mighty slim. Occasionally we went to Hong Kong on bomber-escort missions. These trips were about 750 miles out and the same distance back, all out of sight of land. My logbook showed several missions of over seven-hours duration, cooped up in the cockpit of the P-51. The big engine, which seemed to perform so smoothly over land, sounded like a cement mixer over open water. After listening to it groan and grumble for several missions I took along mystery novels to read. I could keep an eye on the leader, fly the aircraft, and find out who committed the crime at the same time. Then everyone was reading, including the leader, until once we almost missed the Philippine Islands entirely. That put an end to the reading.

We participated in the invasion of Linguyen Gulf, from an airstrip called Mangalden. The fighting was going on in the mountains around Baggio, the summer capital of the Philippine government near us, but we lived a splendid life when we weren't actually flying combat. We had natives build a series of bamboo houses, and in an exotic setting under tall palm trees, we lived like kings for awhile. The water table was three feet below the ground, so it was simple to sink a small shaft into the earth and pump water. We made a shower from three interconnected fifty-gallon water tanks, filled by our underground supply, and took all the showers we needed.

Because porcelain toilet facilities were nonexistent, we had a standard eight-holer which was used by all officers. One of the respected members of the group was Captain John Davis, the Army ground liaison officer. His job was to give us daily briefings on the ground situation to preclude our dropping bombs on friendly troops. Then one night he had an accident that could only have happened in the Pacific.

He had felt the urge shortly after midnight, and flashlight in hand, stumbled outside. It was a warm, moonlit, tropical night, and as he sat he was enthralled by the beautiful scene about him. Someone had forgotten to lower the lid on the hole next to him, and John inadvertently knocked his flashlight into the opening. It was a large, four-cell flashlight he had just received from the States and he was determined to effect a recovery. He lit a long wooden pocket match, then thrust his arm into the hole to see how best to reach his light. Unfortunately, early that morning the group doctor had decided that the eight holes needed to be disinfected. The medical technicians had removed the seats, spread gasoline in the pit, and ignited the whole works. After the smoke had cleared they had put the seats back and taken off. When John struck the match into the blackness there was just enough gas vapor left to blow up with a roar. He received burns serious enough to require hospitalization, and when word of what had happened finally got around, John's life became so miserable that he asked for a transfer and took off without saying good-bye.

Shortly after the case of the exploding latrine we received orders transferring us to an airstrip on the northern tip of Luzon. We knew there were several Japanese within a few miles of the strip, and we were over 200 miles from the nearest friendly troops, but the Japs proved to be no threat, because they were moving into the Cagayan Valley to join General Yamashita, the over-all Japanese commander in the Philippines. Day after day we flew 250 miles to Formosa, ranging far and wide to bomb military installations. Our combat losses were high because of intense enemy antiaircraft fire coupled with terrible weather, and our work was difficult and dangerous. We shot up trains, trucks, cars and anything that moved. One pilot even sank a midget submarine. My own fighter was damaged by enemy fire so often that it began to look like a patchwork quilt. This activity was especially unrewarding because the Allied forces were involved in tremendous air battles over Okinawa and we weren't in on the fun.

One day, after bombing a rail marshalling yard in the city of Tiepe, Formosa, in the face of intense enemy antiaircraft fire, I noticed puffs of white smoke coming from underneath the hood of my fighter when I was about 75 miles from the coast of Luzon. At the same time my wing man, Captain Raymond Clifford, called on the radio to say, "Chief, I think you'd better watch it. I can see radiator coolant leading from your aircraft."

We were cruising at 15,000 feet, so I throttled back, hoping to keep going long enough to reach home base. Although I could see white vapor streaming back over the windshield, 50 or 75 miles didn't seem too far, and besides, there was a lot of coolant to drain out before something serious happened. While gradually descending—or as they say in my business, "losing altitude and smoking badly"—I told all but my flight to zip on home and alert Air-Sea Rescue just in case I didn't make it. I told Cliff to stay close, and then I began to sweat it out.

I had jumped before from damaged aircraft when there had been no other alternative, and for self-assurance I deliberately began to check over my parachute, dinghy and other rescue equipment. My anxiety only increased. For months we had been having trouble with the natives because they would steal anything they could get their hands on . . . especially parachute silk, which made beautiful dresses for their wives and sweethearts. Often we discovered that our parachute packs had been stuffed with rags to replace stolen silk, and now I could just see myself falling through space and pulling the rip cord, only to find myself suspended from an old GI blanket.

Cliff was very close to me, looking intently at the engine of my aircraft. I finally asked him what he thought. "I can't tell, Chief," he replied. "I'd watch it, if it starts getting rough, and get the hell out before it throws parts and starts burning." I checked the engine instruments and noticed that all were well above the peg, indicating the engine was about to blow up. When I began to hear loud, clanking noises I knew I had had it.

I undid the safety belt, rolled the elevator trim tab full nose down, then released the canopy. At the very last moment I told Cliff to take care, I'd see him, then rolled over until the ship was on its back, and let go of the control stick. I was thrown out upside down, clearing the vertical tail by a wide margin.

I counted to three, then pulled the rip cord. It seemed ages before I felt the jerk of the opening parachute—so long, in fact, that I started to claw into the parachute pack, thinking something had gone wrong with the release mechanism. Then I found myself at 12,000 feet, drifting slowly to the water. As I descended, Cliff circled closer until I could see him making the thumbs-up signal. As far as I was concerned my troubles were just starting.

I was 50 miles offshore with only a few hours left before nightfall. A downed airman in a small life raft is a difficult object to spot even if his location is known, so once night fell and I drifted with the current till the following morning I would be far away from my present position and would probably never be picked up.

About 200 feet above the water I unfastened my leg and chest straps and waited until I was 12 feet above to let go of the parachute harness. As soon as I could I inflated my Mae West, but when it filled, one side whistled like a punctured balloon and deflated through a hole about an inch long. I then yanked the lanyard, to inflate my life raft, only to find that as it began to inflate it also began to deflate because of a thumb-sized hole in it. Like the boy and dike, I jammed my right thumb into the hole and watched with relief as the raft slowly became about three-quarters inflated. A moment later, with my thumb still in the hole, I managed to flounder into the raft to survey my position.

I saw Cliff make one low pass over me and then I was alone in the middle of the Pacific Ocean. I began to grope around through the small packages of survival equipment on board my raft. All rafts are equipped with round, wooden plugs designed to seal any puncture. There was a hand pump somewhere which could be used to keep the raft inflated, but I couldn't find anything. I wanted to paddle the raft toward shore, but I could only use one hand and each time I made the attempt I only went around and around. This was no damn good. As I sat there in that soggy raft, trying in someway to make some sort of progress, the shock of bailing out caught up with me and I started crying like a baby.

I couldn't understand why I was in so much trouble again. It was bad enough when I had been shot down in Europe, but, thanks to hundreds of helping hands, I had made it back to safety. Now here I was in trouble all over again, just trying to do a job for my country. I had tried to be a good guy, and I had been trying to do the right things. But somehow God had decided that I should be singled out again. Crying wouldn't help me out of my trouble at all, but as I sat there, crying like a baby, those wooden plugs came floating up between my legs. Moments later a plug was in the hole, the raft completely inflated, and I was paddling madly toward land some 50 miles away. At least I was headed in the right direction.

After paddling for some time I heard high-flying aircraft and spotted twelve P-51s flying toward me at 15,000 feet. I broke out my sea-marker dye and was soon floating in a huge spot of bright green. The guys above must have spotted green immediately, because they boiled down out of the sky and started to circle. My confidence began to build. While the squadron circled I noticed a B-17 heading in my direction. It was a Dumbo, an aircraft especially designed for air-sea rescue. Although appearing to be a standard B-17, it carried a 40-foot lifeboat attached to the underside of the fuselage. When released from the B-17 the boat would parachute to the water to be used by downed airmen. These boats were equipped for either sail or motor, were self-bailing and self-righting. It was possible to sail 800 miles by power and an untold distance by sail.

The Dumbo began to circle me, but would not drop the boat. No matter how I yelled or motioned to them it made no difference. As the first circled, two more arrived on the scene. But they wouldn't drop their boats, and I could gladly have killed every Dumbo pilot in the world as I sat there in a one-man raft while they flew around about me, carrying vessels that would comfortably take sixteen men 800 miles. While I was gnashing my teeth in helpless indignation three air-sea rescue Catalina flying boats appeared and made pass after pass directly over and about five feet above my head. They didn't seem to want to land and pick me up either.

The final blow came when one of the big Cats came flying by close to me while my wing man Clifford leaned out of the waist gunner's big window in the middle of the fuselage, giving me the V for victory sign. I was so mad at him I dropped my paddles and let my hands dangle in the water. And, by God, a fish came up and bit me on the right hand. I couldn't get to those Dumbo pilots, I couldn't get to the pilots of the Catalinas, and I couldn't get to Cliff, but I could sure try to get to that fish. I whipped out my .45 automatic and started to blast away at what was now a school of fish attracted by the smell of blood. After shooting off a complete round of ammunition I couldn't see even one wounded fish and decided to call off my private war in favor of bird watching.

One Catalina began to set up some sort of a pattern. The pilot would circle me and then head off toward the southeast until he was out of sight. Ten or twelve minutes later he would reappear, heading toward me. After circling once he would depart southeasterly again. By this time more flights of fighters, returning from combat missions over Formosa, had joined the rat race above me.

Finally the Catalina dropped a smoke flare some 300 feet from me. Then, instead of disappearing over the horizon, it circled my location. Suddenly I saw the masts of a vessel. Shortly thereafter a 90-foot air-sea rescue boat and a host of guys watched me paddle over to climb up a ladder into safe hands. "Whew!" I said. "I'm sure glad to see you. Those other guys wouldn't do anything to pick me up."

"They couldn't," the skipper told me. "The sea was too rough for the flying boats to land without damage, and by the time the Dumbos arrived the pilots could see us coming and didn't want to waste a boat on you."

The next morning, after a pleasant night on board the rescue boat, a Catalina landed in our cove, and a short time later I was back at the airstrip, trying to find myself a new fighter. A few days later the group medic tried to put me in for the

Purple Heart but 5th Air Force Headquarters examined the regulations and couldn't find a thing that covered fish bites.

Because all of our supplies were sent to us from Clark Field near Manila, 350 miles by air, we were using our C-47 troop-carrier squadron to make daily shuttle runs to pick up the necessary equipment for our private war with the Japanese. In such a remote area, entertainment—especially from Stateside —was rare, but Major Charles James Russhon, now our public-relations officer, was probably one of the biggest operators and scroungers to ever walk the earth. On one of his visits to 5th Air Force Headquarters, Rush learned that Joe E. Brown was visiting the theatre on a USO tour, whereupon he promptly set out to get Joe for a visit to our base. Joe had an extremely tight schedule, but at length agreed to visit us for the day, insisting that he had to be back at Linguyen Gulf that evening.

It took about two and a half hours for Joe to make the trip. Meanwhile we arranged to have all of our troops in front of a makeshift stage during the lunch hour. There were 3,000 of them, plus the usual assembly of natives who always seemed to know when something good was about to happen. When Joe arrived we took him directly to the stage and he was announced to the audience. He seemed to meditate for a moment, then stepped forward to give his famous baseball skit. When he had finished he had done more for those men than anything short of a trip home. The GIs gave him one of the most tremendous ovations I have ever heard.

After lunch Oley and I decided to fly Joe and his party back to 5th Air Force. I asked Oley when he had last flown a C-47. He replied that it had been about nine months ago, in fact it was before we left the States, but he was sure it would be no sweat. As for me, I had a total of about two hours as copilot in one of the crates.

We got on board and Oley and I went up front while the crew chief buttoned the rest of the passengers in the back end. The two of us got seated, only to find out that we didn't know how to turn the damn thing on—a pretty ridiculous state of

affairs, seeing that Oley was a bird and I a light colonel. All of
a sudden the door opened and Joe stuck his head in. "What's
the matter, you guys?" he asked. "Don't you know how to crank
it up?" Just as we were about to answer No he reached over,
turned the battery and ignition switches on, and cranked up
first one engine and then the other. When he had them both
going he gave us a kind of cool look, as if to say "Anything else
I can do for you?" and went back and sat down.

Once Oley and I had a fire started we were able to get to the
runway and take off, although the crew chief had to show us
how to raise the landing gear. When we had been out about an
hour I got a brilliant idea. We sent the crew chief aft to walk
casually past the passengers. We then turned on the automatic
pilot, walked to the companionway, through the door and into
the passenger compartment. Joe was playing gin rummy with
Val Setts, the guitar player, while the rest of the passengers were
either nodding or reading, completely unconcerned. I'm sure
that Joe hadn't told them that the crew was completely out in
deep center field when it came to flying a gooney bird. We had
removed the rear door of the aircraft so that the wind rushing
by would keep the ship cool in the tropical climate. Oley walked
to the door, leaned against the jam and looked down at the earth
below. I sat down next to Joe and said, "Okay, Joe, how about
dealing me in on the next hand?" Joe said, "Sure, bud, fine,"
and proceeded to deal me in. After about three minutes I could
see the mental waves suddenly ignite expressions on his face.
He first looked at me with incredulity, then stared in dismay
at Oley leaning against the door, and finally caught the crew
chief half asleep against the cockpit bulkhead. He jumped up
and shouted, "For Christ's sake, who's flying this airplane?"
and rushed to the cockpit, stumbling over legs of passengers
all the way. When he got there the following scene met his
eyes. There is a flexible hose, about two inches in diameter,
which leads from an outside air vent into the cockpit. We had
tied an old brown leather flying glove on top of the control
wheel. When we actuated the air valve the glove inflated. As
the autopilot gently controlled the aircraft and the control

167

wheel moved fore and aft, and side to side, it looked for all the world as though some mysterious hand with a Martianlike arm was guiding us serenely on our way. Joe screamed like a wounded eagle and shouted, "You dirty bums, get up here and fly this aircraft! I'm too young to die."

Joe spent the rest of the time in the cockpit, keeping a wary eye on us until we were about thirty miles from our destination. We then asked him to go back to the passenger cabin to prepare for landing. When he had gone we noticed a tremendous thunderstorm hanging over the Linguyen airstrip with plenty of jagged lightning streaks shooting to the ground, accompanied by a downpour of rain. Oley and I decided to pull one more gag on Joe before we let him go. We flew directly over the field, right in the middle of the thunderstorm. When in the worst part of the storm we reduced the mixture of gasoline to both engines until they began to run unevenly. As we circled back over the field to line up for the landing runway the crew chief made all passengers put on parachutes and line up at the fuselage door. Oley then went back and made an impassioned address about thunderstorms, engine failure, hazards and bailing out, and put the caper on it by telling the crew chief to start shoving if he heard the alarm bell ring, because we were in an emergency. With that he came up front again. We adjusted the mixtures and made a normal and uneventful landing. When we taxied into the line I never saw a man get off an aircraft so fast. As he did so Joe turned around and said to Lieutenant General Ennis Whitehead, who had met him, "Those dirty bastards will do anything for a laugh." He then turned and shouted back to us, "Anytime you guys want flying lessons, look me up."

We moved the 3rd Air Commandos from the Philippines to Okinawa a month before the atomic bombs were dropped over Hiroshima and Nagasaki. About five days after the Japanese capitulation Oley was ordered back to the United States and I received orders making me group commander of the Commandos. I was instructed to take the entire group to the Island of Hokkaido to a Japanese naval air base called Chitose.

This base proved to be one of the most delightful and beautiful I had ever seen. Situated on a large plain surrounded by tremendous mountains on three sides and the ocean on the fourth, it was like a huge winter resort. We didn't fly often, so there was ample time to investigate the ancient culture of this northernmost Japanese island. We stayed in the officers' quarters on the base, quarters which surpass any in the United States in comfort and convenience. For several months my command seemed like a large vacation.

When I finally received orders to return to the United States I was delighted to turn the group over to Charles Terhune, who had been my deputy for several months. The night before I was to leave, the entire group threw a real blast. I don't know whether they were glad to see me go or just wanted an excuse to have a ball, but we had a fine time. The following day I was honored by a review and parade, then got into my B-25 bomber to fly down to Tokyo for the trip home. As I started the engines a large crowd of men who had become my close friends over the months in the Pacific stood by, waving good-bye. All in all it was a kind of tear-jerking scene until I released the brakes, taxied about two feet, and ran into a portable fuel pump that someone had left just in front of the propeller of the right engine. When the prop hit the pump, pieces of prop and pump flew in every direction. What had started out to be a grand farewell turned out to be a rather small Hello. In fact most of the guys turned pale at the thought of a repeat performance of the party. As for me, I ate dinner as soon as I could, went to bed right after, then sneaked into another B-25 at four o'clock in the morning, before anyone else was even awake.

Once again I got back to the States, only this time the war was over. Without giving it too much thought, I knew that I'd have to take my place in civilian life along with 14,000,000 other guys who were going to revert to civilian pursuits. I arrived in Indianapolis, Indiana, on the night of my birthday—December 5, 1945—and Pat met me at the railroad station. From that moment on I knew that marriage was not a mistake, and I often thanked God that I had managed to live through the war in order to discover finally this sort of happiness.

There were lots of problems that beset everyone who had been in the war. As for me, I had to decide what to do with myself and my life. I was a lieutenant colonel making quite a respectable sum of money, but I didn't have much of an idea of what peacetime military life was like. I didn't have an assignment either, because most of us had been given thirty days to decide whether or not we wanted to stay in the service. I only had two years of college, and more was necessary. I didn't have much money saved up, probably enough to get two more years of school, but then what? There were plenty of jobs mentioned. Pat's dad wanted me to join him in the farming business; Guy Means wanted me to work for him in his Buick-Cadillac agency; it was rumored that the City of Fort Wayne was looking for an airport manager. None of this appealed to me, perhaps because I was still geared to a wartime pace and I couldn't slow down. Above all, that college part worried me.

When the day actually came to go before the personnel people and declare my intentions I told the Air Force, without any really strong conviction, that I wanted to stay on.

After that came a kaleidoscope of events. My first Pentagon assignment; the birth of my daughter Lynn Ann in September 1946; Purdue University from 1947 to 1949; back to the Pentagon; the birth of my son George Marshall; and many other significant things all of which took place in the next five years. Absolutely none of it prepared me for the ordeal I was to go through in Korea. Although I must have been more prepared than others because of my background, I still couldn't forecast what lay ahead. And even had I been able to, it wouldn't have done me any good. Nothing I had ever learned or experienced could give me any advantage—because I now found myself in the hands of a new and ruthless enemy.

170

Part 3: Imprisonment

1.

DEPARTMENT OF THE AIR FORCE
HEADQUARTERS UNITED STATES AIR FORCE
WASHINGTON 25, D. C.

15 May 1952

MRS. WALKER M. MAHURIN

c/o Major Harold I. Williams, Adjutant
George Air Force Base, California

DEAR MRS. MAHURIN:

It is with deep regret that I must officially confirm the notification made to you by Chaplain John L. George, of George Air Force Base, California, informing you that your husband, Colonel Walker M. Mahurin, has been missing since 13 May 1952, as the result of participating in Korean operations.

Our report states that Colonel Mahurin was the pilot of an F-86 type aircraft on a combat mission over Korea. During this mission your husband's aircraft was hit by enemy ground fire.

173

His aircraft was last seen at approximately 6000 feet altitude. Unfortunately, he has not been heard from since.

The Department of the Air Force will continue to hold your husband in a missing status until further information becomes available. He has been recorded in this status only because his whereabouts and exact fate are unknown at this time. When additional information is received, you are assured that it will be furnished you without delay.

Within a short time a Personal Affairs Officer from an Air Force installation will communicate with you. This officer is prepared to assist you in every way possible.

It is regretted that telegraphic notification could not be made to you, but due to the strike of Western Union operators, this could not be accomplished.

Permit me to extend to you my heartfelt sympathy during this time of uncertainty.

Sincerely yours,

JOHN H. McCORMICK
Major General, USAF
Director of Military Personnel

From out of the deadening silence which momentarily surrounded me I became aware of distant voices. North Korean peasants, working in the rice paddies, were running to the scene of my crash. Several were already within a few yards of me. These were to be crucial moments. If I could survive the next thirty minutes, I would be comparatively safe. Most humans are more curious than hostile, and, like animals, react most violently when they or their loved ones are endangered. Luckily I had brought my aircraft down in an area relatively untouched by the war. Now, meeting the North Koreans alone, I had to count on their curiosity overcoming their anger. My only hope was to face them with a smile and make no display of hostility, for if I showed signs of resisting or fighting, they would automatically reciprocate in kind. At that moment the .38-caliber pistol strapped to my leg felt like the largest atomic cannon ever developed.

174

Soon two Korean civilians were upon me, trying to figure out where to grab hold. I smiled as best I could through the layers of mud, and noticed with relief that they smiled back. The older one immediately asked, "Russki? Russki?" It was pointless to do anything but shake my head. My uneasiness returned as a crowd of curious North Koreans gathered rapidly. If I could stick it out until someone in authority arrived, I was certain I would receive a degree of protection, if only because the military would want intelligence information from a United Nations pilot.

In as heavily populated a nation as Korea it is virtually impossible to do anything without being witnessed; furthermore, an aircraft crash is a novelty, especially if the pilot—a white man—comes walking out of the shambles. As the crowd swelled I noticed two uniformed men armed with rifles running toward us, one wearing the uniform of a North Korean soldier and the other a Chinese People's Volunteer. By this time my captors were busily tying my hands behind my back. I protested violently, pointing to my left hand, which was jutting off from my arm at a most unnatural angle. My broken arm then drew an interested audience, and ultimately the group decided to untie me. They next gestured to me to start walking toward a tiny village which could be seen a mile or so in the distance. One of them motioned me over to a nearby rice paddy to wash my face in the water, so that they could see what I looked like. Having some familiarity in the ways of the peasant farmer in Korea and knowing that every Oriental farmer fertilizes his crops with "Night Soil," I bent down to wash my face in the rice-paddy water only with reluctance. When I straightened up there were Ohs and Ahs from the crowd, because it was plainly visible that I was a white man.

The soldiers were not unkind to me, but appeared extremely hostile to the peasants. I learned later that whoever captured a downed United Nations airman was given a substantial reward, to preclude disloyal citizens helping pilots return to our side. In some cases the reward also kept irate loyalists from killing the downed flyer. The soldiers, both of whom carried

175

what appeared to be World War I Enfield rifles, were having the utmost difficulty conversing, and appeared not to know what to do. They kept the crowd from gathering around me, and finally, after making themselves understood in pantomime, directed me to continue to the little Korean village. When we entered the village they took me to a mud hut, apparently the home of one of the village dignitaries, and instructed me to sit down on the floor and wait.

Despite my state of shock, I took stock of my situation as I waited. I was alive, but for how long, I couldn't tell. I was deeply frightened, but fear solved no problems. Being held by the Orientals, I reasoned, placed me in a dire situation, especially because the Eastern mind—of which we understood so little—had now embraced Communism. Here I was, a senior Air Force officer in enemy hands, and it would be advantageous to the Communists to do away with me, for if I lived I might once again fight against them. Although my body was cut badly in many places, I appeared to be in fair shape except for my arm which had begun to give me considerable pain. After I had rested for a half an hour a North Korean noncommissioned officer, who spoke halting English, appeared. His first words were: "Don't worry, we never harm prisoners of war." He took out a small manual of instructions apparently used by all military members. After he had consulted it, his first question was: "Name?" Which I gave him. He then wanted my serial number and I gave that too. He next asked, "What is your rank?" "A full colonel," I said. Obviously he didn't believe me. He said, in effect: "You can tell us the truth. You don't have to worry. Tell us what your rank is." He asked for my unit and I told him that I couldn't answer, so we reached a stalemate. He informed me that higher-ranking officers would be along shortly, then continued his questions.

After three hours later two Russian-built jeeps drove up to the hut, and one of them brought a North Korean Air Force colonel. He took command immediately by informing me that we would move to another place and await further instructions. This was both good and bad. It was good to be in military hands—at least, higher-ranking hands. It was bad to be heading down a dirt road in broad daylight, making dust trails. I could hear fighter aircraft overhead and was certain that once our dust trails were seen some United Nations fighter pilots would drop down and strafe us—after all, I had been using the same tactic that very morning. I asked the Korean colonel if he thought it safe to be driving down the road in broad daylight. He said, "It will soon be dark. Most of the fighter aircraft have started heading back to South Korea. We will not be in danger." We drove for about two hours, arrived at a message center, and it was here that I spent my first night in North Korea.

There were probably eight or ten North Korean soldiers in the message center, operating the communications equipment. I arrived still dressed in my Air Force flying suit with my G suit underneath, completely soaked and covered with mud. The soldiers indicated that I should take off my wet clothes and put on a pair of baggy olive-drab North Korean pants and an olive-drab canvas shirt. I was only too happy to do so because I was cold and miserable and welcomed any chance to get warm. My arm was hurting badly and I would have welcomed a chance to lie down, or at least rest my arm in a comfortable position, but no such opportunity arose. The officers were busy calling, apparently seeking instructions. About three hours later a call came from higher headquarters, ordering them to go back to my airplane to remove the gun sight.

We had know for some time that the Mig-15 was equipped with an inadequate fire-control system. The gun sight was only a slight refinement of those used during World War II. We, on the other hand, had developed the A1CM radar-ranging gun sight which utilized the APG 30 radar, enabling us to determine distance from a target accurately during the initial phase of an attack. In addition to distance, our sight would compute the proper lead gyroscopically, so that steering an indicator on the windshield aimed the guns for the pilot. We were certain that the Russians were anxious to get a gun sight intact, and the colonel's instructions confirmed this fact.

I was led back to the jeep and off we went. It was an exceptionally dark night, yet we drove down the road with our headlights turned on bright. I could hear the sound of aircraft overhead; a night raid was in progress. Just as we started, an alert was sounded over what appeared to be the Communist air-radar-warning net. From a practical standpoint, their warning system was much better than ours. When any of the thousands of soldiers stationed all over North Korea heard an aircraft overhead, he fired his rifle. At the sound of the shot all others within sound range would fire their rifles; thus the alarm traveled essentially at the speed of sound—quite an effective system. But the alert apparently made no difference to my captors, and we barreled through the black night to the scene of the crash.

On the way we met a Russian-built truck loaded with about thirty Chinese Communist soldiers and moving in the opposite direction. When we were even with them they waved and shouted to our driver, who paid little attention. After we'd gone on a quarter of a mile one of the Chinese soldiers picked up a machine gun and fired a short burst, just over our heads. Our driver promptly got the message and ground to a halt. When the truck turned around and came abreast of us all the soldiers climbed down and surrounded our jeep. They immediately began to jostle the North Koreans and crowded around me with obvious hostile intent, all waving their arms, shouting and brandishing their weapons. I was terrified, concluding: Bud, boy, you've really had it now. I believed they were going to kill me on the spot. My captors, however, argued vehemently with the Chinese in my behalf, and though the Chinese and North Koreans didn't seem to understand each other, the North Korean colonel finally managed to pull his rank, whereupon all the Chinese soldiers climbed back into their truck with a great deal of grumbling and drove away. We continued on our course, arriving before long in the little village near my aircraft.

At daybreak the following morning I was escorted to the scene of the crash, amazed to see the sky empty of Allied aircraft. I had half expected to see air-sea rescue craft flying up and down the C'hong-C'hon River, looking for the wreckage of my F-86, but when I reached my mangled plane I was glad that none of our pilots had been able to find it. The Communists had surrounded it with antiaircraft weapons, in the hope that some Allied airmen would spot the wreckage and drop down to investigate.*

When we approached my F-86 we were greeted by a team of North Korean mechanics who had arrived earlier. They had been instructed to dismantle parts of the F-86, especially the radar gun sight. In broken English the head of this team asked me how to remove the sight, but I wouldn't tell him. Undaunted, he and his men started on the airplane with something resembling a hand ax. In their efforts to get at essential equipment they were damaging everything they touched. I watched them until my arm began giving me trouble again, whereupon I asked the colonel if I could go back to the village and rest in the hut. When permission was given I warned, "Whatever you do, don't let them touch anything in the cockpit of my fighter."

Two hours later, as I was looking through the open door of the hut, the chief mechanic came running up, as sore as he could be. Breathlessly he demanded to know what it was in the cockpit that had blown up. Apparently an explosion had occurred and four people had been injured. When I asked him what they had been doing, he told me that they were trying to remove a piece of radio equipment. Obviously one of the mechanics had struck a screwdriver into the IFF set. This highly classified piece of equipment had been engineered to blow up when anyone unfamiliar with the removal procedure tried to work on it, and when one of these boobs tried to jimmy it, this is exactly what happened. I again cautioned him to stay out of the cockpit. Off he went, still angry, only to return three hours later in an even worse temper.

"What was it that blew up in your cockpit this time?"

* I discovered later that 5th Air Force did nothing but search for me for three days after I went down. Not, however, in the area of the crash. They focused attention to the place where I had first been hit.

"You'll have to tell me the story," I said. "I warned you to keep out of the cockpit, but you don't seem to understand." It seemed that, in order to impress the large crowd of North Koreans milling around the F-86, watching the demolition squad at work, one of the men had climbed into the cockpit and pulled the ejection-seat handles. Seat and man had shot out into the crowd, killing 4 and injuring 14 others. The Reds might have captured me but they sure hadn't captured my F-86.

Later that afternoon the remaining experts came walking up to my hut with pieces of my aircraft, radio, gun sight, instruments and many other items. One of them had pulled a box of silica crystals out of the gun sight. These crystals, packaged in a transparent plastic box, are merely used to keep the mechanism dry, but this "expert" was convinced that he had the key to the success of the F-86. He held the box up to the light, repeatedly trying to figure out how it worked as a gun sight. He asked me, through the interpreter: "How does this box work as your gun sight?" "We send people to college for four years to learn how to make that sight work," I informed him, "and now you want me to tell you how it works in two minutes?" The rest of the men nodded. "Yes, yes, that must be right." They didn't ask me about the gun sight again.

Many hours later they came to me saying: "We are now going to take you to an interrogation center." Just at dusk we headed south in a jeep. The mechanics had loaded all the parts from my aircraft into this same jeep, mostly by standing some fifteen feet away and throwing the stuff into the vehicle. Anything which had remained in good condition was certainly broken when it landed in the jeep.

We drove all night, finally arriving in a North Korean interrogation center about thirty miles northeast of Pyongyang, and on the way we stopped briefly to report to a North Korean Air Force general. After jolting along by jeep for many hours over dirt roads, I was grateful for the stop.

The General asked a few questions of no consequence before coming up with one that puzzled me. Through the interpreter he asked why the United Nations B-26 light bombers were dropping pestilence and disease on innocent North Korean civilians. I couldn't imagine what he was talking about and said so. If I was an Air Force colonel as I claimed, he said, I would most certainly know what he was discussing, since our own pilots had admitted carrying out such attacks. The General appeared sincere, as did the rest of the officers present, and he obviously believed the United Nations was conducting germ warfare—but I was so miserable at the time that I paid little attention to what he said.

After the interview with the General we drove on to the interrogation center. Though it consisted of just another group of typical Korean mud huts, a guard group of soldiers had been posted, there was evidence of organization, and I could see a group of Korean officers obviously in charge. A North Korean lieutenant colonel welcomed me in fluent English. I was taken to a well-guarded mud room and informed that it would be my quarters for the present time. The guards gave me an old military overcoat for a blanket and left me alone. By this time I badly needed rest, but before I lay down to sleep I noticed a list of names written in English on the wall at the far end of the room. Other captured airmen had been held in this same room. Each had written his name on the wall, informing those following whom they could expect to join at some future date. I was glad to find Vernon Wright's name along with about twenty others. If I played my cards right, I would end up in prison camp along with fellow Americans.

The next day the Korean colonel, who told me his name was Colonel Kong, came to take me to a nearby hospital to have my arm set. "Nearby," however, became a five-mile walk to still another group of mud huts, each containing some hospital facility such as an X-ray room, an operating room, an out-patient clinic and so on. I saw many wounded North Korean and Chinese soldiers wandering about the huts, and close by I could see a barracks in which patients were recuperating. In one respect the hospital was typical: we were told to wait until the doctor could see us. (Still, I missed the magazines.) While we were waiting we were joined by another North Korean lieutenant colonel who also spoke English. He informed me that he had a severe case of tuberculosis and had been receiving treatment at the hospital. He mentioned that he was not an interrogator, even though he was curious about me and wanted to know my name. He said he had heard of me and knew that I had been leading bombing attacks on the city of Sinuiju. In fact he had been in the city when we pulled off our first raid. Apparently one of our bombs had exploded in a heavy anti-aircraft gun emplacement and killed many troops and civilians. The colonel was angry about this because, as he put it, "There was no warning of attacks. We didn't know the F-86 could carry bombs." I told him, "Those are the breaks; when you fight a war you have to expect a few losses."

When finally called into the operating room, I was astonished to be confronted by a white man who said that he was a Rumanian Red Cross internee. The Red Cross had sent him to Korea to treat the injured, and he was gaining valuable experience toward becoming a doctor when he returned to Rumania. I was skeptical, to say the least. They took me to a crude operating table where preparations were being made to administer ether so that the doctor could set my arm. Having previously experienced ether, I knew that it was possible to babble from its effects, and I was afraid I might say things of military significance. But I wanted to have my arm set and there appeared no other recourse than to do as I was told. When I awoke sometime later the arm was set and in a cast. The doctor told my escort I should be brought back for another examination, but in the meantime I should rest and try not to disturb my arm.

On the way out of the hospital I encountered another Rumanian civilian who was apparently an observer for his government. This man's vehement denunciation of the war gave me an insight into the value of Communist propaganda. He had obviously been subjected to a continuous diatribe concerning the responsibility for the outbreak of hostilities, and had been led to believe that the South Korean had attempted to overrun North Korea but had been repelled by the Communists from the north. He was positive that the United Nations, led by the United States, were the aggressors and that imperialists were trying to take over all of Korea. As incensed as he was, he admitted having no knowledge of the situation other than what he had read in Communist newspapers.

He saw me, a prisoner of war, leaving the hospital with my arm in a plaster cast, and must have reflected that up to this point I had been given humane treatment. Since he had been reading Communist reports of the inhumane treatment inflicted upon North Korean and Chinese prisoners in the United Nations prison camps, his deduction was: If this is democracy, I want no part of it.

When I finally made my way back to my cell at the interrogation center I assumed that I would be allowed to recover from the effects of ether and from the strain of events of the last few days, but this was not to be. I had been lying on the floor for about an hour when two sinister-looking officers walked in, dressed in Chinese Communist uniforms. Both wore heavy glasses; both spoke with what sounded like heavy German accents; and both wrote down every word I uttered. I was surprised that no Korean officer was present when they began asking questions. They, too, were equipped with the same black booklets I had seen before, and their questions were typical of those I had encountered previously. Although I answered the same name, rank and serial-number questions, I was too ill to come up with answers to anything else, so after a short period of time they left, with the admonition that I would see them again.

Later that day Colonel Kong came into my cell with his book and began an interrogation period which was to last twenty days. His line and manner of questioning indicated that he knew little of the military aspects of the Korean War. In fact not one interrogator I talked to had a real appreciation of the military situation. They were all guided by the little interrogation booklet, and were unable to draw deductions from anything I said. They were still skeptical about my rank, for I often heard: "Mahurin, you are much too young to be a full colonel." However, after listening to the Armed Forces' radio from Japan and Korea shortly after I had been in the center and hearing that I was missing in action, they finally acknowledged my identity.

During these tense days my thoughts dwelt upon the possibility that the war would end soon. The severe damage I had seen in North Korea had convinced me that it would be impossible for these people to keep fighting for a prolonged period. The Korean officers informed me daily of the peace negotiations, and I kept hoping that an agreement would be reached momentarily. Admittedly my attitude had undergone considerable change from the days when I was fighting from the cockpit of my F-86. Typical of every man taken prisoner, I prayed daily that I would be released quickly to join my family.

I was especially worried about Pat and the children, hoping the information they would receive from my captors would be enough to convince them that I was alive. When I expressed my concern to the Koreans in charge of the interrogation center, they allowed me to write a letter which they assured me would be sent to my family through Peiping. They further assured me that I would be declared a prisoner of war as soon as possible, in line with the policy of the Communist government. I knew that eventually they might place me on a prisoner-of-war list, but initially—as was the case during World War II—I would be held as missing in action until the Communists saw fit to turn me over to a bona fide prison camp. Meantime I hoped for an early end to the conflict.

I also worried about the questioning. If I could get past this interrogation period successfully, I felt I would be allowed to join other POW's and eventually permitted to go home, regardless of when the war ended. Getting past the interrogators, however, was not going to be easy. I had to be sure not to tell anything of military value, above all anything that could result in injury or death for Allied soldiers. Yet I had to tell enough misleading information to work my way through this center to prison camp. I knew many men who had been POW's during

World War II, and the format the Germans had used was simple. Each man was taken to an interrogation center and kept in solitary confinement until he was ready to talk. Few resisted for more than a month or so. Most had misled the interrogators as much as possible until the interrogators were satisfied that there was little more to gain; then the POW's were sent on to camp. I had to tell as little as I could in order to skim by.

Besides the interrogations, I was especially apprehensive of the food being brought to me. Sanitary conditions in North Korea were deplorable, and this center was no exception. I was sure that the food—especially anything served raw—would give me either dysentery or worms. I was given a minimum diet of fish heads, rice and *kimshee* (a kind of weedlike vegetable dish loaded with onions) and very little else. Once I was offered an apple. Because of my fears, I ate almost nothing. I was sick most of the time, suffering infections from various cuts received in the accident, and my broken arm hurt a great deal. Slowly I began to lose weight.

Early in the interrogation period I was asked to write a biography to be used as reference when I got to the formal prison camp. I had expected this, but had difficulty putting anything down on the form provided. The Communists had surely been listening to American news broadcasts, and equally surely a broadcast giving my background had been made after I was shot down. I was almost certain that my home-town newspaper had carried at least one article, more or less in obituary form, as soon as it had received word that I was missing in action. Our intelligence reports had indicated that most United States magazines and newspapers were sent to Hong Kong by Communist agents and from there found their way to Peiping, and probably to Pyongyang in Korea. I was sure to be questioned about the jobs I had held in the United States Air Force, but nevertheless I limited my biography, hoping the interrogators wouldn't ask for information that I didn't want to give them. Above all I did not mention that I had once worked for the Secretary of the Air Force.

The questions generally involved the force structure of the Air Force. One constant question was: "Tell us the numbers and locations of all the Air Force units in Korea." Having been in Korea for about five months, I only knew the two units I had worked with. When I told Colonel Kong I couldn't help him because I didn't know, he began threatening me with dire consequences if I failed to cooperate. He wanted to know the location, organization, and table of equipment for every numbered Air Force unit in the United States. There are some fifteen involved, and to this date I don't have a clear picture of where and what they are. I don't think that any one person in military service, or any given group of people for that matter, could have sat down and answered all they wanted to know. I couldn't—and wouldn't—regardless of the threats. I gave them a minimum on each question, and when they found out that I wouldn't say more, they'd give up and go on to the next question. This continued for many days—days in which my anxiety and worry continued to mount, even though I seemed to be successfully slithering around important questions.

Interestingly, one day Colonel Kong asked, in the presence of several other North Korean officers, how many Mig-15s I had destroyed. This rattled me. On the one hand, if I told them none, they would be more pleased than if I told the truth. On the other, they had probably heard the news broadcasts and knew exactly how many I had destroyed, and would be angry if I lied to them. When I finally decided to tell the truth and say three and a half I was most surprised to hear them say: "Oh ho! Not bad, not bad." But then they wanted to know something else. How many aircraft was I credited with destroying during both World War II and the Korean War? The interrogation center commander put the question this way: "I have received information through a friend of mine that you are credited with the destruction of 20.75 enemy aircraft during World War II. How did you arrive at that figure?" Immediately I saw a danger signal. About one month before I had been shot down, the Air Force Association magazine had published an article on aces in the United States Air Force, and

I had been credited erroneously with the destruction of 20.75 aircraft. One thing was certain, they had a subscription to *Air Force Magazine*. But this put me in a bind. I could explain by saying that I had actually destroyed 21 German and 1 Japanese aircraft, but then they might consider me a pretty hot article and never let me go home. To put an end to this line of questioning, I maintained a discreet silence, claiming that I didn't know what they were talking about.

A short time later the question I most feared came flying at me. The interrogators came in a group to demand: "We would like you to describe all the tactics your F-86s use to shoot down our Mig-15s. If you don't, we can guarantee you will never see the inside of a prison camp." I immediately replied, "I can't and won't tell you, because if I do I am liable to endanger the lives of my pilots. Further than that, the Geneva Convention rules on treatment of prisoners of war state that this line of questioning is illegal." I added that no Air Force officer would ever give them this information. With that there were many heated accusations on both sides, but, being the prisoner, I was on the defensive. We argued this subject for several days until I said, "All right give me a pencil and piece of paper, and I'll write what you want."

I spent three days writing everything I knew about the Migs: how they took off, how they assembled in formation, how they flew, what altitudes they used, what formations they used, and how they acted in combat. Every time "Mig-15" should have appeared, I inserted "F-86," and wrote about fifteen pages of accurate descriptions on what the enemy Mig-15 aerial activity was like. When I had finished I asked one of my guards to take the fiction to Colonel Kong. A few moments later Kong came to my cell, beaming. "Mahurin, you have done well. I will look this over and be back to see you." He took my papers back to his officer where he spent about an hour looking them over. He came rushing back at the end of this time exclaiming, "This is wonderful, I must get this to the higher authorities." He never again asked me about tactics, nor did anyone else until

187

I found myself in a Chinese interrogation center. For the time, I had managed to stave off the pressure.

During the twenty days I spent at the North Korean center, I was constantly questioned about my background. "What is your family background like?" "Describe your early home." "What did your father do?" "Have you ever worked?" "Were you ever a laborer?" When this question came up I said, "Certainly I worked, I was almost a peasant." I figured I might gain a few points, and they appeared impressed that I had done manual labor during my lifetime. They were also enthralled with my last name. The Luther Burbank of Russia was a prominent scientist whose name was Michurin, a national hero who had done important work in the field of evolution. As a child I had read about him. When they asked me if I had relatives living in Russia, I quickly replied, "Certainly, I have a relative who was quite well known in that society." When I told them the name they replied; "We know him, he is a hero in our society also." This time I had really gained stature with them—until five minutes later when they began interrogating again.

At the end of twenty days some Chinese Communist soldiers in a Russian-built truck came up to my cell and in sign language motioned that I was going to move. I thought to myself, Hot dog! I'm finally going to prison camp. Having heard much about World War II prison camps, I had visions of prison-camp life: a group of barracks, a compound with a wire fence all around, guards patrolling constantly, all the POW's sitting around talking to each other, sweating out the war—and I thought, At last I'm finally going to join the boys.

After I had climbed into the truck we drove for about four hours, finally stopping in another village which surrounded an abandoned coal mine. I later learned that this mine had been in operation during World War II, but that at the end of the war the Russians had removed all the mining machinery and sent it back to Russia. My guards escorted me to the entrance of the mine and down a long shaft about a hundred feet below the surface of the earth. These were to be my quarters, and as far as I could tell they were cold, damp and miserable. In a corner were two sawhorses with boards across; this was my bed. Someone who could speak English finally appeared, and I asked where I was, only to be informed that I was in a Chinese Communist interrogation center. I have never spent a worse night than the first in that coal mine. The guard sat within two feet of my sawhorse bed, and—true to Chinese custom—spit on the floor about every thirty seconds. I didn't mind his being close to me, but his repeated spitting was almost more than I could stand.

The next morning interrogation started all over again, this time by the Chinese. From the questions they asked it was obvious that there was no interchange of information between the North Koreans and the Chinese Communists. The more I saw and heard, the surer I became that they weren't trading anything. My new interrogators hauled out the same kind of black book I had seen so many times before and asked the same questions. Again it was apparent that they had no conception of the military effort on either side, nor any idea of the value of the information they were expected to gather. Altogether I felt it was mere child's play to answer questions by misleading every chance I got and by fabricating in between.

The Chinese used a slightly different method of interrogation. The night I moved into the coal mine a group of nine Chinese officers followed right behind me. They were all interrogators—each a specialist. One had a degree in aeronautical engineering from a Chinese university, another was a communications expert, a third was a political expert, and so on. As my interrogation progressed each expert would deal with me until satisfied, and then another would take his place. I got very little rest.

The radar expert was a surly, squat, extremely insulting Chinese. He had me brought before him in a small room above ground to tell him, as he said, "all about the radar operating in South Korea." I knew very little except what I had learned about Dentist and Dentist Charlie, and I wasn't about to tell him that. I said that as a combat leader I had not been allowed to learn much of a classified nature, since my superiors had

known that there was a chance of my being shot down and captured. This line of reasoning had been successful in the past,
but this time the radar expert didn't seem to buy what I was
telling him. We began arguing violently about my lack of
radar knowledge. I started to yell at him, "By God, I'm not
going to tell you a damn thing! To hell with you and your
threats!" I really had my dander up, and so did he. He finally
threatened: "You are going to cooperate with us or we are going
to kill you." He added, "We control the skies over North Korea;
the United States is no longer the most powerful nation in the
world; Russia is, and you ought to know it. You had better
find your place as a prisoner of war quickly or bear the consequences."

He had no sooner uttered these words than 5th Air Force
started an attack on a little town about two miles away. They
came with every fighter they had in commission, and bombed
and bombed good. My interrogator was petrified. He called the
guards and made them escort me to a bomb shelter about a
block away. These men were naturally yellow complexioned,
but after the first few bombs fell they were white with fear.
For an hour and a half they cowered in the corner of the bomb
shelter, scarcely speaking to each other. When the raid was
over, Mister Radar said, "Go back to your cell. I will deal with
you this afternoon."

About one o'clock he returned, starting all over again. He
repeated that the Chinese controlled the skies over Korea and
ended with the threat: "You must give me this information or
I will see that you are killed." No sooner had he started than
5th Air Force came back to visit the same target. We ran back
to the bomb shelter and hid out as before. Once again he was
terrified; once again he was losing face at a great rate. When the
raid was over he said, more quietly, "You go back, I will see
you tonight."

He came back that night after dark to continue the same
diatribe on radar, when for the third time that day, 5th Air
Force opened an attack, this time with B-29s. For four hours
bombs fell within one mile of my location. At the sound of

190

the first bomb my interrogator departed and I never saw him again. Nor was I ever questioned about radar again.

Sometimes there was humor in the questioning. One day they said: "We know of the white trails your aircraft form in the sky, and we want to know at what altitude these trails form." I answered, "I can't tell you that. It is a ridiculous question. Much depends on the climatic conditions of the atmosphere, how much moisture exists, what the temperature is, and so forth. There is no specific altitude." "Mahurin," they retorted, "you are lying to us. You are evading the question. You must tell us the exact altitude." We argued at length, even though I pleaded I didn't know the answer. At last they began to threaten me, ending with: "You have got to tell us the answer to this point. You are trying to conceal things from us, and it will go hard on you unless you give us the correct answer." With that I stated that the condensation trails form at altitudes above 30,000 feet. But the Chinese replied: "That is not right. We know they form at an exact altitude, and you must tell us what that altitude is." "All right," I said, in desperation, "the trails form from thirty-five to thirty-seven thousand feet." Once again I was told: "That is not right, we must have the correct information." "All right, goddam it, they form at 35,251 feet." "Correct," they said. "We will not bother you on this point again." And by God they didn't.

Shortly after, I was confronted by the communications expert. This man was much older than the rest, but possessed the same arrogance that I was to find during my entire stay in enemy hands. I felt that he was continually trying to demonstrate his superiority over the white man by browbeating me at every chance. As a pilot, I knew very little about frequencies of radio equipment, because these details tend to bore me. But this man was convinced that I knew everything, and intended to extract it from me bit by bit. Frequencies usually involve odd numbers which are hard to remember. For example, the international distress frequency is 121.5 megacycles. The control tower at the Los Angeles Airport is 118.9, while most military control towers are 126.18. I couldn't remember any in South

Korea, although the interrogator insisted that I knew them all. We argued for some time, his argument consisting of threats and mine of denials. I tried every acting stunt I could think of, including tears, to get him off my back—all to no avail. By this time I was mentally and physically tired and suspected that my interrogators were tired too. The interrogation had gone on so long that I was becoming mentally inert, and all I wanted was to go back to my cell for a short rest. I finally told them to go straight to hell. With that the interrogator drew his briefcase over and pulled out a large notebook. "Look, Mahurin, we know all about you. We know who you are and what you have done. You deserve the harshest treatment we can afford." As he leafed through the pages of the notebook I could see that it consisted of transmissions our pilots had made to one another while in combat over North Korea. He finally came to a page on which my name appeared a number of times. He pointed to one of the transmissions I had made—the most incriminating of all: MAHURIN: "All right, you bastards, the next time we are going to drop our bombs on the airfield at Antung." The interrogator said, "You can see by this that we know everything you have done to us." He pulled another document from his briefcase. It was a list of all of the communications frequencies and channels used by every organization in South Korea. He had a thousand times more information about us, from a communications standpoint, than I would ever know.

During the time I was held in the coal mine I was allowed to visit the surface of the earth from time to time to get exercise, and during these small liberties I was usually well guarded by a number of Chinese enlisted men who remained close to me. The fingers of my left hand were beginning to turn black and had started to pain considerably each night. I resolved to take off the cast, and probably removed it just in time. Evidently the circulation had been severely restricted, for my whole lower arm showed signs of infection and had turned black, blue and yellow. With the cast gone, I had less pain and gradually began to regain control of my fingers.

During this time I had the only encounter of my entire stay

which led me to believe that there were elements in North Korea which were friendly to the cause of democracy. For several days I noticed a North Korean civilian who seemed anxious to get near me. He made a point of getting close to me while I was taking my exercise, and once in awhile managed to say hello to me in English. Once he asked me for the correct time, seeing that I was still wearing my Air Force watch. I noticed that the guards and the interrogators were hostile to this man, and he was eventually ordered away from the vicinity. I am convinced that he was on the side of the United Nations.

I had a chance to visit with one interrogator who seemed preoccupied with other things during his stay in the coal mine. He volunteered to talk to me one evening, and since he wanted to discuss social subjects, I found him a welcome diversion. He had been educated in Peiping and was a student of ancient Chinese literature. He enjoyed discussing Chinese culture with me, as long as I prompted him to do so, and I was most interested in him because he was willing to teach me to speak his language. There are eighteen dialects in China—far too many for me to remember the various names. Although most literate Chinese can understand Chinese writing, few can understand more than one dialect. My informant spoke Pekingese as well as Mandarin and was willing to impart his knowledge to me as long as he could. I wanted to learn so that I could understand what my interrogators said among themselves, and felt that this knowledge might be useful to me should I ever manage to escape at some future date. Unfortunately I had mastered only a few words when my tutor was sent back to China.

I had been given two uniforms which I supposed were typical prisoner-of-war outfits. They consisted of high-collar jackets with buttons down the fronts and pants resembling American pajama pants. The material was a cotton dyed the brightest blue I had ever seen. By this time I had been in captivity about sixty days, with no opportunity to wash my clothing, even though I could take an occasional sponge bath in the basinful of water brought to me each day by the guards. I was allowed to shave once a week. I was extremely tired from intense questioning, especially because I had to be alert constantly against telling anything important. Although I had managed to be deceptive, I had to remember each deception so that I would give the same answers if questioned again. Sixty days is a long time without discourse with fellow Americans. I wanted the war to end, but being out of touch with the news, I had no idea what was going on. I knew that the battle was still raging, because I could hear the sounds of jet aircraft overhead many times daily. I was certain that I had not been declared a prisoner of war, because I had not yet reached a prison camp. And though I knew the interrogators were running out of questions—that it must be just a matter of time—anxiety was beginning to consume me.

At the end of forty-five days of constant interrogation by the Chinese I was informed that: "You have completed your interrogations and are now to be sent to join your fellow Americans in prison camp." Boy, what news! I could hardly wait to climb into the truck which was to take us north. After a drive of two days and nights we came into a town called Pyaoktong, which I knew to be the headquarters of the prison-camp area. Located on the Yalu River, this small village is just above the Sun-Ho Reservoir—about as far north as one can get and still be in Korea. I could look across the Yalu River and see Manchuria.

I didn't join other prisoners. Instead I was taken to a small mud farmhouse and assigned to a tiny room which had only a straw mat on the floor for furniture. Next to this room was another in which a guard squad consisting of nine members was billeted. Upon arrival I was told that I would move on to a new location the following morning. But this was not to be. For thirty days I stayed in my cell, constantly guarded by at least one soldier holding a submachine gun in my direction. During this period I just sat and worried myself frantic. I kept thinking that this couldn't be prison camp; there must be something wrong somehow. What was it? Why didn't someone tell me what was happening? I wondered how my family was. Was the war about over? Could I possibly escape? Obviously not—

they watched me too closely. What could I do? Each day I merely existed, going to bed at night, waking up in the morning, and worrying in between. I couldn't even see beyond the group of huts; all I could see were the guards and the buildings. I didn't have any idea where I was, but I felt that some horrible thing was about to happen to me.

2.

SUDDENLY I was moved again. Judging from my new location, the move didn't make sense—it was just more of the same. The Chinese awakened me late one night with a great commotion, instructed me to put on my clothes and pack my things. We walked several miles into the town of Pyoktong, then climbed into a Russian-built jeep and drove off. About an hour later the jeep stopped and I was taken to another cell almost exactly like the first. My anxiety, already at fever pitch, was increased throughout the night by the guard stationed outside my door, who poked his head in my cell every hour on the hour, minutely examining both me and my confines with a flashlight.

The following morning I was exposed to a man whom I would come to know intimately in the succeeding days—a man who called himself Colonel Wong. A short, stout, swarthy-complexioned Chinese officer, he dressed in typical Spartan uniform, complete with small billed cap, and wore heavy steel-rimmed glasses. I disliked him on sight, and because I wasn't saying anything to anybody, he had little chance to make an evaluation of me. He began his conversation by remarking, "I have just had a long session with the high command reviewing your case, and am sorry to tell you that it looks very

195

bad." He then began to review the entire history of my stay in prison camp. He wanted to inquire about some of the things I had told the interrogators in the days back at the coal mine. He gave me a list of simple questions, a pencil, and a sheaf of paper on which to write the answers. Thank God, I had intentionally tried to remember all the lies I had told over a period of almost ninety days. After devising a particular answer to a specific question, I had fixed it in my mind so that I couldn't be caught if asked the same question again. Each day Wong came to my cell to see how I was doing with the answers to his questions, and each day I asked him when I would be sent to prison camp. He always stated that my case was not settled and that the high command had yet to make a decision. However, he would conclude, it looked bad for me.

By this time I was sure that my family had given me up for lost. I worried so continuously about it that I felt I was losing control of my mind. I was in a frantic state, except for the few moments during which I had to control myself while talking to Wong lest I leak information useful to him. In desperation I decided I must control my thought processes or suffer irreparable mental damage, and from the moment of that decision I forced a change in thought every time I began to worry about my family or the state of the war. It was most difficult. I had never practiced thought control in the past, but now felt that I must do it. Although I had lost much weight from worry and lack of food, I tried to relax at night and get some sleep in order to be mentally prepared for Wong's next visit. I was still extremely concerned over my status as a prisoner of war, but my mind had been gradually shaping the conviction that I would never get out of prison camp alive. I didn't want to face this thought, but all events seemed to indicate this final outcome, and I subconsciously began to prepare myself for some sort of untimely demise.

The pencils I had been given were all short and stubby, and I made a big issue of breaking the points often to prolong the writing. Wong grew angrier every time I reported that I had run out of pencils, and one day he gave me a penknife with which to sharpen them. This knife was like our small pocket-knives, with a blade which could slide in and out of a little holder. Shortly after receiving it I contrived to break the blade in three places so that it couldn't be used. When I returned the pieces to Wong with apologies I kept the largest one, a piece about one inch long. I remember thinking at the time that it might prove useful later.

Although the pressure on me was gradually increasing—with guards searching my cell every hour—I was given a new freedom. My cell was situated on the bank of a fresh-running mountain stream, and Wong had given me permission to wash both my clothes and myself there daily. Possibly he agreed to this as a defensive measure, because I was scarcely the most fragrant human in the world. Each day while bathing in the cold water I glanced around at my surroundings. I noticed that there was another hut several hundred feet downstream from mine and another about three hundred feet behind the one I occupied. Each hut was under guard, leading me to believe that each also housed an American aviator. I could hear sounds in the background, indicating a nearby village, but having arrived at this location at night, I couldn't tell much about the surrounding geography. After a few days I saw an American standing at the door of one of the huts, but he was too far away to make any contact. I wanted to talk to him in the worst way, if only to try to get word to my wife after the war that I had been seen alive. Since the Communists had exerted every effort to isolate me, I was sure that they considered me far enough away from other Americans to be unrecognizable.

Following standard practice in North Korea, I used an extremely filthy slit trench about fifty feet from my cell for a latrine. Each time I went out my guard followed and waited until I was ready to return—a most distasteful situation. One day, however, I glanced out of my door (I was not allowed outside the cell except for a specific reason) and noticed, in amazement, another American dressed in prison garb, using the facility. Deciding that this was perhaps the only opportunity I would ever have to make a contact, I quickly wrote a note to

197

give to the American. "My name is Colonel Walker M. Mahurin. I was commander of the 4th Fighter Group before being shot down on May 13, 1952. My wife and family do not know that I am alive, and I believe the Chinese intend to kill me. Will you please remember my name, and when you are sent back to the United States at the end of the war tell my wife that you saw me alive?" I then motioned to the guard that I was sick, and rushed to the latrine. The guard was unable to see the other prisoner, so he paid no attention to my actions. As soon as I got close I threw the note to my fellow American and ran back to my cell. So far so good.

From that moment on I kept an eagle eye on the latrine. A couple of days later I saw my new friend again, sitting on the slit trench. As I watched he took a note from his pocket and placed it in a crack in one of the boards near the trench. When he was finished I asked my guard for permission to relieve myself, and picked up the note. "My name is Robert E. Hammett. I am a B-26 bombardier and a lieutenant in the Air Force. I am being intensely interrogated and threatened with my life. I will inform your wife if I am released and hope you will do the same for me in case you get out."

The next time I had an opportunity I wrote a note to Hammett indicating that I was sure he would be released, because it was unlikely that the Communists would harm men of lower ranks. I told him to keep his spirits high and pray to God for help in eventual release. I told him to learn as much as he could of the Chinese language so that he would be able to get inklings of what was transpiring in the outside world. I asked him to continue passing notes to me, and said that I would do the same. I then hid the note in our private mailbox. Later, when Hammett got my note, I could see him nod his head in agreement.

When I went to the slit trench for the last time at the end of the day I occasionally saw one other prisoner standing in the door of his cell. I tried to attract his attention and eventually managed to get him to look in my direction. When he saw me I gave the international "thumbs-up" signal; he in turn, however, gave me a "thumbs down" which I was sure indicated that he was under great pressure.

With each succeeding visit from Wong I became increasingly apprehensive about my future. I felt intuitively that things were going wrong, without knowing what to do. For many days I had been considering the possibility of escaping, and as each day came to a close I became more resolved to make an effort. I thought that I knew approximately where I was, but couldn't be sure, because we had always traveled at night. I knew I was far enough from town to get some distance away, providing I could make my escape at night before the guards found out that I was gone. Although they opened my door every hour to make a bed check, I could probably pad my bed to make it look as if I was asleep in it. The little stream in front of my hut went somewhere—eventually it would probably empty into the Yalu. If I could get away at night and follow the stream I would probably meet the river, and by following it, eventually reach the Yellow Sea.

However, myriad problems were involved. Obviously I didn't look like a Korean or a Chinese. If my beard grew I would be even more conspicuous, because the natives were generally smooth skinned. Once into the countryside, I'd be forced to either hide from the natives or take the extreme risk of making contact with a friendly one. The first possibility was remote because of the extremely high ratio of people to land. The second was equally remote because the natives were held in check by fear of retaliation by the government if discovered. I could probably steal some clothes, but I'd still have to worry about food. I suppose every man who has ever been captured has thought about the same things in the same way, and to each his thoughts made sense at the time. But in Korea this kind of thinking never made sense and no POW ever made his way to safety.

To attempt to jump one of the guards and either disarm or kill him was stupid. Killing a guard would be like killing a policeman in the United States. All the other guards would be after me with a vengeance. If I fumbled the attack, allowing the guard to get in a shot from his gun, every person within hearing would be alerted. Then where would I be? The best way to sneak out at night would be to dig a hole in the back wall of my hut and crawl out when I knew the guards weren't looking. The Korean family who had owned the hut in which I had my cell had unwittingly helped me in my problem. At the back of it they had constructed a low shelf upon which rested two large chests. I had investigated their contents and found nothing useful in them. However, by moving them to one side at night I could cut a hole in the wall with a sharp stone and at daybreak cover the hole with the chests. I carried the dirt I dug concealed in my clothing when I went to the slit trench.

After a couple of weeks of digging I had a rather respectable hole in the back side of the hut, but I didn't have a chance to look out, because I did all my digging at night. Wong began to show up several times a day to continue his interrogations, and I found the tension building more rapidly than I had anticipated. I'd figured I'd be able to break out in about a week at the rate I was working, so I finally decided to peek outside through the hole to see where I was going, regardless of the risk. After making sure that the coast was clear, I moved the chest aside and stuck my head through the hole right into the seat of a Chinese soldier's uniform. Almost exactly in back of my hut was another containing an American airman. His guard was posted right in front of my hole!

Before I had another chance to exchange notes with Hammett I was moved again. Naturally the move took place in the middle of the night. Again transported by jeep, I found myself in the town of Pyoktong. But this time it was moonlight, and although I could see little of the countryside on the way to Pyoktong, I could make out the rough definition of the buildings where I would be confined. The first thing I noticed was that they were not a prison camp. My guards pushed me through a gate between two large buildings on the other side of which was a somewhat rectangular courtyard surrounded on all sides by wooden buildings two stories high. Facing me was a building with a kitchen room, next to that a livng room, next a room in which I could see more guards, and finally a room which was to be my cell. Above the kitchen on the second floor there appeared to be another large room with windows on all four sides. Altogether this was real confinement.

That night there wasn't much of a chance to look over my cell, but I inspected it closely at daybreak. It was about five feet wide and ten feet long, constructed of mud and straw fashioned into a floor and walls. The building itself had a basic wooden structure, though all the rest was of the same mud construction as my cell. A single light bulb hung from the ceiling. A typical oriental shoji panel, which slid back and forth in a wooden frame, was used for the door. The panel was covered with opaque paper, not heavy enough to keep out the cold but heavy enough to keep out the light.

A woven bamboo mat on the floor kept the occupant from wearing out the dirt underneath, but other than the mat there was no suggestion of furniture. At some time in history an attempt had been made to cover the walls with newspapers written in Japanese, but most of the paper had fallen away or yellowed with age. I could hear my guards talking next door to me, but when the door was open I could see only the one out in front, directly guarding my cell. Most of the time the door was closed, evidently because the Communists didn't want me to see much of my surroundings.

The next morning I had a look at my new guards, the largest Chinese soldiers I had seen to date. There were seven living in the room next to me, and the leader was one of the most brutal-looking men I had ever seen. The guards shook me awake in the morning, making motions for me to dress immediately. I became aware of a speaker system nearby, playing an Oriental song. I heard sounds of city life, and could only suppose that I was somewhere near the center of the city. As the day progressed I found that a North Korean officer, his wife and small daughter, were living in a room in my same building, but we were separated by the room the guards occupied.

I was most puzzled by the speaker system. Although the Communists commonly use speaker systems to take the place of radios, I was amazed to hear broadcasts in English. After the first day I began to listen intently, hoping to hear some useful information. The English broadcasts were coming from inside a prison camp and were being made for English-speaking prisoners. The news emanated from Peiping and had the normal Communist bias; still, it was news and sounded good to me. Besides these news broadcasts there were many speeches made in Chinese, many in Korean and much Oriental music. Interspersed between an apparent program schedule were announcements of the correct time. My surroundings were well organized and I couldn't understand why I hadn't joined other prisoners if I was this close to a bona fide prison camp. It didn't make sense.

Four days after my last move Wong appeared at the door of my cell with a most serious expression on his face. This time there was no hint of pleasantry. He came directly to the point. "Mahurin," he said, "I have been directed by the high command to tell you the following. We now consider you to be an international war criminal. We know you have committed crimes against the people of the world and it is our duty to see that you are punished accordingly. We intend to treat you outside the rules of the Geneva Convention regarding prisoners of war. You must confess to these crimes or you will never leave this cell alive."

My God, what a shock! After all the hours I had spent being interrogated on military matters, after all the days of solitary confinement, I had thought I had finally come to the place where I would join other prisoners—only to be met with this accusation. To have them say that I was now an international war criminal, without giving me an inkling of what this meant, was almost more than I could take. Not understanding what they were talking about, I couldn't see what was behind the charge. They wanted me to confess to something, but what? I was sure Wong wasn't kidding me—he was much too serious. As he put it: "Mahurin, I can assure you I know what I am talking about. We have witnesses and evidence of your guilt. Further, your fellow pilots have implicated you." He went on to reiterate that the Communists were going to bring me to justice and that the only way I could settle my case was to confess to all of my crimes. I replied, "I don't know what you are talking about. I am no war criminal. We are both wasting our time."

What the hell was I going to do now? Suppose I wanted to confess. To what? How would I go about it? Even if I could figure out what to confess, how would I make my confession jibe with others? Suppose I worked up something and it was different from the statements of my fellow pilots? Would the Chinese do something drastic to them because our stories differed? Maybe I was going to be shot or even hung like the Germans and the Japanese at the end of World War II. What could I possibly do? I couldn't help but feel that this was the bitter end, that I couldn't make my way out of this one, no matter how I tried.

Four interminable days later there was a commotion in the courtyard, and shortly my guards came into my cell, carrying a large table and five chairs which they set up in front of me. Soon Wong appeared with three other interrogators, men whom I had never seen before. Once again I was accused of being an international war criminal. This time I reacted by demanding: "You will have to tell me what I am guilty of doing. I haven't the slightest idea what you are talking about." With that the interrogator, who appeared to be Wong's superior, stated: "You are guilty of the crime of waging a campaign of biological warfare against us. There is no doubt. We have all the proof we need. You must confess or be executed. What have you to say?"

Holy Christ! Imagine the effect this pronouncement had on me. I had only the vaguest idea of what biological warfare was. How could they possibly imagine I had anything to do with it? I knew for a certainty that nothing even remotely resembling this type of warfare was being conducted. And how could the F-86 be involved, even if it was being used by the United

Nations? We needed every inch of room we had for fuel and/or bombs! We flew so high that it would be impossible to carry any living microorganisms without freezing them immediately. The whole accusation was impossible. They couldn't mean what they were saying; yet they seemed to be in earnest. If only I had time to think.

But they wouldn't let me think. Questions and accusations came from all sides. I couldn't understand what they wanted nor why they wanted it, but there was no question in my mind that they were dead serious. On this first day they kept after me constantly until well after midnight, then left with the admonition that they would be back the following morning to continue the discussions. That night I was awakened several times by the guards, who caused such a commotion in the courtyard that it was difficult to sleep. At four-thirty the next morning I was instructed to arise and put on my clothes for the start of another day of interrogations. This time six instead of four interrogators came into my room to pressure me continuously. The inquisition lasted until after midnight again, with constant questioning and insults directed at me. Not only were they trying to obtain information along a line I knew to be untrue, they were attempting to degrade me and my nation.

Each day the questioning would begin with the statement: "In our society a criminal is given a chance to redeem himself, but first he must confess to his crimes. We are going to interrogate you, Mahurin, until you have confessed to the fullest." They would usually go on to say, "We have captured Lieutenant _____ and he has implicated you deeply in his confession, so now you have no alternative but to talk."

Then for several hours they would vilify the United States and the United Nations because of what they called the inhuman germ-warfare campaign. They spoke often of the remorse our pilots felt when they had carried out missions in support of the germ-warfare program, and how the pilots who had confessed felt relieved afterward, indicating that they had paid a debt to society by confessing. They always ended up by telling me to talk—talk about anything. "But, Mahurin, you must talk." Each vilification and abuse was coupled with threats of death. If a prisoner didn't confess, he would be executed. Such was the law in Communist society.

The questions ranged far and wide, but were generally directed along the lines of accusations. "Who on your side gave instructions for germ warfare?" No answer. "Did the instructions come from Washington?" Again no answer. "How often were these missions carried out?" "They weren't. It was never done and I don't know what you are talking about." "Don't give us that, Mahurin. Even your own pilots know that you were responsible. You must confess to your crimes."

When I would not talk to them they would grow angry. But I had to find out what they were talking about, find out whether they actually meant and believed in the accusations they were making. It was difficult to think under the circumstances, because such a charge based on what I knew to be a lie didn't make any sense to me. There must be more behind what they were doing. Each night when they finally left, instructing my guards to let me lie down on the floor to get some rest, I was so confused and tired that I could hardly think a rational thought. I knew that they would be at me the following morning, but I couldn't think clearly enough to figure out what to do or say when they came back.

Each night was a repetition of the previous night, with constant noises, shouting and yelling, and sounds of gunfire in the courtyard, to prevent my sleeping. Sleep was virtually impossible. I suddenly realized what was happening. I was being brainwashed.

Years before I had read a book, *Darkness at Noon,* written by a one-time Communist, Arthur Koestler. Eventually made into a play for the New York stage, the book dealt with the story of a Communist commissar who began to deviate from the party line only to find himself arrested by the People's Security Police. Rubashov is confined along with other political prisoners, forced to confess to crimes against the people, and eventually put to death by a bullet in the back of his head. The book is a grim exposure of the inner workings of the police state, and its meaning had been buried in the back of my mind for many years. Now I found myself in a situation closely resembling that of Rubashov and many other people I had heard about over the years. I knew that it was possible for my interrogators to destroy my will to resist telling things I did not want to tell, and I was much too tired and emaciated to withstand pressure of this kind over extended periods of time.

I had obviously been softened up for the kill. First I had gone through a long period of intense interrogation on military matters. Next I had been left alone for a thirty-day period, after anticipating prison camp. I had been given a period of rather intense treatment, warning me that something serious was about to happen—and here it was.

Brainwashing is actually the artificial creation of insanity. The Communists have used the techniques of "Invisible Torture"—inducing uncertainty or fear, forcing sleeplessness, demanding kneeling or standing for long periods of time, using strong lighting and sound effects—to achieve political aims and to eliminate undesirables from their society, ever since it was founded. Through Pavlov they found that variable creation, release of fear, and the maintenance of tension in an indvidual, may induce neurotic behavior and facilitate the acceptance of new ideas. Such techniques make it possible to implant in human minds numerous notions which are not only false as to fact but distort the learning processes. This type of disorientation can produce lasting mental crises or at least serious maladjustments. Individuals who think or act counter to the Communist cause can make trouble—trouble which must be eliminated to prevent the possibility of Communist leaders being overthrown. When a deviationist is discovered he is forced, through brainwashing, to confess to a crime such as treason, which is punishable by death. As soon as a confession is obtained the undesirable is given a public trial, demonstrating to the masses that each has the right of legal representation when accused of a crime. Although the outcome of the trial is a foregone conclusion, the accused is exposed to a string of witnesses for the prosecution who are willing to perjure themselves for the cause. The falsely obtained confession plays a big part too. Depending upon the individual's status, he is put to death, imprisoned or banished from the country. At least he is no longer a possible source of trouble.

God, how I hated to see each day come. I got so I knew almost exactly what was going to happen from day to day. The guards would awaken me at four thirty in the morning. I would be allowed to go to the toilet, and then they would bring a bowl of ice-cold water in which to wash my face and hands. Next I would get a bowl of rice or perhaps a piece of bread and some hot water to eat and drink. About eight in the morning I would hear the sounds of the interrogators arriving to begin the day's activities. I could usually hear them discussing things for fifteen or twenty minutes before I would hear the footsteps of the guard approach my cell to open the door and motion to me to proceed directly to the interrogation room upstairs.

It took me twenty steps to get to the bottom of the staircase, then up four steps, through a door and into the interrogation room. I would finally be facing fifteen similarly dressed Chinese seated in a semi-circle around a small table. A single light bulb, suspended from the ceiling and covered by a green light shade, burned at all times directly over a stool on which I sat while the assembled group directed question after question at me. A guard was always posted directly behind me, though he never took part in any of the discussions.

There were windows in back of the interrogators, and through them I could see rooftops and beyond, the banks of a river. We were too high up to see people, but the sounds of village life were ever present during the day. The interrogators lounged about, smoked cigarettes, and drank tea as they took turns questioning me about germ warfare. Each day at noon the interrogations would cease while the Chinese went to lunch and then took their rest. They would resume questioning about two each afternoon and continue to six. At that time I would be allowed to return to my cell for my evening meal which also consisted of rice, bread or some other meager dish of food. At about seven o'clock the group would return and continue ques-

tioning until perhaps two in the morning. At that time the
guards would be summoned to take me back to my cell until
the next session.

How I dreaded each visit. To watch those fifteen pairs of
slant eyes continually probing for some break in my composure
was almost more than I could stand. Only a few of them could
speak English. The rest asked questions in Chinese which were
interpreted by an English-speaking officer. In turn, my statements had to be translated into Chinese. I complained again
and again that I wasn't going to confess to anything and that
they were just wasting time, but equally as often they explained
that they had nothing else to do but solve my case and that they
intended to do so if it took them the rest of their lives. I tried
to determine whether all of them actually believed the accusations they were making, but it was virtually impossible to tell,
because Chinese facial expressions are characteristically dead-
pan.

Initially the questioning, led by one interrogator, took the
form of direct accusation: "Mahurin, as an international war
criminal you must confess to your guilt before your case can
be solved. We want you to tell us all about the germ-warfare
campaign." The spokesman would then direct: "Since you
refuse to admit that the United Nations is conducting this
campaign, you must tell us what you carry in the external fuel
tanks of the F-86." "Okay," I'd reply, "we carry fuel." "Now,
Mahurin, that kind of comment will get you nowhere. You
must tell us whether you have any men in white uniforms at
your air bases." "Naturally not," I would reply. "We all wear
GI uniforms." "That is not the proper answer either," the interrogators would say. "Our spies have told us that you have
special units at each air base and that the members of these
units wear white uniforms. Further than that, your own pilots
have admitted this to us." No comment!

"Now, Mahurin," they would say, "you can't just sit there and
not speak up, because you are our prisoner and you must confess." Then they would add: "Do you have any decontamination
equipment on your air bases?" "I don't even know what you

are talking about," I would reply. After several days of constant questioning along these lines they produced a book which was a record of all the missions I had flown while carrying bombs. "Mahurin, we notice that you led a bombing misson on the eighth of May. We have obtained fragments of the bombs and pieces of your external tanks. You must tell us what was in the bombs and how those external tanks were made." To all of this questioning I could only say, "The bombs contained explosives and the tanks contained fuel."

After a week or so of this kind of questioning it was easy to see that, once I decided to make any kind of germ-warfare confession, I had been given enough hints to fill it with "facts" which would coincide with confessions made by others. For example, I would have to incorporate comments about how our tanks were compartmented so that they could carry germs. The tanks should also be made to explode on contact with the ground in order to release the contaminants. Each day, through the questioning, I would receive fresh, new hints about what I should write when I decided to do so. There was never a hint of not doing so. To them it was an accomplished fact.

In answer to all my denials and counteraccusations came threats of death. "Mahurin, you are delaying us and the high command is becoming angry with you. You only have a few days left before you are to be put to death." Countless times I was told: "No one knows you are here but us. You are completely in our power, and we can do anything we want to with you. Unless you confess immediately, you will never see the United States or your loved ones again."

Whenever I said that I didn't have any idea of how to make a confession even if I wanted to do so, the leading interrogator would reply, "Why don't you just start? It is like digging a tunnel through a mountain. We start from one end and you start from the other. Eventually, with proper guidance, we'll both meet in the middle." Often they would repeat: "Many other pilots have confessed to their crimes, and each one felt a sense of relief as he threw off his guilt. All have been forgiven by the high command and will be allowed to return home when the war is over."

I was not only exposed to constant questioning along these lines, but I was also forced to listen while they heaped abuse on the United Nations and especially on the United States. They were all certain that the United States had started the Korean War by initially attacking North Korean installations. I am sure that China had been subjected to this sort of propaganda prior to joining North Korea. They portrayed themselves as the innocent victims of aggressor forces. "Mahurin," they would say, "you should know that the United States is no longer the most powerful nation in the World; Russia is. Some day China will be even more powerful than Russia. You are in our hands now, and even the United States can't help you." Often they would accuse me of praying for help in my situation. "We'll guess that you have been praying to your God, Mahurin, to help you from making the confession we demand." They would add: "Go on, pray all you want. It won't help you. We are your God now. You have to do business with us."

By the time I would be released to return to my cell at the end of each interrogation period I would be so confused and mentally exhausted that I would hardly know where I was. I had tried to keep from saying anything, had restricted my remarks to keep from giving them an opening they could use for further probing. I knew that I had to be alert as long as possible in front of them. Once back in my cell, I would be so disturbed over what they were driving at that I couldn't sleep for worry. Remembering what had happened to Rubashov and knowing what was happening to me didn't help matters at all. Almost every night I was conscious of people screaming, guns being fired, and strange sounds coming from the quadrangle. Worst of all, I knew they would be back the following day to continue questioning me. It was all hideous.

I held my own for nearly thirty days until I began to feel myself slipping. I was having difficulty keeping ahead of them, and above all, difficulty concentrating on what they said. I kept thinking that I was unable to stand much more of this—I knew

I could hardly stay awake—yet they hammered away, day in and day out. As the days wore on I felt that I would give anything to get them off my back. I denied all the accusations—I didn't do it; I was sure no one else had. But these were not the answers they wanted.

Finally I knew that I had reached the breaking point. I was called in for an evening session in front of them, but before being seated on my stool I made a babbling statement about nothing at all. The interrogators held a hurried discussion in Chinese between themselves, then directed me to return to my cell for some rest. I was cracking up. The next morning when we began again, I sat in front of those inhuman men in a completely blank state. I was slipping and I knew that I would be unable to keep control of myself as long as they continued to exert pressure on me. All I wanted was to have them lay off long enough to let me get some sleep. If they didn't, I was sure I would eventually say, "All right, give me some paper and a pencil and I'll write a confession." But I knew I couldn't do it. It was an untrue allegation which would reflect discredit on my nation throughout the world. What could I do? I didn't know.

Just before darkness one evening they had been working especially hard to get me to start writing. They could probably tell that I was about to give in. Finally they decided to go to supper and then come back to continue with me shortly thereafter. When they had departed Wong said to me, "Mahurin, you are wasting our time. Go back to your cell and wait for us. We will be back this evening." On the way to my cell I was desperate to the extent that I could no longer think clearly about my situation. I was absolutely through, but I had one extreme course of action open to me—a course from which there was no return.

I still had the little piece of pocketknife hidden in my clothing. The only way I could evade giving in to them would be to kill myself, otherwise they would get what they wanted from me. My cell was arranged with a long table in the center and a chair at one end, facing the door. Except for the light of the single bulb, the room was bleak. In front of the door a guard paced up and down in the quadrangle, but he could not see directly into my cell without standing on a small porch which ran along the front of the dwelling. I had noticed previously that after dark the guards made no special effort to watch me, as long as the light was on in my cell. Once I lay down on the floor to sleep I was allowed to turn out the light.

By now I was in a completely disturbed mental state. This was it and I had to do something quickly. I sat down in the chair behind the table and brought out the small piece of knife. After a few feeble attempts at cutting my leg to determine how much pain was associated with knife wounds, I began to cut my wrists in an effort to find a substantial artery or vein. (I now have recommendations for anyone contemplating suicide. Don't do it by cutting wrists. In the first place it hurts, and in the second place Mother Nature has designed wrists so that they almost defy cutting.) I had trouble cutting past the tendons which make the fingers move, and so for a short time I was unsuccessful in getting a cut large enough to cause a substantial flow of blood. Finally I got down to the blood vessels normally used to take the pulse. I managed to hack through these and wound up with blood spurting several feet from both wrists. So far, so good. I put both of my hands down inside my thick prisoner-of-war uniform as I sat behind the table, so that the blood would be absorbed by the cotton and the guards would be unable to see what I had done. As I sat there waiting for oblivion to overtake me I murmured a silent good-bye to my family, anxious to be on my way now that I had made the decision. Then, just as I began to feel faint, the light in my room went out.

Heretofore the electricity service all over North Korea had been sporadic, because the United Nations forces had been bombing the major power supply at the Sui-Ho Reservoir on the Yalu. As the light failed I reached up to tap the bulb, hoping it had only become loosened from the socket. Nothing happened, so I sat down immediately. The guard came running, flashlight in hand, and began to work with the bulb while calling to all the other guards sleeping next door. In a moment they were all in my room, chattering as the light came on. One guard standing close to the light noticed flecks of blood on the bulb, and came over to look at me. When I had attempted to tap the bulb all the blood held inside my pants had drained out onto the floor of my cell, so I was sitting in a pool of blood about a yard in diameter. Upon seeing this the guards grabbed me in an attempt to stanch the flow. I struggled with them as much as I could, but being in a weakened condition, I was unable to do much more than jump up and down a few times and collapse on the floor. One of the guards who had departed as soon as he saw blood, returned with a doctor and a couple of nurses, who were joined several minutes later by Wong and his fellow interrogators. Wong kept repeating, "Now, Mahurin, this is no way to solve your problem."

Up to now I had been clinging to a bit of foolish pride. Although I had been reduced to a low state and must have appeared as a filthy, dirty animal, I was determined that they would never see me give in to pain. As the doctor began repairing my wrists I tried to act as if nothing had really happened. Even though the doctor tied off the vessels and sewed up the gashes, I acted as if it did not hurt at all. The climax was not long in coming, however, for as he finished he poured raw alcohol on both of my wrists. For a moment I thought I was on fire. As soon as the doctors were finished, Wong and his companions took over. After completely searching my room and my person, they instructed the guards to leave me alone. Then I lost track of time.

For many days I was vaguely conscious of being fed intravenously with glucose. In between times I slept soundly. At the end of what I would estimate to be eleven days I began to feel a bit of strength, even though I was still shaky. Wong and his people came on the twelfth day to ask: "How do you feel now?" "I guess I feel all right," I replied. "Okay, let's go again," they said. Back up to the interrogation room we went as the fifteen members of the team took their places. And we began all over again.

As demonstrated by Pavlov, reflex conditioning must be continuous to achieve results. If there is a break in the process, the procedure must be restarted. Now that I had been given a twelve-day respite, my interrogators didn't bother me any more. No matter what they did or said, they could not alter my decision not to give in to them. Once I had decided to take my own life, no threat they made was horrible enough to change my mind. Thus each time they embarked on a new line of questions I just told them: "I'm not interested. I'm not going to talk to you, nor am I going to tell you a thing. As far as I am concerned you are all wasting your time." I finally reached the point where I wouldn't even talk; I just sat. Day after day they came and tried to pump me. But their hold on my mind was gone; I didn't care any more. I figured that they were going to kill me anyway, so why should I listen to anything they had to say?

From their viewpoint there was obviously a limit. I could see the temper of the group beginning to rise until one day I blurted out, "You guys are ballet dancing with me and you are wasting your time." With that Wong said, "Mahurin, you have been conducting a sit-down strike against us. We will now show you what it really means to sit down." With that I was taken back to my cell and directed to stand aside while they removed all of my furniture except a small, four-legged wooden stool about twenty-four inches high. They directed me to sit on this stool at rigid attention until told to do otherwise. They instructed my guards to keep watch over me and make sure I did not move or relax from attention while sitting with my toes tucked underneath the stool and my arms held straight at my sides. Each morning the guards came in at four thirty to awaken me and to motion that I was to begin sitting on my stool. At nine-thiry each night they would motion that I was to sleep on the floor until the next morning came. Each night I was in absolute agony. I could sit at attention for only a short period of time and would then have to move. Although I still received a minimum of food two times a day, I could gradually feel my body atrophy from lack of exercise.

After my suicide attempt the guards cut a hole in the side of my cell to watch me continuously. They placed a desk behind the hole and stationed a guard at this desk twenty-four hours a day. In addition they opened the door to my cell and kept it open day and night. They had taken everything they could from me except my uniform, and although I had been given a pair of tennis shoes to take the place of my GI boots, they had removed the shoelaces. It was now winter and the temperature dropped as low as fifty degrees below zero during the coldest days. With my feet resting on my toes below the stool, my shoes would pop open, allowing the cold to penetrate right through me. There I sat while my guards warmed themselves with a bucketful of charcoal which they kept blazing just far enough away from me so that I could not enjoy the heat. While they warmed, I gradually froze.

Every time I moved, the guards entered my cell and rocked me back or shoved me around. I was made to lean over backward until I collapsed on the floor, or to hold my hands above my head for so long that I would almost cry out with pain. When they grew tired of pushing me around they put me back on my stool where I tried to sit rigidly. Whenever I saw their attention distracted I tried to move around and adjust my position, but all in all it was a trying experience. By bedtime I was barely able to move to lie down. Once under my blanket I would spend several hours massaging my legs to restore circulation. This went on for thirty-three days.

During the last few days I began to notice that I couldn't restore circulation in my feet, no matter what I did. I also noticed that my feet were turning black in places. When both my hands and feet began to swell I knew that I must do something drastic or eventually lose my feet from gangrene. I would shout at the top of my lungs each time I heard voices or noises outside my cell. At first the guards tried to stop me, but I was desperate enough not to pay attention to them. Since it was impossible for them to keep my mouth covered, I finally yelled frequently and loudly enough to catch the ear of a Communist officer who happened to pass by. When he came into my cell to see what had caused the commotion I showed him my feet, and he left me saying, "I will see what I can do for you, but from my under-

standing your case is very difficult." One day later the chief
interrogator paid me a visit, accompanied by the doctor with
whom I had had previous contact. They gave the guards instructions to close the door of my cell and build a fire daily
under the floor of my room so that I would be warm for the
night. They also gave instructions that I was to be allowed to
get off the stool and sit on the floor of my cell, although I was
not to sleep during the periods from four thirty in the morning
until nine thirty at night. Further, the door to my cell was to
be kept closed at all times. Treatment of this kind was unprecedented for me. I was certain that forces other than those
I had seen to date were about to be brought into play.

3.

DURING the thirty-three days on the stool I was
given a chance to come to grips with what was happening. I
found it impossible to understand why the Communists were
willing to spend so much time and effort to get a confession
from me for something I hadn't done. Although it was obvious
we weren't waging germ warfare in Korea, these people seemed
to believe the allegation. Yet if they were intelligent—and they
seemed to be—they must have known what the real circumstances were, that what they were saying wasn't true. So far all
the interrogators and officers working with me appeared to believe wholeheartedly that the Orient was being victimized by
germ warfare. But they were Orientals, and to me, inscrutable.
I could never really tell by their expressions, their questions,
their actions, what was on their minds. During all the interrogations I had tried to counterquestion to grind out what the
alleged germ-warfare program involved. I tried time and again

to make the interrogators admit that the whole thing was fiction, but a POW, confronted by experts, is always at a disadvantage.

In the opinion of the Communists I must have fallen off the fence of Pavlov reflex conditioning the wrong way. I should have broken down and written and said anything they wanted me to say, but instead I began to defy them. This was not due to my bravery; I just gave up trying to outfumble them. I was the same as dead and I knew it. I found that I had slowed down physically as well as mentally. My body activities were regulated so that I was having bowel movements about every eight days, and I visited the slit trench about three times each day to urinate. I got no exercise other than standing up occasionally while food was brought to me or while making preparations to go to bed. When I was allowed to have heat for my room they apparently decided to punish me by making me build the fire each night in the small hole below the floor of my cell. I considered this a great freedom. Each night I could exercise while blowing on the fire to get it started, and I got a good look at my surroundings—even though there wasn't much to see.

For months I hadn't been permitted to wash my hands and face, nor had I been allowed to shave. When the heating restrictions were dropped I was given permission to wash without soap. All this time I hadn't been getting along any too well with the guards. When given orders I usually kept my morale at least an inch from the floor by snarling back at them. Since they didn't understand English, I could use all the invective I wanted without their understanding what I said. However, I couldn't conceal the expression on my face, and I am sure they knew damn well I hated them—a feeling I am sure was reciprocal. They had only struck me a couple of times in the past, but now they were able to get in a couple of real digs every day. Each morning the entire squad built a fire in the courtyard, to heat water for washing. When they had finished their ablutions they would fill a filthy washbasin with icy cold water, add ice or snow (then lying in quantity on the ground), and bring it to me to wash my face and hands. God, that water was cold. Since I had no soap, it hardly seemed worth the trouble, but the guards stood around to watch, and pride kept me at it. With effort I could wash one hand at a time without making my fingers numb, and I was determined not to show them how it felt, even if my whole hand dropped off.

If they couldn't get to me one way, they'd use another. Instead of continuous visiting, the interrogators now came just once or twice a day. I no longer spent hours sitting under bright lights being questioned by fifteen of them. They began to bring more important military people to talk to me. I now had to face a "Military Tribunal," constituted, they explained, to try me for my crimes. I was no longer taken to the room above my cell, but instead to various buildings in the town of Pyoktong.

Sometimes I would be summoned in the daytime, sometimes at night. The procedure was always the same. The guards would slide back the door to my cell and motion that I was to follow them. They would line up seven strong in front, on either side and in back, to march me through the village. Often our destination would be a half mile or so away, and in the daytime we would have to pass through the North Korean villagers, who always seemed to be out in droves on the streets of Pyoktong.

The guards in the lead, their rifles ready at all times, would either motion or shove the civilians out of our way, and it seemed to me that they were just as alert to the possibility of the Koreans attacking me as they were to the possibility of my attempting to escape. The villagers would often stare, but I never did see any open signs of hostility. I could tell a little about the village, even though I was usually too frightened to absorb too much detail. The streets were mud, the shed-like shops unpainted and flimsy. Though I had been told I was in the central area of the prison camps, I never saw another prisoner or white man as I was marched back and forth. I did notice that there seemed to be a disproportionate ratio of Chinese soldiers to the civilian population, and I assumed that that was because of the proximity of the prisoners.

When we went to the tribunal meetings at night the drill would be the same except that the guards would carry more weapons—Russian "burp" guns as well as pistols. Early each evening there would be villagers in the streets, but on the way home after each session the village would be quiet.

The buildings we visited were usually more permanent than most of their neighbors. As a rule I would be shoved into a doorway that had been covered with a blackout cloth. Then my guards and I would wait until the members of the tribunal had arrived. After fifteen or twenty minutes of conversation between them they would instruct the guards to bring me before them, and the interrogation or trial would begin.

Upon entering I would be confronted by the four to seven members of the tribunal, seated behind a table, ready to conduct the trial. I would stand at attention during the questioning until they chose to send me back to my room. An interpreter was used each time, there being at least one high-ranking member on the board who supposedly could not understand English. The members of the tribunal were different each time.

After confronting the tribunal I would be exposed to an interesting sidelight of Communist practice. The chief interrogator would direct me to write a paper on "Self-Criticism." His explanation was as follows: in the Communist world, when a member of the society commits an act of heresy or has thoughts divergent to the Communist party line, he is severely criticized by his comrades. He is then required to write a paper of self-criticism, outlining in detail his actual and ideological errors. In the paper he must attempt to justify his actions and express his atonement and his intention to live a good Communist life in the future. In Pavlovian theory, a person admitting mistakes he does not believe will eventually be conditioned to correct these very same "mistakes," even though they be nonexistent. Thus is the human mind degraded in order to make the individual change his ways and become more atone with the group around him.

I had to admit in writing that my attempt at suicide was a mistake. I had to say that I would cooperate with my captors and from that point on tell them the truth. But since I realized that telling the truth meant to them that I would say what they wanted me to say, I would never make the self-criticism statements under my own free will. For being rude to the tribunal I was forced to sit on the edge of my stool again for thirty-six hours without sleep with my hands over my head. Finally I could stand it no longer. I vividly recall the last statement in my note of self-criticism: "In the future I promised to tell nothing but the absolute truth about germ warfare to my interrogators. In the future I will behave as a prisoner of war should."

When I had signed my name to the self-criticism I was allowed to return to my cell and rest for approximately sixteen hours. At the end of that time I was again called before the tribunal and told that I must now start to write a germ-warfare confession in accordance with the comments made in the letter of self-criticism. I retorted: "I will tell you the truth, which I have been telling all along. I know nothing of the germ-warfare campaign, and I am positive that it has not been conducted against you. This is the truth and I will say no more. Self-criticisms are for idiots."

Ultimately the continuous strain began to have peculiar effects. When I was alone I could be perfectly calm, yet the slightest unusual happening would send me into fits of shivering. It got to be embarrassing. I wanted to appear to be brave and in perfect control at all times in front of them. But, damn it, every time I went before a tribunal meeting I would shiver and tremble until I was returned to my cell. I couldn't seem to control it. And it was bad enough to display that lack of self-control in front of the Chinese, but much worse when I received an unexpected visitor.

On my birthday, December 5, I was allowed to wash my face and hands with warm water and soap. Shortly after, the guards motioned that I was to go to the room above my cell. When I walked in I saw, standing in the center of the room, a white man about six feet two inches tall, dressed in what appeared to be Russian clothing. He immediately addressed me with a British accent saying, "Hello, how are you?" I replied, as calmly as I could, "I am all right." The man went on to say, "I have been sent from Great Britain as a representative of the British trade unions. I represent a total of nineteen million people in Great Britain, and am in North Korea to investigate the charge of germ warfare. I have been talking to the camp commander, who states that you were the leader in this campaign. I have talked with several pilots who worked for you, and all of them have incriminated you. I understand that you have been interrogated along this line, but have refused to confess. I am here to take your confession, because I want to get to the bottom of the germ-warfare allegation."

He continued to say that he had been informed by the camp commander that I had only two days left to live. If there was no confession at the end of that time, they were going to kill me for certain. He said that there was very little he could do, but he was there to listen to my confession, and if I confessed, chances were he could intercede with the camp commander and I would not be put to death. In the meantime, he said, "While I am waiting for your confession how would you like some hot tea and a cigarette?"

I didn't like this guy from the start. He looked a bit like Hollywood's George Sanders, and was playing a part that would be perfect for that actor. What was a white man doing there in the first place? Although I had a cigarette and a cup of tea with him, he made me so nervous that I was soon trembling all over.

When we had finished our refreshments he said, "Well, all right, let's have the confession." "I have no idea who you are," I said. "I don't know anything, and I wouldn't tell you if I did. I know that the germ-warfare charge is ridiculous; it's not being done. I further don't give a damn what you have heard. I don't intend to confess to you or to anyone else."

We talked for about half an hour while he asked me questions. "Come now," he said, "let's be agreeable about this. What do you carry in your fuel tanks, and how do you conduct this germ-warfare campaign?" For a few moments I tried to answer politely by saying, "I know nothing of what you are talking about." But when he persisted with, "Who started you out on it? We know you aren't responsible, you are just the tool of your imperialist bosses," I got mad at him and refused to answer.

Finally he became provoked and ordered: "Well, you go back to your cell. I am convinced that you are a criminal. I cannot help you. I will go ahead and question more of your pilots. I refuse to be bothered by you any more. It looks to me like you're finished." Then he left and I was returned to my cell.

The next morning the guards took me to a new place to meet the tribunal. When I walked in the door I was shocked to see the Britisher sitting behind a conference table with four civilian interrogators and one military man. I stood at attention the whole day until about midnight that night while the Britisher and the Chinese pumped questions at me continuously. He, as well as they, wanted to know all about bombing with the F-86. They wanted to know where our bombs had fallen and who had participated in the various flights. I stood in front of them saying nothing.

When they finally realized that they were not going to get a confession from me the Britisher spent about half an hour in a fanatic diatribe, telling me what he thought of me, the United Nations, Great Britain and the United States. He was rabid about Russia conquering the world. In his ranting rage he began to resemble a poor man's Adolph Hitler. I had to resist climbing up on the stage and taking a poke at him, despite the fact that the guards, sensing my anger, had moved in close behind me. When he finally finished his tantrum I was allowed to return to my cell.

Not until later did I learn his identity. He is Alan Winnington. Educated at Oxford, a former Fleet Street reporter, Winnington apparently had exhibited Communist leanings for some time before he defected to Russia to take up Communism full time. When I met him he had been in Russia and China for a period of ten years or so. He is now a member of the Anglo-American Community in Peiping, with social headquarters at the International Club, and is a foreign correspondent for the London *Daily Worker*. I personally know this man to be a liar, cheat and traitor to his country. He is the only person in the world I can truthfully say I loathe. I would kill him with my bare hands if there were the remotest chance of it, but I fear that he is beyond return to the free world, and I am beyond going to China to get him.

When the Winnington tactics failed, the Communists thought of something else. Before the tribunal the next day they informed me that they were going to do something they had hoped wouldn't be necessary, but "by your arbitrary actions, Mahurin, we must now show you what you are up against." Dramatically the guards brought in a tape-recording machine and set it on the table in front of the tribunal. The machine was started and I heard the following in English: "My name is Lieutenant—— ——, United States Air Force. I am a member of the Fourth Fighter Interceptor Wing stationed at K-14 in South Korea. I have worked for Colonel Walker M. Mahurin, who was my group commander during the time I was flying combat in South Korea. Colonel Mahurin had been sent to South Korea directly from Washington, D. C., to begin the campaign of germ warfare against the Communist world."

The statement described germ warfare in great detail: how the campaigns were being waged, what was being dropped, how the pilots felt about dropping disease on unprotected civilians all over North Korea and China, and so on. In conclusion the statement said that Colonel Mahurin had been responsible and that all pilots had had to obey his orders.

I listened to four such confessions, and of course recognized all four names as well as the voices on the recordings. At first I thought, If I ever get back home I'll get those guys and beat them to a pulp. Nothing is bad enough for them. But then I began to consider logically what they had tried to do. All four had probably received the same sort of treatment as I had, and they had probably concluded that they would have to make some sort of confession. Obviously a lieutenant or even a captain cannot say that he has initiated a campaign of germ warfare. He is going to have to hang it on someone else—someone higher than he. He doesn't want to accuse his squadron commander, because usually he has too much loyalty for such a man. He can, however, easily name the group commander. Probably none of these guys anticipated my being shot down. Most of the people who had known me at the 51st Wing knew that I would be going back to the United States after ninety days. The lads at the 4th probably thought that I'd finish my missions quickly and be sent home before anything could happen to me. No, these four had had to name somebody, and I was the logical choice. Basically, each man had found a solution to his individual problem. I can't condemn a guy for that. In every case these were very young men from walks of life which would not normally expose them to what they had experienced. In the military service they had certainly had no preparation for what awaited them. Each was a POW in Communist hands—without the briefing, background or training to cope with his situation. Each had to find a way out. On reflection, I couldn't blame them.

After all four recordings had been played the tribunal asked if I was ready to confess. Again I said no, and once again the guards were ordered to take me back to my cell. The next day we began all over again with something different. I was brought in and directed to sit at a table upon which lay pencils and paper. "All right, Mahurin, we have fooled around with you long enough. You must now write a confession of germ warfare." "I won't do it," I repeated for the zillionth time. "I will write a statement of what I did as a combat leader in Korea." "You must write something or suffer the consequences," they replied. With that I wrote a complete ten-page denial of the entire charge, saying that those who had confessed had been forced to do so to work out their own problems. Their confessions were nothing but a pack of lies trumped up by the Communists. Since none of the accusations were true, they were obviously a means of propaganda, and I would play no part in Communist propaganda. When the tribunal took this statement from me they said, "Are you sure this is the statement you want to make?" "Absolutely," I replied. "Further, I am not going back on it."

They answered, "Mahurin, you are only causing your own death." I told them, "I'm sorry, but that is the way I want it."

That night, several hours after I had fallen asleep, the guards awoke me and took me back before the tribunal. This time all the faces were different, except for the man I had been most accustomed to seeing as interpreter-interrogator. When we were well into the question-and-answer game I began to sense something strange. During my imprisonment I had learned a bit of the Chinese language, just by watching and listening. It is easy when one has nothing else to do. For example, if the guards said *"Kivon,"* and one of them went off, returning later with food, it wouldn't be too long before I knew what *kivon* meant. *Chervon,* a Mahurin approximation of a Chinese word, means —to eat. *Ma-man-de* means to wait a moment. *Joshuan* means pilot. And so on. I could ask for what I wanted, could understand a lot of the information coming over the speaker system, and best of all, I could understand much of what was said among the guards. Now I could tell that the interpreter would change my answer around before he gave it to the tribunal. In return when the tribunal asked me a question, the interpreter changed it before it got to me.

I watched this ball bounce back and forth a few times before finally saying, "Listen you bastard, we can stop this right now. I won't answer one more thing unless you give my answers straight to them without changes. What's more I want their questions directly, without your opinion built in." The next few questions and answers seemed to be going through ungarbled. Suddenly the interpreter addressed the tribunal in Chinese: "He understands much of what we are saying. I suggest we switch to Mandarin."

Apparently lying back and forth is standard practice in Communist circles. The members of the tribunal must have believed in the germ-warfare allegations, having themselves been misled by the members of the propaganda agency who knew such charges were untrue. It is highly probable that many responsible authorities inside China and Russia, who should have known better, were actually led into thinking that these charges were true, because of the efforts of their propaganda experts.

They kept after me relentlessly. One night I was awakened by my guards, who carried not the customary old rifles but Russian-built submachine guns. One of them held a very large Russian pistol which he kept pointed at me at all times. In the dead of night, without a sound coming from the village, we marched out of town, well into the country. As we walked I was convinced that they were taking me out to some field where they would blow my brains out—that this was to be the end. I knew that nobody on our side knew for sure that I was alive. Even if they did, it wouldn't make any difference. A guy who is shot down alone in an airplane is in a different position from a GI captured on the ground. His captors can keep him if they want to and not tell a soul. Or they can kill him and claim later that he died in the crash of his plane. Who the hell will know the difference? This time, for certain, my fate was in the hands of my guards.

But nothing happened. Eventually they marched me to a building in which I had never been, and there sat the same old tribunal. This time they were on a platform behind a table draped with a blanket which hung all the way to the floor. Several documents lay on the table, and as I approached I was aware that the guard, instead of assuming his customary position against the door, stepped up to within a foot or so behind me.

The chief of the tribunal began by saying, "Mahurin, we have your written confession here in which you deny any knowledge about germ warfare. We also have another confession which we have written and we want you to read it for us. You must read slowly and clearly so that you will understand what our document contains." God, Almighty, I thought, What can possibly be going on here? I couldn't figure out what they were up to.

They handed me my document to read first. As I silently began to read they directed: "No, Mahurin, you must read each statement aloud." I slowly read the ten pages, one by one. When

226

I had finished they handed me a document I had never seen and directed that I step closer to the platform and read in a loud voice. "All right, you may now read this one," they said. I began to read: "My name is Colonel Walker M. Mahurin, Commander of the Fourth Fighter Interceptor Group. I have been sent to Korea to begin a campaign of germ warfare against the North Koreans and Chinese." It was a germ-warfare confession. As I read slowly and quietly, with my head down, it suddenly dawned on me that they were trying to get a tape recording of me confessing to germ warfare. Further, they were trying to pull it off without my knowing it.

As I read they kept whispering, "Step closer and read in a louder voice." Finally I was only about a foot away from the table, trying desperately to think what to do next. I had read only about three paragraphs of what appeared to be some fifteen pages when suddenly the lights in the room went out. There was much shuffling about while the members of the tribunal groped for a candle which they lighted and placed in front of me. "You go right on reading, Mahurin," they said. "The lights will come back on in a minute." As I started again to read the guard in back of me said: "It won't work without electricity." The chief of the tribunal replied: "That's all right. Let him go ahead; we will try again." Of course these weren't the exact words, but I knew enough Chinese to understand that much.

When I had finished reading they sat back and fumbled around behind the table, talking among themselves. A short time later the lights came back on. As soon as we had light the chief said, "Now, we are not so sure that you understood what was contained in the second document. You must read it again for us." By this time I knew damn good and well that they were trying to get a recording they could use before the world, so I started to read as slowly as I could, in a halting voice. If this thing ever was released I wanted to be sure I didn't sound like a happy-go-lucky arch germ-warfare wager. When I had read some six paragraphs the lights again went out. Although I finished reading the document by candlelight, I could tell that the members of the tribunal were really angry. They were whispering excitedly among each other while they paid no attention at all to me.

When the lights came on for the second time they said, "You have now read these two confessions. In one you deny germ warfare, and in the other you make a confession. You now have thirty seconds to tell us which one you want us to accept." With that the guard in back of me jammed his pistol to the back of my head and clicked back the trigger. I didn't have too many options. I knew that if I picked the honest document they would take me outside and finish me off immediately. On the other hand, if I chose the one in which I "confessed," I would be denying everything that had sustained me and helped me resist in weeks gone by. For the longest thirty seconds I have ever lived I just stood there thinking over my life. "All right, Mahurin, your time is up. Which story do we accept? You are wasting our time." I summoned all the courage I had and blurted, "It is not true. None of it. That denial is the one you will accept. I will not confess."

To my surprise the guard stepped back and uncocked his pistol. The tribunal held a brief, angry conference and then directed the guard to take me back to my cell.

Very late the following night an interrogator came to take me before the camp commander, who, I had been told previously, was a general in the Chinese Army. I got dressed as slowly as I could and followed him with dragging feet to the headquarters building and into a big room. The people present —and there were a lot of them—snapped to attention with all the fanfare possible when the General strode in. He appeared to be of very high social class, and had an extremely light complexion and an intelligent appearance. He ranted and raved at me for about five minutes through the interpreter, repeating the same old lines I had heard so often. "You must confess or we are going to kill you. The tribunal has decided to put you to death, but I am going to give you one more chance. You have no choice in the matter, since you are an enemy of the people. Now what do you say?" I repeated my same old say about: "It is not true and I am not going to confess. I don't know anything." With that the General lost his temper completely and raved at me for five minutes more, finally shouting, "All right you have exactly twelve more hours in which to confess. This interrogator will come to you at the end of that time to take your decision. Go back to your cell."

Twelve hours later, I suppose to the minute, the interpreter came into my cell to say, "The General has instructed me to tell you this is your last chance. What do you say?" Once again I said, "I am not going to do any such thing." With that the interpreter replied, "Mahurin, you are now going to die. We are not going to tell you when or how, but I can assure you that you are as good as dead right now. I am sorry for you."

That took care of that.

4.

I DECIDED to face death as firmly as I could and without any visible show of emotion. After all, I was an American and a senior Air Force officer. Although no one but my captors would know, I intended to show them that I could be brave when they salted me away. But this business of not telling me when it was coming was the worst of all.

I grew hypersensitive to any change in my surroundings. At the slightest unusual sound I'd be sure that they were coming to kill me. If the routine varied just a bit from the previous day, I'd know that this was the day I'd be shot. Probably the knowledge that on X day I would be put to death would have been best from my standpoint, but I had been told that I would never know until the time came. Now I realize that most of the ominous sounds were just normal happenings outside my cell, but at the time I lived in a state of constant fear.

It may be comparatively easy to reconcile oneself to the knowledge that death is inevitable, but it is damn difficult to have it called on and off so many times. The Chinese made a special effort to undermine my nerve. Once every two or three nights I would be awakened and ordered to dress and pack my belongings. We would go outside the village for a short distance, then return to my cell where I would be instructed to lie down and go to sleep. Each time we started I would concentrate on facing a firing squad, or whatever instrument of death my captors had in mind, with a bit of bravery, but once back in my cell the letdown would be terrific. I could barely keep from breaking down. But I was determined that no matter how many times they called it on and off, I would never let them see what it meant deep down inside. Gradually the more they pulled the midnight tactics, the more I realized they'd never get to me this way.

Now Christmas was approaching, and I became convinced that I'd never see my family again for this or any other Christmas. I could handle this thought all right by itself, but something else made it difficult to bear. The speaker which tied into the central broadcasting system was only about a hundred feet from my cell, as Christmas approached, the English broadcasts were increasingly concerned with holiday preparations.

Before I had been shot down I had learned from our intelligence reports that Pyoktong, the center of the prison camp area, was also the location of the largest of all prison compounds. We knew that at the edge of a Yalu River inlet the Communists had established a prison compound designed to accommodate from 750 to 1,000 prisoners. Almost all of the prisoners in this compound were Negroes. They lived in small neat huts with gardens nearby. There were basketball courts and baseball diamonds, along with boxing rings and other athletic facilities. The food was well above the average fare. The prisoners had even been given musical instruments. While listening to the broadcasts I had learned that these prisoners were sending and receiving letters from the states, many of which were read over the local speaker system. Many times as I sat on the floor of my

230

cell I heard groups of them marching by, singing songs and yelling to each other, on their way to the movies or perhaps to a baseball game.

It was obvious why the Communists treated this particular group with special care. The speaker system continually harped on the fact that even though the prisoners had been fighting against the Communists they had been forgiven because they had been forced to fight by their imperialist American leaders. It was continually stressed that under Communism there could be no color discrimination. All men were treated as equals. The propaganda further suggested that all prisoners should remember their good treatment when they returned to the United States, because there they would be discriminated against, forced off the sidewalks, barred from eating places, prohibited from riding in certain sections of busses, and otherwise abused.

Right before Christmas the speaker system began to play Christmas carols. I'll never forget Arthur Godfrey's "On the First Day of Christmas," because I almost learned all the words, just sitting there listening. Crosby's "White Christmas" was just as popular in North Korea as it was in the States. The prisoners themselves had formed a carol group, and they had scheduled broadcasts to sing all of the songs Americans love at Christmastime. It appeared, too, that the Chinese were making preparations for a celebration—perhaps their New Year's Day. All in all these preparations were pretty tough on a man condemned to die.

Thoughts of my wife and family were paramount in my mind. I believed that after a period of grace the government would list me as killed instead of missing in action. I tried to visualize what my little girl and boy were like now and what their mother told them about me. I thought my wife had probably given me up for lost. Perhaps she had remarried. I even dwelt on the fantasy that if—by some strange chance—I returned home, I would find my wife remarried and all that I held dear gone from me.

Once again I could feel my sanity slowly slipping away from me. I worried so much about my family and my life that I found myself frantic from the time I awoke in the morning until I fell

231

asleep at night. I finally decided I had to regain control of my thoughts or really go insane. As long as I concentrated on me and my problems and what was going to happen I was in trouble, so I decided to make definite efforts to put such thoughts out of mind. For about a week this was extremely difficult, but it slowly became a matter of course. If I happened to think of my family or my approaching execution, I consciously switched my mind to dreaming about having been inordinately rich or brilliant or successful. And it worked.

Since I had not had the opportunity to shave for many months, my face was covered with a long, heavy black beard. This worried me. I knew that I could not be recognized with a beard, and although in all probability I would be executed at night, there was a remote chance that I might be shot in daylight hours. The other Americans in the vicinity might see me being marched through town, and I decided to give myself a shave by pulling out my beard. The process was painful because it was gradual, but after a week or so I was relatively smoothly shaven. However, while "shaving" I became aware of something I hadn't noticed before.

As mentioned previously, the guards were watching me twenty-four hours a day through a window cut in the side of my cell. When I started pulling out my beard they became greatly interested and watched me intensely. I noticed that every time I made a move the guard whose face I could see in the window appeared to make a note of it in a thick booklet. I had to check out this discovery for several days before I was sure, but finally I became positive that they had been instructed to record my every single move.

I began to move all over the place. I scratched, stretched, pulled out whiskers, rolled over, groaned, sighed. I put on all the clothes I had, then took them all off seconds later. I tried every movement I could think of and repeated each as often as I could. And the guards wrote furiously. I almost expected them to ask me to repeat a certain action or two because they hadn't quite been able to catch it. At any rate, the book began to fill rapidly. After two days I was sure that they were far behind me, and I could hear them consulting among themselves. Finally they decided to tell their commander what was going on. A few moments later the squad leader returned, grinning, to announce that permission had been granted to discontinue recording my actions. Their sighs of relief were shared, because I was growing just as tired of acting as they were of writing. At least I had won one small battle with them, even though they hadn't known they were fighting.

And now that I had won that one I decided to try for another. My cell was alive with thousands of bugs, mainly those little gray ones that curl up like armadillos when touched. When the guards weren't watching I caught great numbers of them and concealed them in the pockets of my uniform. Twice a day, when allowed to walk back and forth in my cell for five minutes or so, I strolled past the window, and when the guard wasn't looking dumped handfuls of these bugs into the next room. For several days the guards merely complained to each other. Finally the bugs must have started to lift the bedrolls, because the guards took all of their gear into the quadrangle and shook it out. Then they came back with Communist DDT and dusted the room thoroughly. That evening they moved all their stuff back and settled down again. I had them loaded up two days later. We continued this for several weeks and they never caught on. I finally quit when I could no longer find quantities of bugs marching around in my room.

I won still another battle with them. During the holidays they were given a special ration. There were several boxes of apples, plums and nuts, which they devoured as rapidly as they could. There was, however, more than they could eat, and they kept the surplus in a box outside the door of their room. Each night on my last trip to the latrine I pretended to be terribly weak. Stepping from the door of my cell I would stumble and fall to the floor, at the same time reaching over and grabbing a handful of goodies from the box. On the way to the latrine I'd stuff all of it into my clothing so that I could reach for another handful on the return trip. As long as the goodies lasted I managed to get my share. The guards had several fights because they were sure someone in their midst was stealing while the others were not looking.

Like all other prisoners since time immemorial, I tried to keep track of time on a secretly drawn calendar on the wall of my cell. Each day I put a cross through another line. The routine of the soldiers varied on Sundays, and thus I could check myself at the beginning of each week. The broadcasts over the loudspeaker system told me of the hourly passage of time.

Still, I was really not a human being at all. Just an animal. I thought about everything, yet nothing. I couldn't dream about the future, because there wasn't going to be one. I could think about the past, but that didn't help much. I just sat in filth and squalor, waiting for God knows what. Though the weeks went by quickly, each individual day took forever. Through the opaque door of my cell I saw the sun travel so slowly across the sky that it appeared it would never set in the west. Bed and sleep were extremely important to me. Sleep became escapism instead of just a necessary body function. When asleep I didn't have to face the stern reality of being a prisoner condemned to die. And the days became weeks, and the weeks, months—all spent in dreaming, dreaming, dreaming.

I thought endlessly about escaping. Even in the dead of winter. It might have been possible if the breaks had been with me. For one thing, the guards began to bring a chair into my cell to sit on while they watched me each night. It must have been difficult for them to keep an eye on me through the window in the wall, so they sat about five feet away until it was time for me to go to bed. For these evening sessions the guard would leave his rifle in the other room, and hold a large pistol pointed at me.

Usually the guard's comrades would go to bed shortly after dark. As part of my punishment I had to wait until nine thirty before I got the signal to lie down. Often by eight o'clock or so the guard in my cell would be dozing, his pistol held loosely in his hand. One guard was especially prone to dozing. I watched this one closely for several evenings before I decided to make a real effort to escape.

The Chinese had returned the clothing the North Koreans had given me, as well as the two sets of prison-camp uniforms, so I could dress warmly enough for escape. Gradually at first, and then with increasing boldness, I began to put on more clothing each night until I finally worked up to wearing everything I owned. At first the guards were curious, but later they paid little attention to what I was doing. As soon as I could put on every bit of my clothing my plan was almost complete. I could wait until the guard began to doze, kick his gun out of his hand, pick it up and make a dash for the door.

It sounded so good that I almost tried to pull it off. The woods are probably full of guys who *almost* did it. But somehow, in the final analysis, it just didn't make sense. I'm sure I could have liberated that pistol. After that came the uncertainties. At the very least, I would probably have had to shoot the guard in my room. The shot would wake the rest of the guards, who would come pouring out of the room next door. I could probably make it through the outside door of the compound before they gathered their wits, but then what? Once outside the door, I wouldn't know which way to turn. If I could reach the edge of town, I could probably hide out, because I would be dressed warmly enough, but the sound of a shot plus the yelling of my guards would waken every other soldier in town. Naturally they'd start to hunt for me, and I wouldn't be able to keep from making tracks in the snow. Ultimately, after weighing the various alternatives, I gave up the idea. For a time, though, it had served the purpose of giving me something to think about.

One afternoon my guards surprised me by entering my cell en masse and staring at me with critical expressions. Then they began to sweep my floor, motioned that I was to straighten up my personal effects, and wonder upon wonders, brought a bowl of water with some soap and instructed me to wash my face and hands. After satisfying themselves that my room would pass inspection, they brought a high-backed wicker chair and tried it out in various positions. Then they all formed a line in the courtyard, and suddenly an officer appeared—one whom I had never seen before. As he entered the yard the guard squad snapped to attention while the squad leader followed the officer into my cell. After casually walking around my room several times, minutely inspecting everything in sight, the officer sat down in the wicker chair and stared at me. We exchanged glances for several minutes before he broke the silence by asking, "How is your mind?" I immediately replied, "My mind is all right." He glared at me for several moments more, then rose and left abruptly. When he had gone from the courtyard the guards came back to my cell, removed the chair, and all was quiet once again. It was quiet not only for the rest of the day but for day after day after day. When I had finally calmed down sufficiently to realize that nothing new was afoot, I gradually slipped back to my dreaming.

One day when almost a month and a half had passed I heard a commotion in the courtyard outside my cell. The same officer entered again. With an almost identical performance, he looked both me and my cell over, and finally said, "Now, is there anything wrong with your mind?" As before, I said that nothing was wrong. After staring at me for several minutes he departed, but whereas his first visit had frightened me very much, this time I was merely puzzled. His simply didn't seem like normal Chinese behavior. I was sure that something was going to happen, and I was not wrong.

5.

ABOUT one week later the guards whom I had learned to hate so much packed up to leave, and by nightfall I was under the surveillance of a completely different squad. These new arrivals seemed to be fairly decent. If I asked for permission to go to the latrine or get some drinking water, they'd usually comply. Occasionally they'd come to the door of my cell and make feeble efforts to talk to me. Wonder upon wonders, they even brought me a bar of soap! It was only a small hunk of crude brown soap, but it was the first I'd been given in over seven months.

This unusually good treatment lasted for several weeks until, on April 16, 1953, an incident occurred which allowed me to see where it was all leading. There was the usual commotion in the yard, and the guards—obviously spruced up for an important event—looked in to see if I was presentable. Then a neatly dressed Chinese officer, taller and lighter in complexion than most of his fellow countrymen, came bouncing into my cell. He exuded personality and spoke English with an American accent.

"Hey there, boy, how are things going?" he asked. "You look as if you haven't been getting along too well." Although he seemed friendly enough, he scared me to death. This was obviously the beginning of a different technique to get me to cooperate. I didn't trust anyone—especially anyone who went out of his way to be nice. This guy was an enemy, and I couldn't forget it. After chitchatting for a few minutes and walking around my cell to see how it looked he said, "Boy, this is awful. We've got to get you fixed up a bit." He said he could get almost anything I wanted, and yelled to the guards to bring some tea.

237

Sure enough, in about five minutes they came running with a teapot and a couple of cups. He broke out a package of cigarettes, offered me one, then lit up to smoke while we both sipped tea. It was all as casual as could be.

But it was a monologue. I didn't want to talk to him until I found out what this was all about. In fact, I was trembling so much that he asked me several times if I was ill. After about forty-five minutes he stood up to leave and asked if there was anything he could do for me. At that moment all I could think of was that I needed a bath. Even though I had some soap, I hadn't had enough water to bathe in for over seven months.

"Sure, sure," he said. "That's easy, but what else do you want?" When I told him that I didn't need anything else he replied, "I'll get you some tobacco, and some more soap. But let me know if you need other things, because I will be coming to see you from time to time." With that he left.

This initial meeting with Happy Hal started the most confusing period I spent in the hands of the enemy. The following day the guards motioned that I was to put on my clothes and accompany them. This time there were no guns in evidence, and it being broad daylight, I was almost certain that this was not another fake execution ceremony. Just before I walked out of the cell a guard handed me a brand-new towel. We went about two blocks from my cell into a low building which contained a large square tub filled with hot water. Apparently it was the local communal bathing facility. Believe me, that bath was terrific! I don't think I've ever enjoyed water so much. Not only was I filthy, but the clothes I had been wearing for the past seven months were so strong that they could have stood on their own merit. I got a good soaping and then just sat in the tub, soaking up the warmth. After awhile I got out to dress, and as I was putting on my old prison uniform I happened to glance into a cracked mirror on the wall of the bathhouse. What a shock! I had no hair to speak of, and what little I had was almost white. My eyes bulged, and my cheeks were so gaunt that I guessed that my weight had dropped below a hundred pounds. I'm sure that had I walked down the street of my home town my own mother wouldn't have recognized me. Still, there was little I could do to improve my appearance, and after my first chagrin wore off I quit worrying about it.

The following day Happy Hal came back to see me, and this time it was just like a grade-B movie. He was so obviously trying to be a nice guy. He wanted me to take him into my confidence and treat him just like a pal. I knew what he wanted, and I think that he knew it, but we still had to play his little game. And this time when he asked what I wanted I told him that I would like to be able to wash my clothes. He immediately called the guards and gave them instructions to allow me to do laundry once a day. These new liberties overwhelmed me. The next week Happy Hal appeared with some books. He had several volumes of Charles Dickens and a couple of Sir Walter Scott. I presumed immediately that these authors were approved in Communist eyes.

Happy Hal began to pay more regular visits. In fact I think he rather liked to come to my cell just to shoot the bull with me. So far he hadn't tried to put anything over on me. He just seemed to come in to relax for a few minutes, and once in awhile he dropped a few hints as to what was happening in the outside world. He was the son of a once prominent lawyer in Peiping. During the Sino-Japanese War his family had been forced to flee south. They had eventually made their way to Kunming with the Chinese Nationalists. After the war they had returned to Peiping. Hal had been educated at a university just outside Peiping, and prior to the Korean War was a professor of Ancient Chinese history. When the Communists over-ran the city on their way south to defeat the Nationalists, Hal and his family had stayed. Now his father had a menial job and the rest of his family worked at common tasks. It was quite obvious that Hal had chosen to jump on the Communist band-wagon as it rolled by, and now he was in Korea to make a name for himself. I am sure that he was a Communist Party member because he never ceased spouting the Communist line. He did not trust those around him and he was especially fearful that I'd tell some other officer what he had told me. In fact every time he gave me a bit of information he made me promise not to tell anyone what I had heard.

For several days I had been hearing noises in the village around me, noises I couldn't understand. There were sounds of laughter—often American laughter—and the loud-speaker system carried music of a different mood than usual. On several occasions I had heard the sounds of Americans marching through a street not too far from my cell. I decided to ask Hal what it all meant. After peering outside the compound for several minutes Hal came back to whisper that he had news, but he didn't want the others to know that he had told me. The peace negotiators had reached an agreement that the sick and wounded of both sides were to be exchanged in what was dubbed "Operation Little Switch." Hal further confided that this appeared to be the turning point of the war and that the end was in sight.

This news really gave me pause for thought. In the first place I really didn't have to believe Hal, but the sounds in the village supported what he had said. If it was true, then it was possible that other prisoners would soon be exchanged. Especially if the war came to an end. What did this mean to me? In the first place what would a continuing flow of confessions do to change the course of the war? Very little. The harm must have already been done months and months ago. And what about me? I wasn't sure. Suppose the war did end. I was certain that my name wasn't on the POW lists, so the Communists could keep me in North Korea as long as they wanted to.

As I knew he would sooner or later, Happy Hal finally got around to topic A. He began by saying that he wasn't interested in what had happened to me, because he considered it to be none of his business. He felt that perhaps I had been mistreated, judging from the condition I was in, but nevertheless he was not supposed to pry into the past. It was now his job to look after me and several other American airmen as well. He knew that I had been pressured concerning germ warfare, and he admitted that many other people had been pressured on the same subject. He intimated quite strongly that he did not necessarily believe

240

that the allegation was true, but he knew that many of the Nationalist leaders in China did. As a result he said, "You, Mahurin, have a choice to make. Either you confess to waging germ warfare against us, or you never go home. It is as simple as that."

As he talked I found out that the initial germ-warfare charge had been made on March 10, 1952, long before I was captured. Four United States airmen, who had been shot down behind enemy lines in their B-26 bombers, had been forced to make false confessions. A group of scientists chosen from the Communist-block nations had then performed what was touted to be a full-scale scientific investigation which supported the confessions of the four airmen. As soon as a plausible story was generated the charge was brought to the floor of the UN Security Council. We in the combat zone were unaware of the charge, but many, many people throughout the world seriously believed the confessions obtained under duress from prisoners of war in enemy hands.

Once the charge was launched, the Communists bent every effort to obtain false confessions from all who were captured after a certain date. Those who had been captured earlier were no bothered. Naturally, a wealth of confessions from junior-grade pilots was impressive, but what was really needed was a full-scale confession from a senior officer who could shoulder the responsibility for the whole effort and give authenticity to the allegation in the eyes of the world. Hal stated that such a person had been found some time ago, and his confession had been disseminated throughout the world. Now his charges had been substantiated, and thus confessions in quantity were no longer necessary. Still, I had to confess, because millions of people in the Communist world had already been told that I was the father of germ warfare. It would never do to allow me to go home maintaining that these missions had never been carried out. "I can assure you, Mahurin," Hal stated time and again, "your name has not been placed on the list of prisoners of war, and no one on your side knows that you are alive. However, if you do confess," he went on, "your name will be placed on the POW list immediately, and you will be allowed to go home as soon as the war is over."

These statements, which I sensed to be true, bothered me more than a little. It was obvious that Hal was serious. He had instructions from his leaders—instructions which he intended to carry out. He knew that he and his people were generating lies, but he said over and over that there was only one truth in the world and that was Communism. Anything that furthered the Communist cause was good and nothing else mattered. Instead of applying pressure, Hal was seeking to apply logic. Logic was more dangerous than pressure. And having made his initial overture, Hal kept coming back to visit with me. Usually he brought new books with him. At first they were of general interest, such as the complete works of Shakespeare, but later they began to reflect Communist ideology. I read Karl Marx, William Z. Foster and others. Sometimes I was exposed to speeches by Premier Malenkov and other internationally known Communist figures. Quite often the written material depicted the coming decline of democracy and the rise of Communism throughout the world.

Many of the volumes boasted of the industrial growth of the Communist sphere, and Hal continually sought to get me into a discussion of the relative strength of the free world versus that of the Communists. On occasion I could beat him at his own figures. One time especially, when he was trying to tell me how strong Russia was compared to the United States, I managed to dig out a speech Malenkov had made to the top governing body of Russia in which he had estimated the annual Soviet steel production at 38,000,000 tons per year. I then dug up in a book by William Z. Foster—then the leader of the Communist Party in the United States—the fact that in 1953 the annual steel production in the United States was over 94,000,000 tons. When I confronted Hal with this and asked him what he meant when he said that Russia was stronger than the United States, he replied that his high command would not let him

242

discuss this subject. From then on he avoided comparisons of strength.

Hal brought me a couple of Communist newspapers and booklets that were real eye openers. Although I had known for some time that I was in the hands of professional propagandists, I didn't have any idea how extensive their organization was. Now for the first time I realized what I was up against.

Every Communist society had a minister of propaganda. Not advertising, not news, not education, but propaganda. About one in every five people in the population worked for him in some capacity. Further, in Russia alone I learned that there were over 1,400 colleges teaching nothing but propaganda and its uses. One of the largest universities in all Russia was the Moscow University of Propaganda. Propaganda was big business.

Reading between the lines of the material Hal brought me, I could see that the minister of propaganda was responsible for developing plans for the Communists to take over the world— not by arms, but by controlling men's minds. The Reds had an attack—that Communism was good and democracy bad—troops to carry out that attack, and whole campaigns mapped out in the battle for men's minds. Only they referred to it as the cold war.

All this seemed pretty dangerous to me, the more I thought about it. I couldn't see us with any sort of an organization to parallel the propaganda ministry. Not that we'd want to operate in the same way as the Reds, but it would have been comforting to realize that someone on our side was equipped to counter that propaganda, or at least plan ahead in this cold war. And the more I thought about it the more I hoped that our side was on top of that germ-warfare situation. Plenty of time had passed to give our experts—if we had them—the opportunity.

Often Happy Hal and I went walking, and although he made every effort to keep me from coming into contact with other Americans, he missed on two occasions. The first time we were on the outskirts of Pyoktong when we encountered an American coming toward us. I was very surprised to find that he was not under guard. When we met I naturally said, "Hi, how are things going?" "Fine," he replied, "I'm thinking of going for a swim." This I couldn't believe. I had no idea who he was but surely he must have been contributing to the Communist cause in some way to be given such liberties. Later I found out that he was an International News Service correspondent who had been taken prisoner. He was given preferential treatment, partly because he was a noncombatant, but more because he was a useful propaganda device. If the Communists treated him well, they calculated, he would not be critical when he wrote about the entire prisoner-of-war situation upon his return to the United States. Thus they would achieve a propaganda victory. And this is exactly what happened after the war was over.

Once we walked near the major prisoner-of-war compound. We were far enough away so that no one would recognize us, but near enough so that I could see what the compound looked like. It was situated in a depression of land that became a beach on a tributary of the Yalu River. There were many huts within the compound and apparently several POW's living in each hut. I could see a prize-fighting ring, and I noticed several basketball courts in between the huts.

Many of the prisoners, dressed in uniforms similar to mine, were standing around in groups chatting. More were playing basketball, and still more pitched baseballs back and forth. Few Chinese guards were in evidence, and the only restraint seemed to be the several strands of barbed wire around the compound. Most of the prisoners I could see were Negroes, but there were a few whites here and there. Compared with my circumstances, their lot didn't look too bad at all. Hal didn't let me linger long, but at least I'd had a chance to see how the other half lived.

The second American we encountered on our little walks was a POW dressed in the same type of garb as I, and this man, too, was being escorted by an interrogator. As we passed I again said, "Hello," receiving a polite Hello in return, but nothing else. Hal would not then reveal his identity, but later he told me. I found that the man was Colonel Frank Schwable of the Marine Corps, who had been captured about six months after I was shot down. Other than these two contacts, I saw Americans only from a distance.

I sensed, without being sure, that major events were taking place in the war. My treatment was getting better and from Hal's actions I guessed that he was now working against some sort of deadline to extract a confession from me. Although he continued to play it cool each day he visited me I could tell that he was trying harder to get me to sit down and write for him. The climax came one day when he told me that a very important officer from China was awaiting to see me. Hal introduced us and then left us alone. This new guy unnerved the hell out of me. I didn't know who he was but I sure understood what he wanted. Once more I heard the familiar story about confessing or not going home. Once again I was told that I could be kept in North Korea forever if the Communists so decided. Summing up he stated that he was the highest-ranking officer I would ever talk to and that my fate would rest on his decision. Once again I said "Nothing doing."

In my talks with Happy Hal I had mentioned time and again how concerned I was about my family. I was especially bitter about not having been allowed to communicate with my wife. Many times I expressed the belief that perhaps she had given me up for dead and even remarried. Each time the topic came up Hal told me that I had no cause for alarm—a statement I felt he was totally unqualified to make. Finally one day he said, "I have been telling you all along that your wife and children are all right. I will now give you full information. We have captured a pilot who had been living in the United States at George Air Force Base. He knew your wife and children and saw them recently. He told me that they are all growing up well and happy. They occasionally go to the Apple Valley Inn for dinner and swimming, so your little daughter is learning to swim and is getting along very well. Your whole family expects you home when the war is over." Hal then cautioned me not to tell any

245

other interrogator that I had received this information, because he would then be in real trouble.*

Once in awhile Hal would ask if I knew certain people. He wanted to know about Colonel Levi Chase. The Communists were hopping mad at Levi because he had led the bombardment of the power stations at the Sui-Ho Reservoir. He questioned me about Harry Thyng, whom he knew to be my wing commander. I believe that Hal asked these questions out of curiosity, rather than for military information. I think he was just interested in Americans and the United States. One day he asked me if I knew an Air Force colonel named Andy Evans. When I told him that I didn't, Hal said that Andy had been captured a few months previously, and when announcement was made in the American press it was revealed that Andy had worked for the Chief of Staff of the Air Force in the Pentagon about the same time that I was working for the Secretary. Hal couldn't understand why we didn't know each other, and I didn't try to impress upon him that the Pentagon is a rather large place. Another man Hal was curious about was the Colonel Schwable I had seen. He had been Chief of Staff of the 1st Marine Wing in Korea before being shot down behind enemy lines. Once he said that the Communists had just captured a Colonel J. K. Arnold, that Arnold had been flying a B-29 and that his serial number was 1212A. According to Hal, all of these people had confessed to waging germ warfare; and I should do the same. He assured me that all of them had been declared prisoners of war, all had been allowed to write home, and all would be repatriated as soon as the war was over.

Hal finally adopted the practice of holding our little bull sessions in a room across the courtyard from the one in which I was confined. This room, like most of the others I had seen, was

---

* I found out later how Hal had been able to learn so much about my family. My wife, in the blind hope that I was still alive, had been writing to the Chinese prison camp authorities in Peiping and enclosing letters to me. The letters found their way into North Korea and eventually into the hands of my interrogator. He had been reading them all along, probably throwing them away when he finished, then imparting a trickle of information to me.

246

papered with newspapers. When I could sneak in a few glances I noticed that many of the papers were written in English and were, in fact, copies of the London *Daily Worker*. I didn't want Hal to know that I was glancing at them, but I was certain from their rather new look that they contained up-to-date information. Then one day Hal stepped outside to talk to the guards for a moment, and I had a chance to browse. One of these papers confirmed what I already knew—that the germ-warfare allegations had been made in the United Nations on March 10, 1952. This article named the American pilots concerned and gave a few of the details surrounding the charges. Another article concerned the downing of an American F-86 pilot whose name was Lieutenant Colonel Ed Heller. I had known Heller for some time and was shocked to find that he had been shot down. Ed, judging from the article, had been injured quite severely and was recovering in a hospital in Mukden in Manchuria. The article stated that he had been declared a prisoner of war and that his wife had been notified of his state of health and general condition. This really surprised me. Why had Heller been listed as a POW in just a few days, while they had refused to list me?

As soon as Hal returned to the room I asked him why I was being treated this way. He replied immediately, but with considerable embarrassment, "I'm sorry but the high command will not let me discuss the situation with you. You must make a confession if you wish to be placed on the list of prisoners of war and return home." *

Whenever I had free moments from Hal I had plenty of time to think about my predicament. I was no longer being interrogated, nor was I being forced to make a confession. I was still confined, even though I was being treated better than I had been in the past. It appeared that the chances of the war ending and prisoners being returned were better than they had ever

---

* I found out later that poor Ed had been shot down in Manchuria instead of North Korea. In order to exploit this circumstance the Communists held him for almost one year after the war was over. Ed made a dramatic return to the United States, wrote an article or two about his experiences, and is now on active duty with the Air Force.

been. Instead of being killed, it appeared that I was to be allowed to live, but I didn't have any assurance that I'd be allowed to go home. After all, my captors had stressed time and again that, since I had been a successful fighter pilot during two wars, why should they let me go home to fight them in a third.

I was damn sick and tired of being a prisoner of war in solitary confinement. I wanted to talk to someone—anyone—as long as I didn't have to worry about what I said. I wanted to know how my wife and children were. I wanted to fulfill some of those dreams I had spent so much time thinking about when I had been condemned to death. I had missed out on well over a year of my life; I wanted to catch up. I didn't have any confidence whatsoever that I'd be allowed to go home just like everybody else if the war ended. No, I was a special case. Unless I confessed.

I knew that it had been well over a year since the germ-warfare allegation had been made in the United Nations. During that year I had not cooperated with the Communists in any way. Surely by this time there must have been ample opportunity for the United States to develop counterpropaganda exposing the hoax. By this time the entire world must have realized that the Communists were using prisoners of war as propaganda tools, that their confessions had been obtained under duress. The more I thought about it, the more certain I became that the false confessions must have completely lost public impact. Were they still such a big deal? Hardly, after all these months.

If I did make a confession, I could make it as ridiculous as possible. If I wasn't allowed to go home at the end of the war, my silly confession would speak for itself in exposing the hoax. And if I was repatriated, I would be in a good position to exert counterpropaganda against the Communists. I had resisted cooperating for over twelve months, and perhaps I had protected my nation in some small degree. I had suffered some rather rough going in return, and now I was damn lonely for other Americans. Besides, it was high time that I began to think of my wife and family again. Was it fair to them not to exhaust every possible means of returning? Above all I wanted Pat to know what had happened to me and where I had been. After all, I had volunteered to go to Korea in the first place much against her wishes. I had been gone for almost a year and a half, and perhaps she was having a tough time making a go of her life. Maybe I had paid a small debt to society by holding off for a year, but maybe it was now time to pay my debt to my wife and children.

For days I searched my mind frantically to see if there was any other way out of my predicament. Finally, all alone in my cell, without adequate advice, tortured by a longing for my family, condemned by the thought that I would be doing something contrary to my very soul, yet convinced that this was the only way out of North Korea, I decided to make a false confession. It was the most difficult decision I have ever been or will ever be required to make. I noted on my makeshift calendar on the wall of my cell that the date was approximately June 1, 1953.

6.

AS SOON as I informed Hal of my decision he brought pencil and paper so that I could begin to write. He said that he was working with a number of other prisoners and would be coming to see me less frequently than in the past. This was fine with me. I didn't want to write his damn confession anyway, and it wouldn't have bothered me if he had never showed up again.

Now I realized why the Communists had wasted so much time working with me on reflex conditioning. All of the questions, the tape recordings I had heard, all the subtle innuendos, came back to me as I started to write. I began by putting down

249

the mythical interviews I had participated in regarding germ warfare and the phony instructions I had received in Washington before coming to Korea. I wrote of going through Far Eastern Air Force Headquarters on my way to combat to receive further instructions. My confession had to contain references to decontamination units, to white-uniformed attendants, to external fuel tanks. I wrote of carrying fleas, flies and mosquitoes in the external fuel tanks of our F-86s while flying at 40,000 feet, and of how we dropped these tanks all over North Korea. I wrote of how these tanks exploded on impact with the ground and how the insects were released. The more I got into the confession the more ridiculous it became. Imagine how long insects would live with the temperature at fifty below zero and the ground covered with snow. Yet there I was, leading my men into action, dropping insects all over Korea in December, January and February. We were successful, I said, and people up North were being bitten by the insects. I wrote how the tanks were filled up with flies in Okinawa, because that island possessed a temperate climate, and how the tanks were then shipped by air to Korea. I used the names of people who were nonexistent, or who had been dead for hundreds of years, or who were in places far removed from Korea. Everything I wrote was completely implausible, and I knew that anyone who saw my statements in print would find them laughable. For a week Hal let me alone. Then he took the copy I had written and departed with the admonition that he would return in a couple of days.

My mind reacted in a rather curious way as I wrote the confession. Having searched my soul so thoroughly, then having suffered all the pangs of remorse after my decision, I now found that the actual fiction wasn't too difficult to write. The more I wrote, the more ridiculous the story became and the more I knew it would appear as fantasy, even to a reader of minimal intelligence. In fact I actually convinced myself that I was helping our cause. I had already started to think out what an advantage it would be after the war for my nation to display my confession with its fantastic story, then to display me to refute it, thus demonstrating to the world the lies and deceit of Communist propaganda. The more I thought about this aspect the more junk I put into the confession, as a useful investment for the future. I had big visions of being one of the principal spokesmen against the Communist treatment of prisoners, if and when I got back home.

It was during this period that I saw my first aerial combat from the ground in North Korea. Late one afternoon I heard the sounds of aircraft overhead and asked my guards for permission to go to the latrine. On the way I looked to the north toward Manchuria to see if I could spot any activity. Sure enough, there were about forty condensation trails parallel to the Yalu River, heading to the Sui-Ho Reservoir for the standard turn south into North Korea. At the same time I could see two tiny little trails flying up the river on the North Korean side. It was obvious that the big gaggle of aircraft were Migs, and the other two were F-86s. As the Migs made a right turn on a southerly heading, the F-86s dropped in behind their formation. Suddenly the Mig fighter leader must have spotted the two F-86s, because the whole Mig formation exploded. It was fantastic to watch. What had once been a beautiful formation of high speed, high-flying aircraft, now became a beehive of Migs, all trying desperately to make a 180-degree turn and scurry back across the Yalu into Manchuria, with the two F-86s chasing and shooting all the way. I was certainly proud of the United States Air Force as I trudged back to my cell.

The afternoon after the dogfight my guards instructed me to gather up my belongings. It was time to move again. At night I was escorted to a waiting Russian jeep, and after about a two-hour drive I was led into a small hut and imprisoned again. When I looked out of the door the following morning I discovered that I was in a small valley near a tiny village, and in a good position to see a rather large river some distance away. There were a few huts near mine, but I couldn't tell whether I was in a prison-camp area or just a small community. I was, needless to say, disturbed by the move until Hal showed up. He told me that the move was temporary and that I was in what was called the Gold Mine prison camp. It seemed that the Japanese had established a gold mine on the banks of the river that I saw in the distance. At the end of World War II the Russians had removed all the heavy mining machinery and transported it into Russian proper. Now all that was left was the skeleton.

Hal still wanted me to work on my confession. He had taken what I had written to the high command and it had been unfavorably received. Now I must make some changes. He began spending more and more time with me while I tried to work up some sort of a paper that would please everyone. I had moved in the third week of June, yet since I could still hear the sound of the aerial combat, I knew that the war was still going on. It couldn't be that Hal was personally anxious for my confession. He must have been pressed by his commanders to complete my work as rapidly as possible.

We bargained back and forth a good deal. Hal wanted me to elaborate on a mythical conference I was supposed to have had with the Secretary of the Air Force before coming to Korea. I had supposedly suggested to the Secretary that fighter aircraft be used for the purpose of germ warfare. Okay on this one. Especially since we had to fly so high that carrying anything in our fuel tanks besides fuel would be idiotic. Then I had to write about a conference with a general officer in which I was given instructions to start the bacteriological-warfare program in Korea, and so I related a mythical talk with General Wyland, the Commander of Far Eastern Air Force, and General Everest. To all this I agreed.

I wrote about briefing pilots of the 51st Wing. I wrote of the fuel tanks which I said were compartmented so as to be able to carry fleas in one compartment, flies in another, and mosquitoes in a third. I described two missions I supposedly had flown myself in which the tanks were released at high altitude to fall to the earth in North Korea. Hal tried his best to help me devise a story that would be acceptable to his superiors. In fact, he even started bringing me parts of my confession that he himself had written. Each time he brought one of his bits

252

of jeweled prose he would say, "Now here, Mahurin, is something that you just copy down and add to your confession. The high command will like this." On several different occasions I hid the sheets of paper containing his versions in his own handwriting. Most of the time, however, he asked that I return what he had written as soon as I had copied it.

About the 21st of June I witnessed an event which showed just how far the Communist propaganda agents would go to obtain a desired result. There were many hundreds of Chinese soldiers in the general area of the Gold Mine camp, and often I could see them drilling and playing games. One day about noon an aerial dogfight took place overhead. Although I could not see the action from my cell, I knew the Migs and F-86s were hard at it by the sound of the machine guns and cannon. Suddenly I heard a strange whistling noise, and when I leaned out the door I saw an F-86 external fuel tank hurtle to the ground about 300 feet from my hut. Within a moment or two, many of the Chinese soldiers were on the scene, and shortly a group of officers arrived to remove the tank. Since the food for all the soldiers was prepared in a central location, each guard squad sent a representative at mealtime to bring the food back to the hut in which the squad lived. But this night, shortly after the guards had finished eating, they all fell desperately ill. Many of them collapsed in the dusty paths surrounding the little community, and there they lay. No one offered to help the fallen, and I saw no evidence whatsoever of any medical aid. Those who fell stayed in one spot until they were well enough to get up, and some of them were there for as long as twenty-four hours. It was only a matter of minutes, however, before truckloads of guards from another camp rolled in to replace those who were ill. It was strange that even though I ate the same food as the guards, I didn't get sick. Nor were any of the villagers stricken. It seemed obvious to me that one of the propaganda agents had managed to contaminate the guards' food in order to implicate the fuel tank of the F-86. No effort was spared in the propaganda campaign.

The first of July, as I sat at the door of my cell I heard the sounds of drums and symbols and singing, and much to my surprise saw a large procession of North Korean natives and Chinese soldiers marching down the dirt road to the center of the village. At the head of the procession were standard-bearers carrying large pictures of Comrade Mao and Comrade Kim Il Sung. I had never seen the natives so cheerful nor had I seen them parading before, and when Hal came to see me the next day I asked him about it. "Oh that," he replied, "a prominent leader in North Korea has just had a birthday and the people are celebrating." They do funny things in a Communist society, but this seemed unusually odd. For several days now I had not heard the sound of aircraft flying overhead. Hal refused to comment, once more stating: "The high command will not let me discuss this with you."

I finally finished writing my confession about August 8, but Hal told me that I had to make a few more changes, and these took several more days. When it was finally finished Hal wanted me to back-date it to May 10, 1953, saying that the high command would not accept it otherwise. I absolutely refused. We argued violently on this point for several more days, and he finally gave in. I dated the confession August 10, 1953.

I was confident that I had provided any number of loopholes for our counterpropaganda agency, should the Communists ever publish it. I was also absolutely certain that the other guys who had written confessions had done the same thing. Once the transcripts were studied, it could be shown to the world that they had been obtained under duress. Also they could be shown to other airmen to warn them what to expect if they were ever shot down. The more I thought about it, the more it began to look like a pretty good propaganda gimmick for our side.

I made a big point of the date. For one thing, Hal's insistence that I date it well in advance of the time I actually started to write made me suspicious. When I flatly refused to use his date he wanted me to leave the last page undated. I agreed. Hal then claimed that the high command wanted two last pages, one with a date and one without. At the time I didn't realize the importance of the dates.

254

I was left alone until August 26. During that time my guards occasionally allowed me to go to the river for a swim. Once in awhile on these excursions I could see other Americans from a distance, but the Chinese made a special point of keeping me isolated. One time I saw an extremely thin prisoner taking a bath in a small branch of the river, a man so bony as to be frightening. The river was delightful for swimming, even though it was extremely cold. Many times one or two of the guards went in with me while I bathed, but there were always others on the shore to stop any feeble attempt I might possibly make to escape. In any event, this new liberty was most welcome.

On the 26th, Hal came to tell me that the high command still considered my confession unsatisfactory. I was again forced to make revisions, but this time only minor ones. Hal practically wrote the whole thing in his anxiety to get it finished. I tried to beat him down on every point, and again we argued about the date of signature. I absolutely refused to put down anything but the 10th of August, and he finally told me to leave the date blank. After dinner that evening Hal took me to a large building where I was required to read the entire confession for a tape recording. I mumbled as much as I could, stuttered wherever possible, and mispronounced as many words as I dared while completing the recording. About three o'clock in the morning I was escorted back to my cell.

Three hours later I was awakened by the guards, who instructed me to pack my belongings and prepare for a move. Everything I owned was taken outside and minutely inspected. I even had to take off all my clothes. The pages of notes that Hal had written for my confession were discovered, and like the big fish that got away, I lost the only tangible evidence that such things had ever transpired. When Hal came along later the guards turned the notes over to him. "Oh, ho, Mahurin, you have been trying to put something over on me," he admonished. "It wouldn't do for you to get away with that."

About eight thirty on the morning of September 3, a white man in a prisoner-of-war uniform came walking up the path toward my cell. When he came within earshot he said, "Hello, my name is Frank Schwable. I am glad to be able to talk to you." It was the first time that I had been allowed to speak freely to an American in over sixteen months.

The war had been over since June 27.

Part 4: Homecoming

1.

EVEN though Frank Schwable was an American in prisoner-of-war garb, I was slow to trust him, being suspicious of everything and everybody, and judging from his restraint, he felt the same way about me. I did find out that he had also been in solitary confinement since the time of his capture. We talked—guardedly but politely—for about half an hour, and then Colonel Andy Evans, the emaciated man I had seen taking a bath a few days previously, walked up the path toward us. Both Frank and I were glad to see Andy, though neither of us had known him before. All three of us, Hal explained, were to start for the city of Panmunjom in the neutral zone of Korea, and from there we would be sent to our own side of the battle line. We would depart shortly, but in the meantime we were to have breakfast with our captors.

The Communists really put out a spread for this breakfast—for propaganda purposes. The table was laden with food, and around it were seated many of the interrogators who had worked closely with us. As we ate, Communist press protographers took pictures which, we were sure, would be distributed throughout China as evidence of the good treatment afforded high-ranking prisoners of war.

Just after breakfast we were escorted into a building and thence to a tribunal room. Many North Korean officers of various ranks were present, and what appeared to be a three-man tribunal sat behind a desk. As soon as we were brought in the senior member of the tribunal gave a long-winded harangue through an interpreter about the seriousness of waging biological warfare and how the leniency of the North Korean People's Republic had decided that we were to be returned to our homeland even though we had committed crimes against the people. After the familiar concluding insults we were dismissed. But that meeting forcibly brought two things to my mind: (1) the North Koreans had had very little to say about the treatment of captured fliers and were merely being given a chance to save face by "convicting" us as we left; and (2) they obviously believed that they had been victimized by germ warfare.

Shortly after, we were escorted to a Russian-built dump truck which was to take us south. The three of us rode together, escorted by Happy Hal, and followed by approximately six more trucks filled with other prisoners. Once we started we found we could talk together without interference from Happy Hal. It turned out that Frank Schwable had been shot down several months after I had been captured. At the time Frank had been fourty-four years old and had not been in good heath. The Communists had worked on him—during roughly the same time they were working with me—in an effort to get one high-ranking officer to confess to germ warfare, and they had brainwashed and maltreated Frank so badly that he was now in extremely poor condition. An older man, he hadn't been able to take the physical strain and had finally capitulated. Since he had broken before I did, the pressure on me was now relieved somewhat. Frank, however, was deeply concerned for his own future.

Andy, on the other hand, had been downed some six months

before the war ended. Because of the short time element, the Communists had worked on him hardest of all. A United States Military Academy graduate, he had been harder to break than Frank and I; yet the Communists wanted to get his confession and they did. All three of us were examples of what could be accomplished if the enemy wished to exploit prisoners for propaganda purposes. Andy had refused to eat during the days he was being pressured, and as a result he was in very poor shape, physically and mentally. Altogether we were a sorry sight. Of the three, I was perhaps in the best health.

As we headed south we discussed what to do when we were turned over to friendly hands. Hal tried to hear what we had to say whenever he could, but the noise of the truck made eavesdropping difficult. We knew that we would be exposed to intense questioning by our press representatives when we reached Freedom Village, but we were quite sure that our government would help. Surely there would be instructions for us, telling us what to do and say. My strongest single emotion during the ride was my constant fear that we were not actually going back home. Frank, because he had been allowed to write to the United States while a prisoner, was an acknowledged POW, but neither Andy nor I had been declared. It was entirely possible for our captors to change their minds at any time.

In our guarded conversations we worried about the reaction which would await us back in the States. I could not believe that we'd face any serious problems—that is, other than coming up with the best way to meet the press and to exploit our experiences to the advantage of the free world. Nonetheless, all three of us were emotionally disturbed about going home; it was rather like getting a last minute reprieve. I hadn't talked to anyone for so long that, once the barriers of caution were down, I couldn't stop asking questions, sharing experiences, and discussing the future with Andy and Frank. It was impossible to sleep or even rest in that damn truck, and the excitement of the situation gave me a terrific headache. When I actually found time to think about going home and what I'd do once I arrived,

I became all the more anxious to play my cards right these last remaining moments in capture.

One thought was paramount in my mind. I wanted revenge. I had often fantasized about being able to jump into the cockpit of an F-86 and fly back to those various interrogators' headquarters with plenty of bombs and ammunition, but now—a little more realistically—I contemplated a more peaceful kind of revenge. The more I thought about it the more I felt my turn would come at last when I told the outside world my story. I didn't know how many Americans had confessed to what, and neither did Andy or Frank, but we knew that we weren't alone, and we were sure that every last confession had been forced. Personally I was looking forward to a chance to get even.

Altogether the trip to Panmunjom took three days and two nights, and it was no doubt the worst traveling experience of my life. Bouncing around in the back of a truck is bad enough, but these roads were murder. During the day the driver could at best make about thirty miles an hour, with much lower speeds at night. There were no stops for rest, and it was impossible to sleep.

But there were plenty of things to see. We passed through both Anju and Sinanju on the way, and I realized why I had been hit so many times by antiaircraft fire. Never have I seen so many antiaircraft gun emplacements concentrated in one place. Then for one entire day we passed hundreds of thousands of soldiers squatting in the roadway, hammering big rocks into small stones. The hills alongside the road swarmed with others carrying baskets of dirt. This backbreaking effort was road construction in its crudest form, for the Chinese were attempting to reconstruct the highway system in North Korea. The three of us were both amazed and appalled. On occasion we passed over finished stretches of roadway only to find that they were just slightly superior to the unreconstructed road. When I think now of the communal mode of life behind the bamboo curtain, I can visualize those miles of roadway swarming with human ants, reluctantly doing the bidding of a few leaders who bask comfortably in some quiet place far removed from hardship.

262

Farther south we passed through the North Korean capital of Pyongyang. The convoy stopped on the outskirts for several hours, obviously waiting for nightfall so that we prisoners wouldn't be able to see the city as we passed through. The night was so bright, however, that we were still able to get a good view. Pyongyang was a shambles. Not one single building of consequence was standing. Most of the inhabitants lived in hovels constructed of rubble; they were perhaps the worst-clothed, worst-fed civilians imaginable. None of the faces bore any enthusiasm, interest or evidence of happiness. Once again I was reminded of a swarm of ants trudging in a line.

We reached Panmunjom on the evening of the third day. The town was crowded with representatives of nations monitoring the peace negotiations, and all of us were surprised at the intense activity. Naturally we wanted to leave the truck at the first opportunity, but Hal explained that we would remain under guard until we were transported to the American side. For the benefit of the prisoner-of-war exchange, the Communists had constructed a huge tent city on the outskirts of town. When we arrived to be escorted to our tents we could see hundreds of other prisoners waiting to be exchanged. Our tent held about eight guys, and for the first time we were exposed to others who had come down from the Gold Mine camp with us. The other five men were captains and lieutenants—among them three whose voices I had heard on tape recordings while in camp. For the first time we could talk freely, because there were no interrogators in the vicinity. It turned out that all those who had confessed to waging germ warfare were to be released at the same time. Further, it seemed that we would be exchanged on the very last possible day. As we talked to some of the other men I was surprised to hear several say that they had been told by the interrogators only the day before we started south that: "We have Colonel Mahurin in captivity, and we have not yet made a decision whether to turn him loose or not."

At about nine o'clock that evening, while we were waiting to go to sleep, the Communists pulled another of their typical propaganda tricks. All of us were carrying the same old piles

263

of junk we had been given when first captured, but now we had to turn in everything we owned. Our captors issued each man new towels, new clothing, a new toothbrush, candy, cigarettes and other items most of us hadn't seen for months. After the clothing issue, a guard sorted me out of the crowd and to my dismay motioned that I was to follow him. I felt a terrible, irrational premonition that they had decided not to let me go after all. Following a short walk, however, I found myself in the presence of a white man. As I entered his tent—which I must say was posh for a tent—he introduced himself: "I am Wilfred Burchette, and I'm glad to know you. I am especially glad to see that you are going back to the United States."

I was surprised. I hadn't expected to find a white man here and I felt that Burchette, along with all the rest of the people in the Communist sphere, was going to try to get something from me. But he didn't. I think, in retrospect, that he must have been lonely for someone to talk to. An Australian, he had been a war correspondent on General MacArthur's staff during World War II. He mentioned the names of several American friends with whom he had corresponded from time to time, and he wanted to be sure that I said hello if I ran into them upon my return. Then he wanted to know about my treatment at the hands of the Communists. Not wanting to jeopardize my situation, I merely told him that I was still alive and that this was enough for me. Then I asked if he knew Alan Winnington. He replied that he and Alan were good friends, and wanted to know when we had met. I dodged the question by asking if Winnington was on the scene at Panmunjom.

"Oh, yes," replied Burchette, "he's here. Do you want to talk to him?" I said that I'd like nothing better, but perhaps a peculiar expression on my face tipped my intention, because Burchette excused himself for about five minutes and then returned to say, "I'm sorry, but Winnington is not here. He has gone to Peiping where I am led to believe that he will marry a Chinese girl. Sorry you two can't get together."

Like hell he had gone to Peiping. When I reached our side the next day I found out that Winnington was in Panmunjom, covering the exchanges along with the other press representatives. I can only gather that he didn't want to see me—and with good reason.

The following day we were all awakened bright and early. Probably for the first time since we had been in enemy hands we were only too happy to get up and face the day. After breakfast we were given Chinese bowltype haircuts, and some of us were even shaved so that we'd look halfway presentable when we were returned. About noon a large procession of trucks pulled up in front of our tents, forming a convoy for the trip into Kaesong. Frank, Andy and I were taken out to a shiny jeep and the rest of the prisoners were led to very fancy Russian-built trucks with padded benches on either side. After the trip south in those miserable trucks it was amazing to find padded seats for a mere fifteen-mile ride. This was another fine example of Communist propaganda tactics. By God, they seemed to think of everything. As we climbed into our vehicles some thirty Communist cameramen began to take movies of us. I got a big kick out of Andy Evans. He had to walk around the jeep to get into his seat, and as he did so he put his thumb to his nose and held it there until the procession moved off. His gesture must have spoiled several thousand feet of good film for the Communists, and they were hopping mad, but Andy casually ignored their protests.

The three of us sat in the back of the jeep and a Chinese driver, an interrogator and a guard rode in front. We were followed at a distance by the trucks. Shortly after we left Panmunjom there was a hurried consultation in the front seat, and suddenly the interrogator waved for the rest of the convoy to stop. I was instructed to leave my seat and exchange places with Andy. Once this was accomplished, off we went again. About five miles from Kaesong we began passing truckload after truckload of North Korean soldiers, ex-POW's also being repatriated, but in the opposite direction. We were amazed to see them tearing off their American clothes and throwing them to the ground. The roadside was littered with GI gear for miles, and Communist photographers were taking pictures all along the route. Later we found out that these were the same hard-core North Korean Communists who had allowed themselves to be captured in order to foment trouble in the prison camps at Koje-Do. They were now putting on a demonstration which would be exhibited throughout Communist societies to show how anxious these loyal comrades were to return to their homeland. The passing trucks held perhaps thirty soldiers each, all singing North Korean marching songs in unison, all waving their right arms and brandishing clenched fists in time with the music. Interestingly enough, hundreds of North Korean civilians were brazenly picking up the discarded clothing for their personal use.

As we approached Freedom Village we noticed much construction preparing the neutral zone for the controlled peace to follow. Our hearts were warmed to see hundreds of big American bulldozers and auxiliary road-building machinery knocking down hills and making roads at an unbelievable rate. What a contrast to those hundreds of miles of Chinese soldiers making little rocks out of big rocks in order to build a meager path!

Finally we circled a small hill and approached the receiving area where we were to park. There must have been thousands of military observers from many nations, not to mention hundreds of photographers and reporters. An American band was playing, and there were even American girls in uniform on hand to greet us. Overhead the big old Stars and Stripes waved proudly above the whole scene. Several large, trim, military policemen directed us to pull up in a line in front of this mass of people. Our driver must have been confused by the noise of the crowd, because he pulled about three feet past the point where the biggest of the MP's had motioned him to stop. The MP, like any good cop, came back and chewed that poor Communist soldier to pieces. God, what a beautiful sound!

Suddenly it dawned on me why I had been ordered to exchange places with Andy Evans. I was comparatively healthy, while Andy looked like death warmed over. Almost all of the photographers were on my side of the jeep, and the Communists

266

wanted them to take close-up pictures of me rather than Andy. The bastards! I turned my head away from the cameras, giving them only a beautiful shot of Frank Schwable, a fine one of poor Andy, and the back of my head.

We had been stationary for perhaps one minute when a long-time friend of mine, Colonel Ed Stirling, came rushing up to hug me saying, "My God, Bud, this is the first time we knew that you were alive." Another old friend, Brigadier General Ed Underhill, joined us immediately, pumping my hand for all he was worth. He was vice-commander of 5th Air Force and had come over to Freedom Village for that particular day in the hope that he'd either see me or at least find out whether I was still alive. Altogether, the scene rapidly became too damn emotional. I was asked to get out of the jeep and walk over to an ambulance which was to take us to a large building for processing, and as I got in and sat down, all those many months of strain caught up with me and I began to cry like a baby. Frank came in right after me and sat down, crying as uncontrollably as I was; and when Andy came in crying, too, even the driver of the ambulance began to wipe his eyes. God, what a relief! What a really and truly welcome relief. We were finally free.

When we entered the big building we were given forms to fill out, indicating whether or not we wished to talk to the press. This one threw me. I figured that by this time someone would surely have instructions for me, but it now appeared that I had to make the decision myself. I knew that I had a hot story, but I wanted to be sure that I told it in a way that was satisfactory to my government. I was being hounded by reporters who wanted me to give them statements, but I didn't have any guide lines. I called to Ed Stirling and asked him what he thought. "Geez, Bud, I don't know what to tell you to do," he replied. "Wait here a minute and I'll ask Ed Underhill to come over." But Ed was just as baffled.

At that moment our participation in the germ-warfare confessions was still unknown to the press. All the newsmen wanted were answers to questions like "How does it feel to be back on our side?" or "How long were you in prison camp?" Someone had told them about my previous combat record, and I suppose I was considered a newsworthy item. I was pretty darn sure that there were representatives from all the major newsservices in the world in the vicinity, and if I really wanted to blast the Communists I would probably never have a better sounding board. Now that I was among friends my courage was mounting by leaps and bounds, and since no one seemed aware of the enormity of what had transpired I came to a fast conclusion.

The way I saw it, this was my big opportunity. If the Communists had been putting out this baloney for over a year, it was high time somebody stood up and told the world how it was done. As ashamed as I felt for having confessed to something that wasn't true, now was the time to stand up and blast, even though I might be castigated for it later. If I could get my story out right now, then the Communists would be hard put to make any sort of propaganda hay—at least for this one particular day.

I looked around for Andy Evans and discussed the situation with him. He agreed to appear before the press with me, but by this time he was shaking so badly that I thought he might faint. He wanted me to do the talking. If he were asked any specific questions he'd answer, but otherwise he couldn't trust himself to talk much. When we had agreed on our course of action we looked for Frank Schwable, but he had left the room. Next I located the chief public information officer and told him that we'd meet the press.

I wasn't quite prepared for what happened. We were taken into a room which contained, at the minimum, over 350 correspondents and cameramen. Not only did we have a conference, but motion pictures were taken which were later shown on television in the United States. I guess Andy and I were before the cameras for as long as forty-five minutes. Looking back now, I realize that my statement must have sounded slightly garbled, but I was so anxious to get the word across and stop the damage done by the false confessions that I couldn't think of anything else. I told my story as well as I could. Then I told what little I knew of Andy's treatment, gesturing at him from time to time to illustrate a point. If there was anything in the world at the moment which lent mute testimony to what I was saying, it was Andy. He had just about had it.

"The Communists had absolutely no evidence on the ground," *U.S. News and World Report* of September 18, 1953, quoted me as saying. "They explained it in this manner—in their society a confession is a fact. If you confess you've done it, they have no scruples about the circumstances involved in your confession. And not only your confession. If another pilot from your organization confesses, then he has of course also made you guilty."

"Their big hold on those guys," I went on to say, "the big thing is, when a guy goes down alone he is listed as missing in action. If you were convinced in your own mind that nobody saw you go down, then it is obvious that they can do anything they want with you. In Andy's case he thought that his people saw him go down. But a lot of these youngsters around—nobody knew they were down. So that's a tremendous wedge for them to get this confession business out."

In answer to a query from one correspondent regarding what was actually contained in a confession, I replied, "The basic thing was that we said we were dropping fleas, flies and mosquitoes that were infected with everything we could think of; and a lot of us had stuff that isn't carried by fleas. For example, one boy said his fleas, flies and mosquitoes were infected with tetanus. Of course tetanus is blood poisoning. But they bought that. And they bought typhoid. I think typhoid is borne by water; you drink typhoid in water."

As soon as we could get away from the press we were taken to a shower—a wonderful shower—where we bathed, threw our prisoner-of-war uniforms away, and put on brand-new uniforms of the United States Air Force. This was an especially proud moment for me. I found that officers' clubs all over the combat zone had donated money to purchase uniforms for each officer who came out of North Korea. We couldn't pay for a thing. To me this was a wonderful gesture, and I'm sure none of us will ever forget it. As soon as we were clean and dressed properly we were taken by helicopter to a large station hospital at Inchon to spend one night prior to boarding a ship for the trip home. I think that the Air Force made a smart move in treating us as hospital patients, because most of us were too weak to do much moving around.

The hospital was excellent. Imagine—after sixteen months I found myself sleeping in a bed with real sheets and a real pillow! As soon as we were settled we were given the necessary forms to fill out, plus the opportunity to wire home to our families. I can't remember what I said in mine, but I tried to tell Pat that I was alive and well and would be home shortly. After a brief physical check-up we were allowed to draw some money from the finance office for use on the way home, but I had been without money for so long that I had to have the finance officer's advice before settling on $200. Next, armed with all that money, I went directly to the Post Exchange to see what I could buy for the family, and ended up with—of all things—a desk radio for my daughter.

After a quiet and restful night we were advised that we would be boarding a troop transport that afternoon. All of us were looking forward to going home, but we couldn't understand why we weren't being flown. The medical people told us that it would be best to go home slowly: first to get our health back, and second to prepare ourselves for joining our families. After being in prison camp for so long, we were told, we weren't in shape to stand shock after shock right away.

While I was waiting for transfer to the ship I was visited by the commanding officer of the 4th Fighter Wing, Colonel D. P. Hall. He brought about ten of his senior officers with him, and I was delighted to see them. It was just like old times. Naturally I was full of questions about the air war in Korea, and they in turn asked about POW life.

In our conversation one interesting fact came to light—something that amused me more than a little. When I was first questioned by the Communists on the tactics the F-86s used to shoot down Mig-15s, I had gone into a detailed description of the mistakes the Migs always made while trying to take evasive action. The worst mistake of all, I had said, was for them to try to climb away from the F-86s, because in climbing the Mig became a perfect target. I suggested that the best way to avoid attack was to make a sharp level turn, changing direction as rapidly as possible. In so doing, the F-86 pilot would be given the worst possible target and the Mig pilot would soon have the advantage. I hadn't really expected the Communists to swallow this advice, even though they had insisted that I write a detailed description. From our standpoint, the worst thing the Mig pilot could do was to climb, because his plane had a climb advantage, and the best he could do was to try to turn with us, because we could outturn him every time. Now, out of idle curiosity, I asked Colonel Hall whether, at any time during the war, the Migs had shown a tendency to try to turn with the F-86s. He replied that they had adopted this tactic some three months after I had been shot down. For about a month they had turned instead of climbing, and our lads had shot them down almost every time. They had finally given up in disgust and resorted to their old tactics. This welcome news was too good to be true, even for me, but I checked it later in the States, and Harry Thyng confirmed Hall's report.

When the time came for me to leave for the ship and for the boys from the 4th to return to K-14, Lieutenant Colonel Sam Sartor gave me a present which moved me greatly and which I remember to this day. It was a cigarette lighter with the slogan, FOURTH BUT FIRST, engraved on one side.

2.

UP to this time my fears about the American reaction to germ-warfare confessions seemed to be groundless. The press representatives who listened to us when we were released appeared to be very sympathetic. When D. P. Hall and his troops took time out to come up to visit me, I couldn't help but feel that they, too, were glad to see me and glad to have us back. I was so anxious to turn this situation into a victory for our side that I gradually paid less and less attention to the possibility of adverse comment when we returned home.

So much kindness was displayed everywhere that at times I found it difficult to hold back the tears. Naturally, thoughts of my family were uppermost in my mind, even though I was trying not to think of them constantly until I got nearer to the United States. I didn't relish the thought of spending sixteen days at sea, but powers above me had decided that we wouldn't go by air, and that was that. (Andy Evans had been sent on to Tokyo and would fly to the States three weeks later. But if anyone needed special care, Andy did.)

We were going home with several thousand GI's, but as hospital patients we were given what might be considered "first-class" accommodations. Frank Schwable and I were allowed to eat in the captain's mess, and the rest of the guys used the ship's officers' mess. To those of us who had lived for month after month on chicken heads and rice, this was good living. The cooks made every effort to give us anything we wanted, and the daily menus were something to behold.

A couple of days after we settled on board we were given physical examinations, to see if we needed medical treatment. I was in good shape except for intestinal worms—a common enough disease in the Orient.

The third day out I found that there was a psychological warfare officer on board—a man who was to take depositions from all of us who had made germ-warfare confessions. As soon as possible I looked him up to find out if he had received any instructions from the government regarding our activities. When we docked at San Francisco I was certain that we would be met by a large contingent from the press and I wanted to make sure that we would not say anything uncomplimentary to our country. We were all in a unique position—the Communists' tactics were without parallel in human history—and the eyes

272

of the world would be focused on us. Unfortunately this officer didn't have a clue. Because we were not supposed to use the ship's communication system, I asked him to wire Washington for instructions. He promised to do so, but throughout the trip—despite his repeated efforts in our behalf—no answer came. Little by little it dawned on me that the United States had not, after all, developed a positive course of counterpropaganda. In the meantime, as the highest ranking Air Force officer on board, I called a meeting of all other returnees to try to explain our position, and after a long discussion we decided that I would be the spokesman for the group, although it was clearly understood that I wasn't in any way trying to establish a military command. We were all supposed to be having a vacation and this was scarcely the time for military discipline. All of the men were concerned about their futures, but they could take a load off their minds—for the time being at least—by letting one man do the worrying.

Frank Schwable was perhaps the most diffident of the people in my circle. Perhaps because of his maturity he anticipated more trouble at home than we did, or perhaps he had been given some indication of the problems he would face. Whatever the reason, he just didn't seem to unbend as much as most of the others.

As for me, when I did take time out to think about the future I was anxious to put all of my ideas in motion at once. I had lost one and a half years of my life—years that I'd never get back. I'd have to make every moment count in the future. I wanted to continue my military career—it was the life to which I was dedicated—and I especially wanted to begin flying again. Some day I might be called on to fight again for my nation against the very same enemy I now detested, and I wanted to be ready for any eventuality. My false confession, I thought, might be a problem for awhile, but I had a lot to offer as a pilot and an officer, and if I did my job well my career shouldn't suffer because of my prison-camp experiences. And most important of all, at long last I was going to have another chance to get to know my family.

273

As time passed I became acquainted with the experiences of others in our group. Approximately twenty-five of the officers had been together as prisoners. This group was headed by a Marine lieutenant colonel named Gail Thrash, who was generally regarded as an exceptionally fine man. Somehow, during the months of hardship, he had been able to inspire faith in those around him, and though they had been sorely tried, most of the men in their small POW compound had maintained some degree of sanity.

Commander Ralph Bagwell, another man in our group, had been on a dive-bombing mission in a Navy propeller-driven AD when he had struck a cable suspended between two mountains. The cable had ripped off his vertical stabilizer and he had flown into the ground at a speed of well over 300 miles an hour. He had regained consciousness to find himself several hundred feet from the cockpit of his demolished machine, but miraculously he had been injured only slightly.

Another who had been captured under unusual circumstances was Commander Doc Richardson. He had been hit by ground fire while flying a Grumman F9F jet fighter. Doc, too, had hit the ground at full speed. Somehow he had been thrown clear of the wreckage, only to find that his arm was broken in several places. When the Communists captured him they made no effort to set his arm, and it was badly misshapen.

A third man I came to know well on the voyage was Lieutenant Colonel John Giraudo of the Air Force. John had been strafing a convoy well up the North Korean peninsula when he was hit by antiaircraft fire. He had bailed out at low altitude, landing on a hill near the convoy. When he hit the ground two North Korean soldiers had run toward him, firing machine guns as they ran. One bullet had struck John in the chest just below the shoulder, and although the resulting hole was small in front it was very large in back. The Communists had refused to give him medical aid, and he had almost bled to death. Somehow he had been strong enough to recover, but he still had a tremendous hole in his back where the bullet had left his body. I liked John on sight. He had not been pressured to make a false

274

confession, but he was keenly interested in the fate of those of us who had.

In shooting the bull with other ex-prisoners of war on the ship I heard many unusual tales indeed. The human mind has an interesting ability to slough off distasteful memories, and now our conversations centered on the lighter moments of our imprisonment. Since Gail Thrash's compound held the largest number of POW's, they had managed to keep each other's spirits up, and though most of them held relatively high ranks and were therefore prime targets for Communist conversion attempts, they had resisted stanchly.

One day they had decided to put one over on their captors. Someone had found a dead rat, and they cooked up a plot to see just how much the Communists would fall for. They printed an Air Force serial number on two sides of a small square of white cotton cloth. Next they fashioned a small harness for the dead rat, and then tied string from the harness to the cloth so that it resembled a small parachute. At night they took the rat into the middle of the compound and placed it on the ground, exactly as though it had dropped from the skies via the parachute.

The next morning the first Communist interrogator who spotted the dead rat cried out in alarm, and soon a large group of guards and interrogators assembled. One of the first men to see the rat rushed off, then returned stripped to the waist, his entire torso covered with iodine. He picked the rat up with a pair of tongs and put it into a paper bag. Later the interrogators returned to call a general assembly of the POW's in order to brief them on this horrible device that the United Nations had dropped on them during the night. And still later the Communists made excursions to other prison camps to tell about the dead rat in the parachute. They kept up their briefings until the rat became too decayed to be exhibited.

This same group subsequently decided to stage a "Crazy Week" to confuse the prison-camp authorities. Bright and early one Monday morning they had one member draw a large rectangle in the dirt in the middle of the compound. During the night others had fashioned two paddles out of "requisitioned" material. The rectangle was to be the deck of an aircraft carrier, and one of the officers was to use the paddles to act as landing signal officer. The rest of the men were to be pilots flying jet aircraft.

The first guy who had to go to the john began warming up his engine vocally while still in his hut. Then, with his arms out to simulate a swept-wing aircraft, he taxied out to the take-off end of the rectangle. The landing signal officer took his position, waved a go-ahead with the paddles, and off he took, accompanying himself with jetlike sounds. Upon returning from the latrine he flew around the carrier, prepared for a straight-in approach, and landed to the violent arm waving of the landing signal officer. Once landed, the prisoner taxied back to his hut and shut his engine down.

To put it mildly, the Chinese Communist guards had been nonplused. They were so confused that an emissary had been sent for the head interrogator. The next man to go to the john had repeated the same process of being a Navy jet-fighter plane, and the next, and the next. As soon as the interrogator arrived he grabbed the first prisoner he saw, to find out what was going on, but the man wouldn't speak to him because he wasn't a prisoner; he was a jet airplane. The interrogator promptly had him put into the local jail. When the next prisoner wouldn't answer the interrogator had him put in jail too. Finally the jail became so crowded and so many more customers were waiting that the Communists decided to let everyone go back to the compound, even though they couldn't find out what had caused the madness.

The boys had continued the charade for a full week, during which time the Chinese became convinced that their captives had all completely lost their minds. At the end of the week, when the prisoners stopped being aircraft as abruptly as they had started, the Communists were thrown into confusion once more. Again they started throwing the Americans into jail, and again the jail became overloaded. The affair of the imaginary aircraft carrier left the prisoners in complete control of the battle for their minds. The Communists never bothered them with thought control again.

As the days passed by, life on the ship grew more and more relaxed, but in spite of the good food and rest most of us continued to worry about what was to happen when we reached San Francisco. On the fifteenth day at sea the ship slowed down perceptibly. As spokesman for the Air Force men on board, I asked the ship's captain about the delay. He explained that there was to be a welcoming ceremony at the dock at Fort Mason in the shadow of the Golden Gate Bridge, and that the ship had to make land at precisely the right time. The captain went on to say that we would anchor outside the harbor until late at night, then proceed to dock first thing in the morning. This was tough for all of us to take, but there was nothing we could do about it. Nearly all of us spent several hours topside that evening, watching the glow of San Francisco in the sky.

The following morning, as we slowly moved up to the pier, the ship's railing was lined solidly with GI's searching the shore for their loved ones. John Giraudo, Ralph Bagwell and I were as high up on the bridge as we could get without interfering with the captain when suddenly one of the guys, who had been watching the opposite side of the ship, came running over to me to exclaim, "For God's sake, Bud, look what's coming down from the north in the sky." When I looked around I saw a flight of sixteen F-86's formed into a big letter "M," flying toward the ship at about 1,500 feet. This big "M" circled the ship several times in perfect formation and then headed north in the direction of Hamilton Air Force Base. I found out later that the flight was led by Major Vince Gordon who commanded the 84th Fighter Squadron. He knew I was on board, and he and Harry Thyng—who by this time was director of operations of Western Air Defense Force—had cooked up the flight in my honor. Next, to my surprise, I saw a large ocean-going tugboat heading toward the ship. As it drew closer we could hear the sounds of music; the Hamilton Air Force Base band had come to entertain us as we docked. For nearly an hour they played all the songs we wanted to hear, not stopping until the gangplank was down and we were disembarking.

As we neared the dock John Giraudo came out with the captain's binoculars in hand and began to look at the large crowd assembled dockside. Suddenly I saw him stiffen and gaze intently at something for a few minutes. Then he turned to me and said, "Here, Bud, take these glasses for a minute." As he turned away I could see that he was crying. He had spotted his Beth in the crowd. For my part I began to search the crowd for Pat. When I spotted her she was looking up intently, but I could tell that she was unable to distinguish any of us. I watched her for a minute and turned around, crying myself, just in time to hand the glasses back to John, who had recovered his composure. We must have traded glasses and tears back and forth for twenty minutes until the ship was finally tied to the pier and we were given instructions to go down the gangplank.

When I stepped ashore and managed to get Pat into my arms it was all I could do to keep from crying all over again. Only one thing kept me from it. There were at least thirty-five of my old friends from Western Air Defense Force surrounding us to wish us well. What a wonderful surprise! I couldn't say much to them, because there just wasn't time, but once again Harry Thyng was behind it all. He had arranged for them to take time off and come down to the ship.

Just as I had managed to say hello I got another surprise. George Welch and his wife Jan broke in on Pat and me to wish us the best. It seemed that Dutch Kindelburger, the chairman of the board of North American Aviation, and Lee Atwood, the president, had decided that George should fly my wife to San Francisco to meet the ship. Since Jan was one of Pat's best friends, she had decided that she would come too. George was to spend the night with us, then fly us all back to Los Angeles the following day. Upon our arrival in L.A., Pat and I were to go to the Beverly Hills Hotel and stay as long as we wanted to as the guests of North American.

I was so darn glad to be home that I was virtually speechless. For the moment my cup was running over. But it was too good to last. A couple of reporters broke in on us, and suddenly we were surrounded by hordes of them, all asking questions regarding my prisoner-of-war experiences. By this time almost all of the other guys had disembarked and were in the same situation. I didn't know what to do or say, because we had still received no instructions. Fortunately John Giraudo bailed me out. He barged his way through the crowd, grabbed my arm, and hustled me into a waiting bus. As soon as the other guys jumped into the bus, off we went to be processed into the United States. But there was still another hitch. It seemed that four of us were to depart for Parks Air Force Base on the other side of the bay for some sort of secret meeting. None of the people at Fort Mason knew what was up, but they had received orders for us and had a staff car waiting outside to take us to Parks. So far, at least, we had been spared the press, but it was easy to see that the reporters were suspicious. If we were being kept from them deliberately, they wanted to know why.

Upon our arrival at Parks we were ushered into the office of the director of intelligence and asked to write brief statements of our experiences. It took me about an hour to write the following:

> I was confronted with the allegations of having waged bacteriological warfare against the Korean and Chinese People's Volunteers about two months after I had been captured. I was told that I had the choice of either confessing to these allegations or being killed; further, they intended to get a confession from me, no matter what.
>
> By using extreme mental and physical measures they were able to reduce my power of resistance to a very low level. I attempted to find out exactly what it was they were trying to develop, and I did so by making fantastic comments in regard to the activities of my wing in Korea, in order to see what the reaction of my interrogators would be. I quickly found out that any statement I made would be accepted without question, although I myself knew that the statements were absurd. I knew that they were rigging a forced allegation which they in-

tended to foist upon the people throughout the world. I refused to acknowledge such a charge and refused to state that what I had written was true, because it definitely was not. Because of this refusal, they began to subject me to a series of what I would call "subtle physical tortures" including sitting at rigid attention on the edge of my bed for 38 hours, sitting on a stool 15 hours a day for 30 days.

During this period, which occurred during the latter part of 1952, I suffered frostbite on my feet because they took away my shoelaces and would not allow me to close the door of my room; nor did they allow a fire to heat my room. They kept me in solitary confinement until the middle of April 1953. I started to cooperate with them in the middle of May 1953, in order to try to return to the United States and bring my story to the thinking people of the world.

The statements that I made and the alleged confession that I wrote were absolutely ridiculous and absolutely without basis in fact. By no stretch of the imagination could it have possibly been supported by evidence on the ground unless such evidence was planted there; yet this confession was accepted without question.

In order to satisfy the problem, and, as the Chinese interrogator put it, ". . . take advantage of our lenient policy regarding prisoners of war," I was required to make a tape recording of the so-called "confession," giving details of things that happened and missions that had been performed. I finished writing this confession, in what the interrogators referred to "acceptable form," on the 3rd of September, 1953, the same day that I started south for Freedom Village. I was not informed that the Korean War had ended until about the 9th of August, 1953, and found, after the war was over, that I was still being interrogated and was still being told that the chances were excellent that I would *not* be allowed to return home.

As to my treatment while a prisoner of war in the hands of the Chinese Communists, I can definitely say that it was not in accordance with the Geneva Convention. In fact, my interrogators told me, at the beginning of my interrogation, that they considered me to be a war criminal and that they intended to treat me outside the rules of the Geneva Convention. On this point alone they gave me their word. I lived in solitary confinement all the time I was in the hands of the Communists.

The charge of bacteriological warfare is preposterous. In fact, my interrogators questioned me closely regarding the highly explosive bombs I dropped and then turned right around and accused me of the allegation that these very same bombs contained infected insects. The most ridiculous thing of all was that they accused me of having dropped insects on them during the winter of 1952. It is common knowledge that insects cannot possibly live in temperatures that range from freezing down to 50 degrees below zero, and such temperatures were common in North Korea at that time.

I have never, as accused by my Communist interrogators, participated in this type of warfare. I know it was not done and they know it was not done. The entire allegation was an attempt to besmirch non-Communist societies and was absolutely without foundation. The United Nations did not wage such warfare. Any person who believes such has not carefully examined the facts.

Next we sat before a motion-picture camera and each of us read our statements while our pictures were taken. I asked several times for an explanation, but each time I was told that our statements were required for a highly classified project and that we would be told later what the project was all about. It was about five-thirty in the afternoon when we finished, and a staff car took us back into town. Pat, Jan and George had taken rooms in the Mark Hopkins Hotel, and I immediately joined them. On the way through the lobby I picked up a newspaper which told of our landing in rather unglowing terms, placing special emphasis on the fact that Colonel Mahurin and others were spirited away from the representatives of the press and were apparently being kept under official wraps. The general tone the press seemed to take was that we had something to hide; it was even intimated that maybe there was truth to the germ-warfare allegation after all.

After a tall Scotch and water—dynamite to me because I hadn't had a drink for so long—we decided to do the town. Pat had thoughtfully brought several suits and a uniform for me, and I chose the uniform. I don't think I have ever been as proud as when I was pinning my medals on that uniform. I felt good all over. I had gained weight on board ship and by this time I was up to 126 pounds. When I put on my trousers they almost fit, being just a little bit loose. I quickly rushed over to show George and Jan that I wasn't so skinny after all, then rushed back to my room to put on my blouse. The blouse hung on me like a tent. I couldn't possibly have lost that much weight. It almost reached my knees. For a moment or two Pat and I pondered the sight, and then I looked at the label. I bought all my uniforms at a place called Wilner's in Washington, D.C., and this one came from Shinbaum's in San Antonio, Texas. It turned out that Major Bill Evans, six feet, three inches tall and two hundred pounds, patronized the same tailor we did at George Air Force Base, and that somehow our blouses had been switched. That ripped it. I wore civilian clothes that evening.

I don't remember too much about it—my first night in the United States in twenty-two months. All I know is that I was happy—plain happy to be home. I do recall that as the evening wore on we began to run into more and more of the ex-prisoners who, with their wives, were celebrating just as we were. More than a few were showing their drinks, and I realized that none of us were the two-fisted tigers we had been before. Still, it was wonderful.

On Sunday we flew back to Los Angeles. The weather was clear and bright, and George let me fly for awhile, although I was very much out of practice. We landed at International Airport, then hustled to the Beverly Hills Hotel. More partying. And this time it included Lieutenant Colonel Tom Queen, one of my 1st Group Squadron commanders, and his wife Glee. All in all it was a fine weekend, but I was anxious to get on to George and see my children. Pat and I lasted until Monday and then packed for home, much to the disgust of George Welch. "Goddamn it," he repeated time and time again, "why don't you stay around for a couple more weeks?"

Great as the prospect seemed to be, I wanted to leave for the desert. And off we went.

3.

SEEING the children was the absolute best. In twenty-two months Lynn had grown till she was now almost a young lady, while Marshall was a little boy instead of the baby I had said good-bye to. They were both handsome children, and I was so proud of them I almost burst. Patty had moved out of the large house we had occupied when I was fighter group commander, because rank had its power, and, since I was no longer commander, another man had moved in. Pat had been living in an apartment building we shared with three other families. It was perfect to be home at George once again, and to my delight we were visited by many old friends who were glad to see me back. For my part I couldn't seem to stay away from the children, nor could I stay away from the refrigerator. Nothing delighted me more than being able to pull up a chair in front of the gleaming white box, in order to stare at all the good things inside.

Classed as hospital patients, all POW's were given thorough physical examinations in order to get complete records of the effects of living in the Orient under adverse conditions.

For the first time in the history of our nation we were trying to get total physical and mental information on all returned prisoners of war. Previously, in World War II and before, POW's had just seemed to migrate home or to duty stations

after the war, and it had been virtually impossible to get sta-
tistics on their conditions. In the Korean War they were relatively few in number and all were kept under close surveillance,
making it easy to keep accurate records. Eventually it would be
possible to predict behavior patterns of future prisoners of war.

After my physical exam, which took three days, Pat and I
decided to fly to Fort Wayne to visit our parents. Arriving in
Chicago in midafternoon, we discovered—much to our consternation—that we had forgotten to bring any cash. We were
worrying about attempting to cash a check or wire home for
train fare when we met a young man neither of us knew. He
introduced himself, saying that he was the pilot of an airplane
which had come from Fort Wayne to take us home. We were
amazed. Dick O'Connor, the chairman of the board of Mag-
navox Radio Corporation, had sent his posh executive transport
to pick us up.

Being back in my home town was great and I had the same
emotions I always feel when I go back to the old stamping
ground. Naturally I didn't return to any hero's welcome, nor
was I asked to participate in any World War II-style parades.
For several days we were visited almost continuously by our
friends, plus our parents' friends and many well-wishers. To
my surprise I found that one of my best friends, Bob Bacon,
had been sitting in a bar when the news of my release had been
broadcast on the radio. Bob had put his head down on the
bar and cried. I haven't yet decided whether he was loaded or
whether he meant it, but this touched me plenty and I'll never
forget it.

By this time the press was full of comments pro and con
pertaining to the twenty-one defectors—the men who had decided to stay in Communist hands. Also there was much comment regarding those who had made false confessions. Almost
everyone I talked to in Fort Wayne was interested in my story,
so much so that I was contacted by one of the large radio
stations, which wanted to be able to give its listeners my first-
hand account. I was only too glad to appear, and I talked for

a half an hour. Though we received many congratulatory phone calls and letters after the broadcast, I was still conscious of a pervading doubt, because I sensed that my situation would get worse before it got better.

Most of the press comment had been on the fence regarding the brainwashing situation, although there had been quotations from various columnists and statements by various lawmakers that tended to point the finger of accusation at us. Especially at me, because I was talking and I was a high ranker. Naturally my concern grew with each unfavorable comment. Though the press in Fort Wayne—and for that matter in Indiana as a whole —was extremely favorable, I was, after all, a native son.

The unfavorable ones jarred me to the bone. I suppose this is always the case—nobody likes to be shot at—but in my mind I seemed to magnify the bad comments all out of proportion. Worst of all, I had followed the exploits of General Dean, who had been taken prisoner early in the war, quite closely and I knew that he had been accorded a hero's welcome. This was as it should have been, and there was no doubt that our situations were different, but playing the villain, as I seemed involuntarily to be doing, was a new and tough role for me.

Furthermore I didn't have a job. Colonel Bob Delashaw, the base commander at George as well as the commander of the 479th Fighter Wing—a unit of Tactical Air Command—seemed to be quite anxious to have me in his command when I talked to him about it, and said that he'd be glad to go to his superiors to see if he couldn't arrange an assignment. One of our next door neighbors, Captain Jack Martin, was married to the daughter of Major General Ted Timberlake, the commander of 12th Air Force, the parent unit of the 479th. Shirley and Pat were good friends, so the next time Ted Timberlake came through George I asked him about working in one of his units. He, too, seemed to cotton to the idea. Still, I received no orders. From what I could gather—which was damn little—the requests for an assignment for me were going to headquarters through official channels. There they'd either be delayed for some unknown reason or the reply would state that additional time was required before an answer could be given. I deduced that no one was anxious to do much about me until some sort of official statement declared that I was either a good guy or a bum.

In the meantime Brigadier General Don Hutchison, the commander of the 27th Air Division at Norton Air Force Base, called several times to ask whether I wanted to join his organization. I knew that the job Don had to offer would be a desk job, and I didn't want to accept it until I had exhausted all other possibilities of staying in the flying game.

Throughout the country the press had been carrying many more articles regarding POW's. It appeared that the Marine Corps was preparing a full-scale investigation of Frank Schwable's activities before a board of superior officers in Washington, D.C. General Pate, Commandant of the Corps, had made public statements indicating that the conduct of some officers in prison camps had been less than desirable and that he wanted this situation investigated. I, myself, had been contacted by the Office of Special Investigation to see if I would have any objection to being interrogated on my prison-camp experiences. The cloud over my head seemed to be darkening.

Since I was sure that the criticism leveled at me had something to do with my not being able to get an assignment, I decided to write to my old boss, General Everest, who at that time was Chief of Staff for Operations in the Pentagon, asking if he could arrange any job for me in the tactical field. Several days later I received a reply which had evidently been researched by the personnel people at headquarters. General Everest observed that, since I had been a tactical commander for so long, it was time I was given a desk job, which, he added, would probably be best from a career standpoint. Following receipt of this letter, I heard rumors that, because of my experience in prison camp and because my future in the service seemed to be in question, Tactical Air Command did not want me in any capacity.

Most of the stuff circulated in the press was read by people at George Air Force Base. The more candid of my friends wanted to know what I would do if I had to get out of the service. I never talked to anyone having direct dealings with the situation, but I knew that the Air Force was considering the establishment of a board to consider the cases of all POW's. I further knew that a board of officers had been constituted in Washington to devise a code of conduct for future POW's. All this news seemed ominous for me. I try not to run scared if I can help it, but I was beginning to lie awake nights, worrying about the future. The first few great weeks had now dissipated into a series of rather dim days.

With this sour information in my hip pocket I went to San Bernardino to talk to Don Hutchison. He not only wanted me in spite of the uncertainty of my case, but he had visited Head-quarters Air Defense Command to seek approval to assign me to his unit. He had orders already typed out and was merely waiting for me to say yes before he had them published. He wanted me to be his chief of staff (for me a really responsible position) until I could get back into the old familiar way of doing business in the Air Force—then he would move me over to become his director of operations. At last I had found a home.

Although still on leave, I received a call from Hutch one day, inviting me to give a talk at Hamilton Air Force Base. It seemed that all the senior officers of Western Air Defense Forces were assembling for a division commanders' conference and I was to be the principal speaker. I was glad to go, because I felt that it would be best for me to explain what had prompted the germ-warfare confession to as many people as possible. At the time I was especially concerned because a letter written by Senator Richard Russell of Georgia to the Secretary of Defense, Mr. Charles Wilson, had just been released to the press. Senator Russell was the ranking minority member of the Senate Armed Services Committee, and had been chairman of this august group. His words were bound to carry weight in the Pentagon, because the military services try not to antagonize those who control appropriations for the military establishment.

Senator Russell had written: "My views may be extreme, but I believe that those who collaborated and the signers of false confessions should be immediately separated from the services under conditions other than honorable. From what I have been able to observe in the press since the exchange of prisoners started, it is evident that the defense agencies under your direction hold other views. I respectfully submit, however, that at the very least to preserve the morale of future forces, as well as to accord the proper respect to those who have sacrificed for their country, some definite tribute should be paid to those who sustained themselves and their country's honor in the face of privation and war." Later the same letter went on to say: "If such reprimand or punishment is not contemplated, please advise me as to whether the fact of such 'Confessions' will be placed in the files of those officers for consideration when they are considered for promotions."

On his part Mr. Wilson had replied: "We do not as a general principle condone those who made false confessions contrary to the interests of their country, or whose actions caused their fellow prisoners added misery. Such cases will be carefully and sympathetically examined by the services concerned, to ascertain whether in any of them there had been unreasonable failure to measure up to the standard of individual conduct which is expected even of a prisoner of war, or deviations from standards of behavior prescribed by law."

Naturally Mr. Wilson's comments appealed to me slightly more than did those of Senator Russell; still, I felt that I should talk forthrightly to as many people as I could to explain the power of Communist propaganda agencies. It appeared that the United States, having fallen into the trap originally set by the Communists when the false confessions first came out, was about ready to fall into another. When the Communists accused us we went into a tail chase with them, trying to deny something that had never happened. They figured that we'd have trouble working out just the right approach to such a denial, and we did. Up until that time we were still in a tail chase. If a decision was made to separate from the service all of us who had made false confessions, the loss in dollars alone would be tremendous. Including training and flying time, about $300,000 to $500,000 had been spent on me alone. Add all the others, and the United

States had an enormous investment which would be lost if board action eliminated us from service. Just what the Communists wanted. Perhaps if I could get to the right people I might be able to do some convincing.

When I appeared to speak, General W. E. Todd, the commander of Western Air Defense Force, was present with 75 to 100 of his highest-ranking officers. For about four and a half hours I told exactly what had happened and how I felt about it. For the first time I postulated a theory which had been in my mind for some time, even while in prison camp. Why should we not train our men to be useful to us even though captured, just as the Communists had done? Why do we take youngsters fresh from small communities, send them to flying schools, send them to wars with the possibility of their being shot down, and then expect them to behave with steel determination when they have had no such training and when they are exposed to people who have been trained to break them down? There must be a better way. I recalled that our briefings had never been specific when it came to what to do if captured. Sometimes it was said: "Give your name, rank and serial number only." Other times: "We can't tell you what to do or say." Still other times the instructions were: "Tell them anything they want to know." If you were fresh out of Kendallville, Indiana, with a year or so of college, and received these conflicting instructions, would you know what to do? Why hadn't we been appraised of the false confessions when they first came out? Who was better entitled to know than those of us who might possibly be shot down behind enemy lines and then exposed to a society capable of forcing captured airmen to admit to something that wasn't true?

Who knows but what a POW could be useful to his nation even though in the hands of the enemy? What if the major operating command devised phony threats against the enemy? If every captured pilot talked about impending atomic attacks in the near future, it would give the captors cause for serious thought. If a group of people put their minds toward plans to make POW's useful, instead of letting them shift for themselves, some sort of beneficial result might be achieved. The main thing was that there should be some planning and instruction for potential POW's other than "Name, rank and serial number."

Anyway, as I stood there making my little speech to the officers of Western Air Defense Force I felt that I was at least outlining the possibilities of future action—a much more productive course for the country than trying to find things we could do to our own prisoners of war who had been forced to give in to the enemy for propaganda purposes. I mentioned only a couple of possibilites; there might be many more ideas which could be effective if someone was thinking them up. But until our nation came up with some clever, intelligent ideas of its own in the propaganda field we would always be behind the Communists in the fight for men's minds.

When I finished talking General Todd, whom I respect highly, came to me to congratulate me on my return and to ask a question. He felt that my talk had been a good one and that I had some ideas which might be of value if considered fully by someone of importance in the intelligence field. "I'd like to arrange for you to appear before the Central Intelligence Agency and then before representatives of the State Department," he said. "Would you have any objections?" Naturally I didn't. I had sat on my duff in prison camp too long, thinking of what I would do if involved in propaganda war, to maintain silence now that I was back in the United States where someone might listen to me. But somehow the time was not right. Several days later General Todd called me to say that the trip to Washington had been postponed. I never heard about it again.

When I got back to George I received a call from Headquarters Air Defense Command, informing me that the Director of Intelligence, Brigadier General Woody Burgess, would be paying me a visit to talk about my experiences. He arrived the following day, and we talked while sitting on a sofa in my living room. I told him all I had told the people at Hamilton Field, and when I finished he wanted to know if I would object to

290

telling the same story to the people at ADC Headquarters. Of course not. But I heard no more. I guess I was getting too hot to handle.

My opinion of my situation was confirmed shortly thereafter. I received a call from a friend—a very important national figure —who invited me to be his guest at a hunting lodge in Pennsylvania. It seemed that General Le May, General Twining, their wives, and many other notable couples, would be assembled for a weekend and that I was to bring my wife. The plans called for me to fly by military aircraft while my wife's airline ticket would be arranged for her.

We were delighted with the invitation. It was a fine opportunity to mingle with some of the nation's leaders, and it seemed as though it might be a vindication of sorts. I arranged for airline tickets, Pat took care of the baby-sitter problem, and we both shopped for new clothes. Then, the day before we were to leave on the trip, I received a call from my friend's secretary. With many profuse apologies, she explained that the party had been canceled. It seemed that one of the important guests had become ill and the party would be reorganized at a later date. About a week later I found out that the party had indeed gone off on schedule. It was just that my wife and I were not welcome.

We didn't mind too much though, because we both could understand. It was just that we would have liked to have had this news straight from the shoulder instead of in a roundabout way, but each individual sees his own actions in his own particular light. It was a great shock to know that my situation had such a profound effect on our social status.

Just after Halloween, Colonel Gabreski and his wife Kay invited Pat and me to bring the children to San Bernardino to visit for a day. Gabby was working for the inspector general's office at the time, having returned from Korea shortly after I had been shot down. We had a wonderful time visiting with the Gabreskis, but on the way back to George our car was sideswiped by another, resulting in a terrible accident.

291

Prior to the impact Pat and I had been chatting about how considerate Gab and Kay had been. All of a sudden I saw the glare of headlights, heard a shattering crash, and then realized that I was upside down inside my car. Pat and my daughter had been thrown out on the pavement while my son and I were scrambling around inside, trying to help them.

Fortunately there was much traffic on the highway, and in the shortest possible time police were on hand and an ambulance had been called. I was so busy trying to fill out the necessary reports, exchange insurance information, and get Pat and the children into the ambulance, that I hadn't notice the pain in my left side. As soon as the ambulance departed with screaming siren and flashing red lights, I had a chance to look at our car—a new Pontiac Pat had bought a month or so before I returned from Korea.

It was totally demolished. Turned completely on its back, the doors flung wide open and the wheels cocked in every direction, it suddenly represented Colonel W. M. Mahurin and what had happened to his life. The bad luck that had shot me down in Korea, followed me through the sixteen months in prison, caused me to face a critical government at home and possibly a court-martial in the near future, had struck yet another blow. I felt that I was personally demolished, too, because I didn't know whether my wife and children—the only things I had left—were injured or safe. It was just too much.

Somewhere in the crash one of the seats of the car had been thrown behind on the pavement. I walked back to the seat and there, in the glare of literally hundreds of automobile headlights and with hordes of onlookers, I sat down. Things had piled up on me and mine until I couldn't take any more.

The police came to my rescue and insisted that I go to the hospital to find Pat and the children. At the hospital I found that they were uninjured; but I wasn't—I had ruptured a kidney. For twenty-four hours I waited as the medical staff contemplated removal of the damaged organ, an operation which would have ended my flying career. I didn't mind so much for myself, but to have things happening time and again to my family just didn't seem fair.

Two weeks in the hospital gave me a lot of time in which to relax and think. I decided that I shouldn't worry too much about what was going to happen in the future; what happened would happen, and that would be that. On the other hand, I would try my best to do a job for the Air Force until my country decided that it did or did not want me. If I was booted out I could always do something somewhere for a living. My spirits were bolstered in the meantime by the number of people who came to visit me. Almost the entire gang from the 94th Fighter Interceptor Squadron came in on various occasions. Colonel George Laven, the commander of the 479th Air Base Group, visited every day. Naturally Pat and the children came as often as they could. It was nice to know that there were people in the world who would stick close, even though association with me might possibly be dangerous. Colonel Randy Holzapple made a special point of visiting me while he was on a trip to Edwards Air Force Base. George Welch came up as often as he could, and Bill Wahl visited often with his wife, Madelin. Still the specter of a court-martial seemed to be ever present.

The Schwable case was receiving great publicity in the news. The hearings were closed, but information was somehow leaked in driblets and magnified in the papers. Though it had been stated by the Marine Corps that this was an investigation and not court-martial, it appeared to me to have all the trimmings if not the name. What was happening to Frank could very easily happen to me, and in all honesty I didn't welcome the prospect.

After my release from the hospial, representatives of the OSI made an appointment to debrief me on my experiences with the Communists. It turned out that all released prisoners of war would be given a chance to testify to the OSI so that this data could be added to the medical history already obtained. For my part I wanted to tell my story in detail anyway, and this would be the best opportunity.

293

I spent about two weeks with OSI agents. We started on a rather lumpy basis, because the first request they made was: "Tell us what you know about other prisoners of war. We want to know about those who have done things which would reflect discredit on the United States or those who have done things harmful to other prisoners." I was aghast at this question. I had a head full of information which was valuable from an intelligence standpoint, yet here they were, disregarding what was important and trying to get me to tattle on other POW's. Not only did I know a lot of military information pertaining to the Chinese Communists, but I also knew of several prisoners who were still being held by the Communists. It was important to get this story into the proper hands, but when I broached the subject the OSI agents said that their instructions didn't call for that kind of an investigation. They were only interested in nailing other prisoners who might have done something wrong in prison camp.

After a fast go-around with the agents, I finally convinced them to call Washington for instructions on the kind of information to ask me. For several days we were at an impasse until word was received from Washington to look for items of both military and intelligence value. The teletype stated that now all prisoners would be interrogated on military matters. My arguments had finally done some good. But still, I was amazed and totally disheartened that my own nation hadn't been interested in gaining military information useful in case of another war or in case of a rekindling of the war in Korea. All they wanted to do, it seemed, was to be able to crucify this man or that man because of his actions while under duress in North Korea.

During the OSI investigation I did almost all of the talking. The agents had no Korean experience, so they didn't know exactly what to ask me and they only stopped me when they wanted to clarify a point. I started by telling them that I didn't have any firsthand knowledge of the activities of any other prisoners, because I had lived in solitary confinement all the time I had been up north. I wasn't about to tell them anything

294

I had overheard, because it would have come from a Chinese interrogator who could well have been lying. I spent days elaborating on the difference between a political interrogation and a military interrogation and why it was so important to tell our future pilots what to expect if shot down in Communist hands. All of the things I had thought about while in confinement I now brought to light for evaluation and perhaps for use. I had had experience in this line in France during World War II, so it was easy for me to recall almost all of the things I had seen and heard which could possibly be of value from a military standpoint. When I had finished testifying I dictated about 175 pages of single-spaced typewritten copy. I could do no more.

(Many years later during an Air Defense Command rocketry competition at Tyndall Air Force Base, I was shooting the bull with Gabby, J. C. Meyer and a host of other guys, when the conversation turned to Korea. Somehow I started talking about my experiences, only to find that J. C. knew all about them. He had been an instructor at the Air War College at the time, and told me that he had read all of my OSI testimony. It seemed that the document was being used as a study manual for students going through the school. Not too long ago I tried to get a copy for my own edification, but I was told that in all probability it wouldn't be made available, so I gave up the idea.)

On the 6th of November a most significant event transpired. Dr. Charles W. Mayo, a member of the Political Committee of the United Nations, reported to the committee regarding the harsh treatment afforded prisoners of war in efforts to obtain false confessions. Dr. Mayo projected moving pictures of four of us who had made statements at Parks Air Force Base, and then gave a carefully worded speech covering detailed information regarding other prisoners who had been subjected to inhuman treatment. At the conclusion of his report Dr. Mayo said: "Thus we can surely say that in Communist doctrine and practice, behind the iron curtain and in the past, the concepts of truth and morality which are sacred to the tradition of free men are totally subjected to the success of the Communist movement. Any means, any deceit, any brutality, is justified by the

295

Communists if they think it contributes to the victory of Communism."

At that moment Communism lost face throughout the world. Heretofore millions of people no doubt believed the United Nations guilty of waging bacteriological warfare in Korea. Now Communist propaganda was exposed; the treachery of Communism was on the table for all to see. Uncommitted peoples throughout the world could look carefully at the evidence and say to themselves, If this is the way rulers in a Communist society behave, is this the way I want to live? Although it was a tremendous moral victory, it was late in coming. We were not prepared for the allegation in the first place, and it took us a long time to get around to exposing it for the lie that it was.

On the 10th of November I received orders transferring me from the 479th Medical Group to the 27th Air Division (Defense), and on the 18th I was instructed to remain at George Air Force Base for flying training with the 94th Fighter Interceptor Squadron. Within thirty days I was fully combat-ready in the North American F-86D, the nation's leading all-weather interceptor. As soon as qualified I asked to be assigned to Oxford Air Force Base—another unit belonging to the 27th Division—in order to become qualified in the Lockheed F-94 Starfighter, a two-place all-weather interceptor. Within fifteen days I became combat-ready in this aircraft also. My purpose was twofold.

In the first place I was home and free, although living under a cloud, and I wanted to be combat-ready in as many different fighter aircraft as possible. If war erupted in the world anywhere, I was ready to go. I could serve my nation once again, and if asked, I had every intention of doing so.

In the second place, I was interested in continuing my career. The best way to do it was to become proficient with the tools I had to use in doing my new job effectively and well. As chief of staff of the 27th Division I was tied to a desk, but I could still take my place in the cockpit with the younger men. Further than that, I found that I was the only colonel in Air Defense Command qualified to fly two different combat aircraft. There was some satisfaction in this.

After looking all over Orange County, Pat and I finally bought a home in Redlands, some ten miles from Norton Air Force Base and the 27th Air Division. I think the children liked the move as well as we did, although they began to be questioned about me by the neighbor's children. One night Lynn came home to ask: "Why were you in a jail?" When I pumped her for more information it seemed that some of the other children had been teasing her with statements about jail, which led her to believe that I was sore sort of criminal. The other children had apparently been listening to their parents talk about me and had only picked up the information about my being a prisoner. Putting two and two together, they must have figured that I'd been in San Quentin or some such place. Lynn was crushed, because she had never heard her daddy referred to in such terms.

After this episode I began to listen and watch what went on around the neighborhood. Some people were rather cool to us, though most were warm and friendly. Once in a while I heard a snide remark, but generally we were treated with respect. Since the whole affair was in the current periodicals, I expected as much. As far as the officers and men of the 27th were concerned, I couldn't have been treated better, and after all, that was what really mattered.

Then, too, the Schwable case had just been concluded. Though I had never been directly involved in what was going on, I watched with close attention. When announcement was finally made regarding the outcome, the newspaper story said that the recommendation had been made that Frank be restored to full duty. However, the board further recommended that he be assigned to positions which did not involve command responsibility. Though not knowing the inside story, I concluded that Frank had been given the shaft. I knew how he must have felt, because I was afraid the same thing would happen to me and I knew how I'd feel under the same circumstances.

It had been made public that a board of general officers had been constituted to examine the records of all Air Force personnel who had been prisoners. I anticipated that the board would conclude its findings some time after the 8th of February. How long after I didn't know, but at least something was going on which would result in a settlement of my case. Whether its conclusion was good or bad, knowing that I wouldn't be kept on the fire too much longer was some small satisfaction.

4.

I HAD been extremely worried over the pronouncements of Senator Russell, mostly because his sentiments were shared by a number of other representatives of the government and the press. Often a new newspaper article or statement would appear, condemning prisoners for their activities. Even though Dr. Mayo had scored heavily in the United Nations, this did little to ease the anxiety of waiting until the Department of Defense made its final determination.

On February 20, newspapers across the country carried an article written by George Gallup, Director of the American Institute of Public Opinion. The contents were as follows:

Should American soldiers who broke under Red torture and made false germ warfare confessions be punished?"

The public's verdict, by the commanding ratio of 3-to-1, is "No."

That's what interviewers for the Institute report after talking to typical citizens from coast to coast about the problem now under study by high military authorities in Washington.

Among the minority of 20 percent believing that the men who "confessed" while war prisoners of the Communists in Korea should be punished, 4 percent think they should be court-martialed. Another 4 percent think they should be given a prison sentence.

298

One percent believes they should be given the death penalty.

One of the most widely publicized episodes of the Korean War, the germ-warfare "confessions" by American soldiers were familiar to three of every four persons questioned in the survey— a remarkably high figure in opinion studies on knowledge of news events.

The Air Force recently appointed a five-man board of high-ranking officers to recommend whether the individuals should be cleared, what future they should have in the Air Force, and whether court-martial charges should be brought.

Today's survey sounded out opinion on the issue by using a battery of three questions. The first:

"Have you heard or read anything about the American prisoners of war in Korea who were forced to make false confessions that the United States had used germ warfare against the Communists?"

> Yes 75%
> No 25

The second question:

"Do you think the men who made these false confessions should be punished, or not?"

Here is the nationwide vote:

> Yes, should 20%
> No, should not 61
> No opinion 19
> ──────
> 100%

The feeling that some form of punishment should be meted out to the war prisoners is somewhat higher among persons who attended grade school than it is among those who attended high school or college.

The last question, asked of the 20 percent who believe the soldiers should be punished, was:

"What punishment do you think these men should be given?"

Here are the replies:

299

Should be court-martialed 4%
Given prison sentence 4
Given light punishment 3
Denied citizenship 1
Given dishonorable discharge 1
Given death penalty 1
Demoted in rank 1
Other 1
Don't know 4
% Saying Punish Them ... 20%

Surprisingly, after publication of this article, the number of adverse comments directed toward prisoners of war dropped off to zero. Condemnation, it seemed, had become an unpopular cause.

In the latter part of March I received orders from Headquarters Air Defense Command to attend a senior officers' school at Sandia Base, Albuquerque, New Mexico, a school which had been set up to instruct those who had a valid need to know about the nation's newest nuclear weapons. The course, though short, involved highly classified information only recently available, because we had just exploded our first hydrogen bomb. The security requirements were stringent, and I considered myself fortunate to be allowed to participate while still under fire because of my prison-camp experiences. I couldn't help but feel that this was a good sign.

Upon return from Sandia I received a message relayed by Base Operations at Norton Air Force Base from Brigadier General Bill Hudnell, a long-time friend from World War II days in the Pacific, who had passed through Norton on his way to San Francisco. Bill had left word to "Tell Bud 'No sweat and I'll contact him later.' " This was encouraging, but I couldn't be exactly sure of what he had meant. A couple of days later I received another message—this time from Hamilton Field— which General Monroe McCloskey, the commander of the 28th Air Division, had relayed: "Tell Mahurin not to worry; he'll know what I mean soon."

Early in April I was notified to appear before a board of officers which was investigating fourteen Air Force officers under the provisions of Air Force Regulation 36-2. This regulation is designed to eliminate officers whose service has been questionable, yet not sufficiently questionable to warrant dishonorable discharge or court-martial. In actions involving AFR 36-2, it is necessary for the officer concerned to show cause why he should be retained in the service. If unable to show sufficient cause, the officer is given the option of resigning his commission or facing official action to separate him from the service under conditions other than honorable. Usually the individual elects to resign.

When I received these orders I was immediately worried because they did not specify why I was to appear before the board. I had been contacted on several occasions by lawyers who represented officers involved in false germ-warfare confessions, and in each case the lawyers had wanted me to testify in behalf of their clients. I had replied to all such requests that I had no knowledge of individual activities other than my own while in prison camp and felt that I could do little to aid any one man who was in trouble. Now it appeared that I might be required to testify. Although I was not one of the fourteen and I was not to be examined by the board, I began to sweat.

In the meantime General Hutchinson had been transferred to North Eastern Air Command, and his replacement, Brigadier General James W. Andrew, had arrived. Jim and I hit it off immediately. I had discussed my situation with the new boss on several different occasions, and he had heard me address the officers at Western Air Defense Force. Now he promised to find out what was transpiring at Scott Air Force Base. Jim made several long-distance calls, then told me to go ahead as I had been directed, assuring me that everything would be all right, though he couldn't inform me at that moment of what I could expect.

I flew back to Scott in Belleville, Illinois, alone in a T-33 jet trainer. It was a long and lonely flight. Many thoughts rushed through my mind on that trip. I wasn't on trial, but still I was involved. The only thing possible was to state the truth.

301

After that, if trouble came I would meet it as best I could. I was worried for my family, and naturally worried for my future.

I landed at Scott in the early evening, and after parking my things in my quarters, went to the officers' club for dinner. At the bar I ran into a long-time friend, Brigadier General James Howard, one of the few Congressional Medal of Honor winners alive and walking. (At the height of the air war in Europe, Jim had singlehandedly attacked a large formation of enemy aircraft which were shooting at our bombers. He had destroyed seven and repulsed the rest—a tremendous accomplishment. He was now on reserve status, living in Washington, D. C.) After an exchange of greetings I asked him what had brought him to Scott. "Hell, Bud, don't you know?" he replied. "I'm on the AFR 36-2 board. In fact, I'm the one who wanted you to come out here." It turned out that Jim had suggested that the board listen to my case. They were aware that I didn't have information on anyone else, but they wanted to hear my story so as to be more competent in judging others. When I breathed a sigh of relief Jim said, "Gee, if I had known that you'd be worried about those orders I could have had them written differently."

The following day I appeared before the board and all I was asked to do was to tell my story, which I did gladly. At the end of my testimony the chairman held up a document which was a transcript of my false confession. It seemed that on the last day of prisoner-of-war exchange the Communists had started to broadcast recordings of all the confessions from Radio Peiping. Further, they had published all confessions, apparently hoping that the free world would condemn those who had made them. In this the Communist aspirations backfired. Our people now had a chance to see what we had written, and especially to find out where we had made erroneous and misleading statements. It was now clear how ridiculous the actual charges had been.

For the first time I was happy that I'd made the decision a long time before my release that I'd always tell the truth. I had nothing to hide, and besides, I wanted to get back at the Communists. Telling everything straight out was the only way. Once in awhile I'd considered clamming up, but it would have done me no good; and I had to live with myself, no matter what.

Altogether I appeared before the board on two separate occasions before the chairman told me that I would no longer be needed and could return to Norton Air Force Base. What a relief! The trip home seemed to take only about thirty minutes, because I could hardly wait to tell Pat what had happened. She had been consumed with anxiety when I took off for Scott, but now would be overjoyed to know that we didn't have to turn in our suits just yet.

After the Scott episode I began to investigate my situation actively. There had been 89 Air Force officers of various ranks involved in false germ-warfare confessions, as well as in other questionable acts while in enemy hands. After review by competent authority it had been determined that 14 of the 89 should show cause why they should be retained in the military service. After the results of Jim Howard's board were in, 4 men of the 14 were asked to resign their commissions. Naturally it was impossible for me to obtain any details concerning these 4 men, though while I had been in prison camp I had overheard my interrogators talking about a couple of these cases. One of the officers before the board had written articles for a Communist-sponsored prison-camp paper called, *For Truth and Peace*. I had never seen the paper or the articles, but I was told they consisted of a confirmation of germ warfare, as well as a series of discussions as to why soldiers of the United States were fighting a war that was not in the best interests of the nation. Anyone is entitled to personal opinion, but the Communists had paid this officer for his articles; in fact he had returned to our side with several thousand Chinese dollars in his possession. This was going too damn far. In another case I was told that an officer in one small compound had been treated almost as a guest by his captors while other men in the same compound were starving. This clearly smacked of collaboration.

On the 16th of May, 1954, I arrived at Division Headquarters at the usual time to find General Andrew and several other senior officers seated in my office, waiting for me. After the

303

usual good mornings, General Andrew suggested that I look at my mail basket to see if there was anything new. On top of the stack was the following:

HEADQUARTERS
AIR DEFENSE COMMAND
ENT AIR FORCE BASE
Colorado Springs, Colorado

7 May 1954

SUBJECT: POW Status

TO: COLONEL WALKER M. MAHURIN, 8658A
THRU: Commander
        27th Air Division
        Norton AFB, California

1. Reference is made to message from Headquarters United States Air Force, dated 7 January 1954, which clarified the duty status of ex-Korean prisoners of war. A special board convened to consider those ex-Korean prisoners of war whose conduct while in the hands of the enemy left a question as to their future usefulness to the service. Those concerned have been notified by separate action.

2. In view of the above board action, which was announced publicly on 8 February 1954, you and many other ex-prisoners of war have in all probability been apprehensive as to your future status.

3. This is to reassure you that no official reservation exists regarding the propriety of your conduct while a prisoner.

cc: WADF

FREDERIC H. SMITH, JR.
Major General, USAF
Vice Commander

When I read Fred's letter I almost laughed at Paragraph 2. Apprehensive was hardly the word. But thank God for him; coming from that man, above all, it was really welcome.

Jim Andrew, for his part, had added a letter of his own:

304

SUBJECT: POW Status

Hq ADC

27 COMDR (7 May 54)   1st Ind

HQS 27TH AIR DIVISION (DEF), Norton Air Force Base, California

TO: Colonel Walker M. Mahurin, 8658A, Headquarters, 27th Air Division (Defense), Norton Air Force Base, California

1. Noted with pleasure and forwarded for inclusion in your personal file.

JAMES W. ANDREW
Brigadier General, USAF
Commander

5.

AS far as I was concerned, the edict from Fred Smith opened the door to a normal service life. Without the worries of the past I could concentrate on the future, and it looked bright. Jim Andrew assigned me to be operations officer of the 27th Air Division. I caught up on my flying, and in fact represented the division as the team captain of the 27th Division rocket team at the annual world-wide rocket meet in Yuma, Arizona. Living in Redlands was especially delightful because I was close to my work and Pat was among friends.

After a year our deputy division commander, Sam Agee, was promoted to brigadier general and transferred, so I was assigned the duty of vice commander as well as operations officer, a job which lasted over a year. Naturally Jim and I tried to make our division the best in Air Defense Command, and we were pleased with the results. Meanwhile Pat and I had a third child—a boy whom we named Michael Randolf after General Randy Holzapple. Gradually, people began to forget about prisoners of war,

305

and for the most part, forgot about the details of the Korean War.

Things went well until the early part of 1956 when I received orders transferring me in June to the Air War College at Maxwell Air Force Base in Alabama for one year of advanced schooling. At almost the same time I was offered a position in the civilian aircraft industry. The Air War College assignment was significant from a careeer-officer standpoint because it is one of the steps which lead to promotion to general-officer rank. It was especially significant to me because I was on the list somewhat ahead of my contemporaries. Pat and I had known that we would have to leave California someday—this is service life; but we hadn't even thought of school again.

On the other hand, a position in the aircraft industry was most attractive from a number of angles—especially the one that said "More money." Of course that wasn't the only reason. There were many others, even if the salary increase would be somewhere in the neighborhood of 33 percent. The offer was made by a man I respected highly, and it came from a reputable contractor in the industry. I hadn't sought the job—they had come to me—and it was a mighty difficult problem to decide what to do.

I mulled over the situation for many weeks. In an effort to find out all I could about the pros and cons, I called all of my friends whom I felt could give me good advice, including such illustrious persons as General Carl Spaatz, General Ira Eaker, General Emmett O'Donnell and many others. But in the final analysis Pat and I had to make the decision.

Regulations pertaining to promotion to general officer were rigid, because to be eligible an officer had first to be a permanent full colonel. With 14 years of service I was a temporary full colonel and had been one for 5 years, although I was a permanent major. In 1956 the Air Force was promoting 150 majors to lieutenant colonel and 100 lieutenant colonels to colonel each year. My promotion-list number—the number of people who were ahead of me in seniority—was 2,500. Unless the situation changed drastically, it would take me 44 years to be eligible for promotion to permanent colonel and then general. That's a long time.

In industry I would be associated with men who were in my same age group and I would do the type of thing I had been doing all my mature life—dealing with the Air Force and aircraft. It seemed to me that the opportunities for advancement were excellent. If I elected to join industry, I would eventually be in a financial position to send my children to the best schools and to live in one area permanently instead of being required to move about every three years, as Pat and I had done while in service. As another consideration, I could accept a reserve commission, continue military flying, and rejoin the Air Force in the event of war. After careful deliberation Pat and I decided to leave the Air Force.

Initially we really enjoyed civilian life. Several of the people working for the same company lived near us, and we found that we belonged to an interesting group. We loved our home in Pacific Palisades, and the children blossomed at a school near home.

I enjoyed my job immensely. There were fourteen men working in my organization, almost all of them pilots. In addition to my normal administrative responsibilities, I was also an experimental and production test pilot for the aircraft being produced by the company. I applied for a reserve commission in the USAF, was given the rank of lieutenant colonel and the command of an air-rescue squadron equipped with SA-16 flying boats. To a guy with a fighter-pilot background this was a bit less than a challenge. But all of it was fun ... for awhile.

After nearly a year in industry things began to go sour. For one thing, the Mahurins adjusted. The extra money we thought we'd have each month disappeared—as it had in service life. Several of the happy couples around us started divorce proceedings, and we found that our bright and shiny house needed repairs, just like every other house. I had to give up my rescue-squadron duties because the required summer active-duty tour interfered with my job. But that wasn't all; without realizing it, I was not fitting into industry.

The company I worked for had been in business a long time before I reached the scene. And it had been getting along fine without me. Still, I considered that my experiences stood me in good stead to advise on appropriate courses of action for the company in future Defense Department dealings. They didn't see things my way, and all of a sudden I realized that I was trying to steer an ocean liner with a canoe paddle. I knew that I was right as rain, but try as I might, I didn't seem to be able to convince others. Something had to give, and it was Mahurin. Though I left the Air Force a colonel, I was only a second lieutenant in the private-industry hierarchy and I had a lot to learn. Late one afternoon, eighteen months after I had left the service, by boss called me into his office and said: "Bud, I'm going to have to let you go." I replied that I knew he was under pressure and if my leaving would help I'd be glad to go. (Besides, I didn't have any choice.)

Somehow I thought it would be easy to line up another job. I figured that my background should be useful and that someone among my many friends in industry would decide that I was just what he wanted. But that wasn't the case. Word gets around, and I didn't seem to fit into any given slot.

For three long months Pat and I sweated it out, day after day. I could see the money dwindling every moment, a situation which was extremely critical because we had amassed no great savings in our years of service life and especially because both of us had become accustomed to security after fourteen years in the service and insecurity was a new thing. I could only plug away, hoping.

During this time I had plenty of interviews with friends and acquaintances. Most were interested, but the big stumbling block always seemed to be where to put me. I told everyone I talked to that I had been fired, period. There wasn't any sense in trying to make up any kind of story that wasn't true. But, thank God, a friend of mine, Dan Darnell—a former test pilot with North American Aviation—finally came to my rescue and introduced me to a man who decided that I was just what he wanted for a sales engineer. At one point this man asked me, as many others had, why I didn't go back into the service instead of staying in industry. All I could say at that time was that I had made a decision to stay in the aircraft industry and intended to do so if I had to build airplanes in my own garage.

I learned plenty in my new responsibility. For one thing, I was even more impressed with that fact that I was only a second lieutenant in industry. For two and a half years I beat the bushes, selling electronics equipment. It was a challenge and it was fun. Inside the plant I had a little cubbyhole office with a chair and a desk, but the friends I generated made up for the Spartan accommodations.

The next step up the ladder came when I was offered a position which involved establishing a West Coast office for a Midwest corporation. Since I had reached a plateau as a sales engineer, I welcomed the chance to add to my experience in another field. Best of all, it was a chance to become acquainted with the nation's space programs.

Running an office a thousand miles or so from the parent corporation is interesting and demanding. I enjoyed the work and enjoyed monthly visits to the home office to "Get the word." But I missed people. I couldn't get up from my desk and go a few feet to find out what was going on, because there weren't that many people in the office. Thus, when an opportunity came to switch jobs once again and go with a company even more heavily involved in space programs, I again made a switch.

And that's where I am today. I have found what I want and I have been moving ahead slowly. The space business is plain fascinating, and often, when I am deep in discussions about trips to the moon and beyond, I think back to Korea only to find it a long, long way behind me. Still, the Koreas as such haven't disappeared, even though we have had John Glenn in orbit and the Russians have had their Nikolayev. Unfortunately there are Korea-type problems in the world: Laos, Viet-Nam, Morocco, the Congo and many other hot spots. In all these places there is a possibility that there will be more Mahurins,

309

Schwables, Deans and the rest. I hope that we have learned some lessons.

I was proud of the way my old Air Force came through when the chips were down. I thought it used a lot of "smart" after the Korean War by giving each case individual attention. We could have been treated differently if our superiors had adopted the hard-nosed attitude that we were guilty—period. But the Air Force went one step better. It established an escape-and-survival school at Reno, Nevada, to try to simulate as closely as possible the conditions many of us experienced. Now it is practically mandatory for pilots to spend some time at Stead Air Force Base, being "brainwashed" and shoved around almost exactly as they would be under actual conditions.

Of course, no matter how long a guy is cooped up in a cell in Reno he knows that one day soon he'll get out. No matter how many threats his captors make, he knows that they don't mean it in the long run. But still, the school is a good start. I know one Air Force colonel who became so involved in the game that he actually picked up a log and put the slug on an enlisted man who was trying to take him prisoner. (He got away, too.) And even though the colonel's zeal is uncommon, nevertheless a guy can't help but be more prepared than I was when he has finished the Reno survival school.

I was frankly disappointed with the committee that established the "Code of Military Conduct for Prisoners of War"—a code which came out shortly after the dust had settled in Korea. To the best of my knowledge none of the committee's members had ever been a prisoner of war. Experience might have led them to different conclusions.

They decided that a prisoner should only give name, rank, and serial number to his captors. This is fine—up to a point. These were the instructions during the American Revolution, I'm sure, and during the Civil War as well. But in the meantime science has gone a long way. If the enemy really wants to find out what the prisoner knows, all he has to use is a shot of sodium pentothal. If he wants to get a prisoner to confess to something and has enough time, he can get any human being to break. Under the circumstances perhaps the prisoner should be instructed to hold out as long as possible and then tell only enough to satisfy his captors. Most of us didn't know too much anyway. Maybe a good rule of thumb would be to tell only that which will not result in harm to one's fellow soldiers.

Somebody in our government is already thinking along these lines, or Powers wouldn't have been given the instructions he received. I watched the Powers case with great interest and was especially sensitive to all the adverse comment that was made about him before he returned to the United States. He was compared—unfavorably of course—to Nathan Hale, the comment being that he shouldn't have confessed to being a spy pilot. But there is a mighty difference between brave utterances on a gallows trap door and in a Russian court of law. When we were all made aware of the instructions Powers had been given, it began to appear that he had done the right thing at the right time and served his nation well. In time, I think, we'll be changing our instructions to our soldiers in the field, because we seem to be involved again in small wars, whether we like it or not.

Changing our instructions to soldiers in the field, however, is not enough.

Most of us have been brought up in a society of winners, but somehow we have forgotten all about winning in our last several skirmishes. A soldier is bound to have a different attitude about fighting and dying in a war just to "contain" an enemy. But the same soldier will have a real rock-'em sock-'em attitude when the goal is to win a war completely. One thing is for sure—he won't pull out a poison needle and kill himself if he is taken prisoner during a containment war, because he knows it will be over one day and he will come back home again. Yet we had plenty of evidence of guys who did practically that very thing in the Pacific to avoid capture during World War II. When we Americans are out to win, there is no stopping us. And as long as the Russians know that, they won't take chances pushing us around.

I was extremely disappointed several years ago with our national shrug of the shoulders when the Russians put the first

311

satellite into orbit. Only recently have we developed an attitude of "Let's beat them, by God" and "We'll do it, too." But it took a change in outlook on the part of our government to start us out on that winning path. We all know that Gagarin was the first human in orbit, and we all are aware that Titov was the first man to stay in outer atmosphere for a long period of time. Yet the welcome for John Glenn as he rode down the streets of Manhattan should be a clear indication that the United States of America is solidly behind a winner.

We still have plenty of chances to beat the Russians in the space race, as well as on the ground. They'll probably have the first two-man capsule in orbit; but quite possibly we'll be the first nation to change men from one vehicle to another in outer space. It will be a neck-and-neck race to see who puts the first man around the moon. But the big one—the blockbuster of this age—we should win if we don't get complacent. When the United States of America has a flag proudly flying on the surface of the moon and our astronauts are standing there waiting to greet the Russians as they come in for a landing, then I'm going to say to myself—Maybe that Korean experience was worth while after all.

I think that we can win in other fields, too, if we have the right national spirit. I'd like to see us establish a national objective of "World-Wide Democracy" to match their objective of "World-Wide Communism." I'd like to see us form a development-planning department to carry out this objective. Mr. Kennedy had the right idea when he appointed Edward R. Murrow as his director of the United States Information Agency. But that isn't enough. Whoever has Mr. Murrow's job must do development planning to carry it out, and if so he ought to be in the President's Cabinet.

I have frequently deplored the fact that military men who resign from the service often feel obligated to let out a public blast at those with whom they have had differences. Somehow it seems to tarnish the luster of a military man when he pops off, often without too much skill, about his nation and its administration. We can't criticize him for thinking—he has a brain just like everyone else—but I do think that he is obligated to adhere to the general policies of his government, regardless of his position in or out of the service. For these very reasons I long kept myself from writing a book about my experiences in North Korea. I suppose I would have blasted away at any and all targets in the latter part of 1953 and the early part of 1954, but for several years I was too busy doing other things to even think of such targets. Now, perhaps mellowed by time, I am much more interested in helping fellow Americans learn about Communism and how to fight it. This is the main reason I have written this book. If one single reader is more adequately prepared to face capture should he some day have to fight in some Communist-inspired war, it will have served its purpose.

I am getting too old to hop into a fighter aircraft again to do combat with the Russians or the North Koreans or the Red Chinese. But I'm not too old to outthink them if I get a chance. For that matter, neither is any other American. With the right kind of guidance I am confident that all of us will get together and outsmart the Communists, just as we have other enemies of democracy throughout our history.

Library of Congress Cataloging-in-Publication Data

Mahurin, Walker M.
Honest John / Walker M. Mahurin.
p. cm. — (Wings of war)
Originally published: New York : Putnam, c1962.
ISBN 0-8094-9645-3
1. Mahurin, Walker M.
2. Fighter pilots—United States—Biography.
I. Title. II. Series.
UG626.2.M33M34 1993   358.4'14'092—dc20 [B]   93-19934 CIP

Published by arrangement with Walker M. Mahurin.

Cover photograph © Carl Purcell
Endpapers photograph © Rene Sheret/After Image